"There Must Be a Pony in Here Somewhere"

"There Must Be a Pony in Here Somewhere"

Twenty Years with Ronald Reagan

A MEMOIR

John A. (Jack) Svahn

Langdon Street Press

Langdon Street Press
212 3rd Avenue North, Suite 290
Minneapolis, MN 55401
612.455.2293
www.langdonstreetpress.com

Cover photo from the White House.
All photos are "White House photos" with the exception of the first image on page 177 which is an "SSA Photo".

ISBN-13: 978-1-936782-66-6
LCCN: 2011940098

Distributed by Itasca Books

Cover Design by Alan Pranke
Typeset by Nate Meyers

Printed in the United States of America

For my mother Esther, who throughout life always told me to just take it one day at a time

Contents

Preface ix

1 – The Ronald Reagan I Knew...1

2 – The Beginning...17

3 – Welfare? I Think That I Know How to Spell It.........................27

4 – The Blue Book..40

5 – All Out War..50

6 – Be Careful What You Wish For...68

7 – Let's Wrap This Up..83

8 – Off to Washington...91

9 – Transition...106

10 – The Third of Something..120

11 – What a Mess!...144

12 – Saving Social Security..169

13 – Let's Put a Heckler in the Cabinet 205

14 – The White House..230

15 – Life in the White House..267

16 – 1984..290

17 – Reagan's Biggest Mistake 323

18 – A Different West Wing..334

19 – End Game...356

Acknowledgments 369

Preface

It was spring in Washington, D.C. My wife Jill and I were on our way from our second home on Kent Island on the Eastern Shore of Maryland to meet Lee Verstandig and his wife Toni. Lee and I had been suite-mates on the second floor of the White House's West Wing during the administration of Ronald Reagan. Lee was the Assistant to the President for Intergovernmental Relations and I was the Assistant to the President for Policy Development, the President's chief domestic and economic policy advisor.

It was June 11, 2004. We were going to the National Cathedral to attend the state funeral of the fortieth President of the United States. Ronald Reagan had passed away on June 5 at the age of ninety-three. We had known for years that this day was coming and in some respects it was a time for joy. When all of Reagan's key staff attended the dedication of the Ronald Reagan Presidential Library in Simi Valley California in 1991, someone made the prophetic comment that it was probably the next to the last time that we would all be together. It was just three years later that the former President was diagnosed with Alzheimer's disease and had handwritten a poignant letter to the American people telling them of his diagnosis, closing with:

"I now begin the journey that will lead me into the sunset of my life. I know that for America there will always be a bright dawn ahead."

Now, after ten years of a progressive and debilitating disease, the journey that he wrote of was over and we were glad that it was. It was the end of an era, the passing of a great man, and the end of a chapter in my life that had begun thirty-eight years earlier.

Ronald Reagan was an optimist; he never saw a half empty glass. One of his favorite stories, one that most White House staffers heard a hundred times during their time there, involved two young boys who were twins. One was an optimist and one was a pessimist. On their birthday, the parents gave the pessimist a room full of very nice presents, but when they went to see him in his room he was crying. When asked why he was crying, he told them that he was afraid that his new toys would break. The other son, the optimist, got nothing but a huge pile of manure. When his father found the child, he was digging frantically in the pile. His father asked him what he was doing, and the little boy replied, "With all this manure, I know that there must be a pony in here somewhere!"

When I left the White House, there was a good riddance reception given for me and my family in the Roosevelt Room. As was customary, the guest list was a combination of friends and colleagues. When we entered the room from the Oval Office, the President began his remarks. He went on and on about our time together and how great a guy I was. It was beginning to get embarrassing. So I waited until he paused for a breath and I said, "There must be a pony in here somewhere." It brought the roof down. The President was laughing so hard he almost couldn't finish his comments.

This book took me many years to write. I am prone to recounting events of the past—it is an inherited trait; my father was very adept at it. Listening to my stories, many friends and associates would urge me to write them down, to write a book. This book is an attempt to put over twenty years of working for Ronald Reagan into some context and preserve what one person saw during that time.

When I finally got serious about writing a book about my front row seat to history, I visited the Reagan Library in Simi Valley, California, to do some research. I had been to the Library when it was dedicated in 1991 but this was my first visit to actually look at papers. Not that there is a large collection of my papers at the library. I adhered to the mantra laid out by former Vice President Dick Cheney when he was the White House Chief of Staff for President Gerald Ford. "I learned early on that if you don't want your memos to get you in trouble some day, just don't write any." It was on this first visit that I found out that I could not even see my own limited collection of papers, let alone any others.

Under the Presidential Records Act of 1978, people seeking access to any records in the library must file a request under the Freedom of Information Act. That applies even if you wrote the material yourself. When I filed my request, the formal answer that I got back from the Library indicated that the staff could begin reviewing my request in approximately twenty-one months. This has not been an easy project.

Most people say that they first became aware of Ronald Reagan, the politician, as a result of the nationally televised speech that he gave on October 27, 1964, supporting Senator Barry Goldwater's bid for the Presidency. That speech, a last ditch effort for Goldwater, ignited a movement that still is a potent force in American politics. Conservatives simply refer to that appearance as "The Speech." In it, Ronald Reagan laid out what he saw as the problems with our country and his thoughts on how to cure them. I thought at the time that it was good. I agreed with what he said, but even more, I liked the way he said it. As it was, I wasn't the only person to like The Speech. Little did I know the impact it would have on my life. I was twenty-one that year and was going to vote in my first election. I was a political science major at the University of Washington.

Two years after Goldwater lost, Ronald Reagan was running for Governor of California and I was getting ready to go into the Air Force. Having some spare time before I reported for duty, I spent the fall doorbelling for Reagan in San Diego. He got elected and took over the reins in Sacramento at midnight January 2, 1967. I went off to Lackland Air Force Base in San Antonio to become an officer and navigator and probably to eventually wind up flying in Vietnam. (I didn't, but that is a whole different story.)

So I became a "Reaganite" in 1966. It is an appellation that I have to this day. I served in four Reagan Administrations and played a role in some of Ronald Reagan's most controversial and successful domestic initiatives. At some times in my career, being a Reaganite has been used against me and at other times, it has been used admiringly in my favor. Today, like Ronald Reagan himself, being a "Reaganite" is held in high esteem by a majority of Americans.

John A. (Jack) Svahn
Reno, Nevada

Chapter 1
The Ronald Reagan I Knew

I have always been upset with the way that Ronald Reagan was portrayed by the media and by his political opponents. The liberal left despised him and was constantly deriding his intellect, knowledge, and work habits. Clark Clifford, Lyndon Johnson's defense secretary once referred to Reagan as an "amiable dunce." And Tip O'Neill, exhibiting the two-faced nature of Massachusetts politics would at times try to joke with Reagan and at other times make scurrilous personal statements about him.

There are many stories about how Reagan and Tip could argue during the day and then sit down and have a drink together while they told each other jokes, and those stories are true. Ronald Reagan was a gentleman. He could be civil to almost anyone. He sat down with emissaries from the evil empire and had pleasant conversation. So too, could he sit down with O'Neill and make small talk. But if you had ever listened to O'Neill rail against Reagan, right to his face, you would know that they could not be friends.

I recall a Joint Leadership meeting in the Cabinet Room when the President was talking about the welfare mess and O'Neill exploded, "That doesn't sell when you talk to real people, not those rich people you hob-knob with!" Then he backed off saying, "I have the greatest respect for the Presidency." The President responded, "You just don't like the incumbent" and he wasn't joking.

Reagan rarely complained about O'Neill, even in private other than to indicate that he didn't like the way that O'Neill politicized everything. You couldn't say the same about Tip. In public O'Neill was once quoted as saying, "He knows less than any President I've ever known." At times, even some of the guys on our side of the aisle occasionally made uncalled for derogatory remarks. Of course, now every one of them is a big Reagan fan, "always have been." Today, you have a hard time finding a Republican who wasn't a "foot soldier" in the Reagan Revolution. None of these characterizations by his detractors was accurate. Reagan was the most intelligent, caring, and hardworking public official that I met in twenty-four years of public service.

Decision-making was an area where he was routinely derided and underestimated. Ronald Reagan was not afraid to make a decision. He actually reveled in it. Time and time again, he proved he was his own man and comfortable in making decisions. Yes, like any good manager, he delegated a lot. The same people who said he delegated too much are the ones who criticized Carter for not delegating enough. Carter was consumed by the minutiae. Ronald Reagan worked with broad, well thought out brush strokes.

Reagan never shirked from his duty to make decisions and once made, he stood by his decisions. This is a part of his personality that many staff members never understood and it led to a lot of handwringing in the halls of the West Wing. On occasion, he could be influenced by a personal plea from a friend or a sad story, but usually he had a good sense of what was right and what was wrong and that would guide his actions. Woe be it to the staff guy who tried to tell him that a decision he was about to make wasn't "good politically." He was confident and he had something that a lot of people seem to leave in their hometown when they come to Washington: common sense.

On more than a few occasions, the President made decisions with which I did not agree. He was after all the boss and that was his prerogative. Mine was to make my argument and once the decision was made, to just salute, say, "Yes Mr. President" and do my best to carry out his decision. Two issues where he made a decision against my recommendation remain problematic to this day. One dealt with airline safety and the other was a Medicare coverage question. In both cases, I think that his decision was based on personality and friendship rather than on the facts.

I had raised the question of safety in the sky with him at an Issues Lunch, a weekly Monday luncheon that we had, and suggested that it would be a good time to plan and implement a long-range upgrade of the FAA's Air Traffic Control System. I had the staff do some homework and just having come through the grueling task of trying to update the social security system's major computer systems, I knew that even though we had the best air traffic operation in the world, neglect over a period of time would change that situation.

At both the state and federal level, I have found that government agencies go in fits and starts when it comes to major systems. They wait until a data processing system is almost ready to collapse and then spend big dollars bringing it up to modern standards. That is when the real problem arises because they do nothing to *keep* it modern. Instead, they spend a couple of years patting themselves on the back for replacing the old system and then turn to some other priority. After a period of years the crisis strikes again and the cycle repeats itself. In terms of computer systems, the government cycle is usually about twenty years. Think where you would be today if you were at the end of the cycle and were using fifteen-year-old computers and software.

It wasn't going to happen on my watch, however. We scheduled a meeting in the Cabinet Room on the subject and Elizabeth Dole, then Secretary of Transportation, came loaded for bear and wearing a bright green suit. She didn't want any part of it. If she said, "Mr. President, we have the best Air Traffic Control System in the world" once, she said it ten times in the hour we had for the meeting. I didn't get my plan for an update of the ATC system. Reagan always had an eye for an attractive woman.

Today, the FAA is scrambling at the end of their twenty-year cycle, trying to update a sadly overloaded ATC system. It comes home to haunt us sometimes. On one occasion, during an approach to Dulles Airport in Washington, D.C., I personally listened to an air traffic controller tell the pilot of a jumbo jet, on which I was traveling, that the ATC radar was out and he had no idea where the aircraft was nor who else was around him. With bad weather all around, the pilot insisted that the controller give him a direction and an altitude for flying. The controller, obviously exasperated, asked the pilot what his current heading and altitude were and then told the pilot to fly that heading at his current altitude. And he said for the pilot to "let me know if you see anyone else out there!"

The Medicare issue involved whether or not Medicare would cover heart transplants. Medicare does not cover procedures that are considered experimental in nature. If Medicare covers a procedure, then most private insurance plans will recognize it and provide coverage.

Otis Bowen, then the Secretary of Health and Human Services wanted Medicare to cover heart transplants without any qualification. Otis was a physician and he had been one of the few Republican Governors during the last two years that Reagan was Governor of California. They knew each other then and Reagan liked the doc. It was hard not to like Otis. He was a quiet, friendly fellow but he did have opinions on certain matters and heart transplant was one of them.

I was concerned about the precedent that would be set by declaring heart transplants no longer experimental for Medicare reimbursement. There is an old adage in government and crime—follow the money. I had seen a similar good idea go off kilter in the past. Back when Caspar Weinberger and I were at the old Department of Health Education and Welfare, Congress had added coverage under Medicare for End Stage Renal Disease (ESRD), kidney dialysis, and transplants. During the deliberation on the legislation, much testimony was given about the number of people who would be eligible and the overall cost of the program. The ESRD program was never expected to exceed $220 million. What no one counted on was another old Washington saying, "If you pay for it, they will do it." Instead of a small no growth program, the ESRD program spawned a boom in new providers. Because of the payment methodology, patients in the process of dying were also dialyzed. The program grew out of control. By 2004, the ESRD program accounted for almost $18 billion of Medicare expenditures. Many dialysis patients being paid for by Medicare were the elderly who were near death from cancer or stroke.

I had been visited in my office in February 1986 by Dr. Robert Jarvik, the inventor of the Jarvik artificial heart. Jarvik's Jarvik-7 artificial heart had been successfully implanted in a human being in November of 1984. Jarvik was convinced that he could successfully improve the artificial heart to where it could become a valuable tool in the cardiologist's bag in treating heart disease.

One of the most memorable recipients of Jarvik's heart was William Schroeder. Schroeder lived for over 600 days with the Jarvik artificial heart. In the first few days after the implant, President Reagan called Schroeder to congratulate him on the successful operation and to wish him well. Schroeder took the opportunity to talk with the President to complain about not having received a Social Security disability check. Schroeder told Reagan that all he got from the Social Security Administration (SSA) was "the runaround." Reagan promised Schroeder, "I'll get on it right away." And he did. I didn't get many direct calls from Reagan but I did that day. The next morning two SSA officials showed up at Schroeder's bedside with the check.

I could see that just like the ESRD program, a Medicare heart transplant program could grow into something that was never intended. I told the President that we didn't do heart transplants on people over sixty-five, they had to be experimental. And I told him that if Medicare paid for it and if Jarvik ever perfected his artificial heart, we would see wards of the elderly all hooked up with artificial hearts and awaiting transplants. Good old Doc Bowen carried the day however. He just told the President that he thought it was a good idea and Ronald Reagan agreed. I am still waiting for Dr. Jarvik to perfect the artificial heart.*

But I really didn't get to know Ronald Reagan until I worked for him in welfare reform in 1971. Prior to that, I had only met him twice. But after March 3, 1971, I spent a lot of time observing him. He took a very active part in the welfare reform issue and I was there watching and listening.

I, like most staff, never did get to be really "personal" with him. In the twenty years that I worked with Ronald Reagan, I only saw a handful of people who were "personal" friends of Ronald Reagan. Most of them were older contemporaries from his previous life, people like the Bill Buckley's, the Walter Annenberg's and Earl Jorgensen's. They would get together periodically to socialize. And of course, members of the old California kitchen cabinet like Holmes Tuttle were long-time friends. But Washington, D.C. had never been high on Reagan's travel agenda, even when he was Governor. So, by the time he got to be President, he had very few personal friends in Washington. Other than Charlie Wick, Bill Clark, Ed Meese, and Paul Laxalt, most of the people in government were just part of the cast. Even with Ed and Bill, it still appeared to be more of a business relationship than a personal one. Mike Deaver had a special relationship with both Reagan and Nancy. Because of the years spent with them, they treated Mike almost

---

* In fact, Jarvik's invention was approved by the FDA for trials as a way to buy time for heart transplant patients! The push is already on to approve Medicare payment for the artificial heart. When that comes through, we may well see those wards full of the elderly awaiting heart transplants.

6

like a son. I always got the impression that during the time that they were in the White House their friends were really Nancy's friends.

I spent a lot of time with the President in the over three years that I was in the West Wing but we were never pals. We told jokes to each other and usually met in scheduled meetings a couple of times a day on average. I always tried to give him my best advice even if sometimes it wasn't to his liking. Throughout the years he was always most courteous and pleasant, but sometimes you had to ask yourself if he really knew who you were or whether you were just another nice staff person.

The press corps used to kid the senior White House staff by asking if they had passed the "name test," which meant Reagan knew your name and used it. There is the old story about when he was greeting a group of mayors in the White House and the next in line was his Secretary of Housing and Urban Development, Sam Pierce, Reagan greeted him as "Mr. Mayor." Unfortunately, it actually happened. That little incident created quite a hullabaloo in the pressroom and among some members of the Administration. But it not only happened to Sam Pierce, it happened to a lot of people. It was as though if you weren't in the position he expected, he couldn't associate you with a name. It happened to me when I returned to the White House after having been gone only two months. I was attending a meeting in the Roosevelt Room with my former deputy, Chuck Hobbs, and Governor Tom Kean from New Jersey. The President came in and went around the table shaking hands and when he got to me, I had to introduce myself. We both laughed. I didn't take it personally; it was just Ronald Reagan. Don't get me wrong, Ronald Reagan was a really nice person and he always treated staff and guests alike in a most cordial and polite manner, but he wasn't personal. In my case, it could well be the thirty-two-year age difference between us that contributed to this feeling. I was only twenty-seven when we first met and had just turned forty when I moved to the West Wing.

I am not the only one to recognize this trait. On one occasion, I was visiting Bob Tuttle at the Embassy in London where he was serving as President George W. Bush's Ambassador to the Court of Saint James. Bob is the son of the late Holmes Tuttle, a successful Southern California businessman who was one of the individuals who originally convinced Reagan to run for Governor. During the Reagan Administration, Bob served as the President's personnel director having taken over from John Herrington. Bob and I sat at the dining table at the Embassy having lunch and swapping stories about the old days, marveling at the "boss" and how he treated us. We both revered Reagan but also commented on the fact that we were never close to him. Bob observed "Jack, neither he nor Nancy ever got over the fact that we were 'the kids'." Maybe that was the explanation.

When he was Governor, he was younger and he had more people around him that were closer to his age. He always liked to be "one of the guys" even if everyone else knew he was the boss. The guys in the Governor's office used to sit around and tell stories and listen to his stories of his days in Hollywood. He didn't tell as many Hollywood stories in Washington and when he did, the story was usually related to an issue before him, not some semi-ribald discussion of his days between marriages.

Because of security concerns resulting from the assassination attempt early in his first term, he couldn't do things as President he could do when he was Governor of California. I recall one afternoon a group of us were in the Governor's Office discussing some issue of welfare reform implementation when the Governor pushed back from his seat and stood up. "Fellas," he said, "just keep going on here. I'm going to have to leave a little early today and run an errand." With that, he pulled a letter out of his pocket and read it to us.

The letter was from a U.S. serviceman who was stationed in Vietnam. He had written to the Governor that his unit had been transferred to Sacramento and that his wife and family had already moved there in his absence. Her birthday or their anniversary (I don't recall which it was) was approaching and the serviceman didn't know anyone in California to ask to get her a present. The serviceman had enclosed a check in the letter. In the letter, he asked if the Governor would have someone on his staff send her some flowers. Reagan said he thought that it was a good idea. "So that is what I am going to do. Pick up some flowers and take them to her on my way home." And that is what he did. No fuss, no fanfare.*

In one meeting during the legislative battle for welfare reform in California, he read a letter to us from a man who was the sole caretaker to his mentally retarded adult brother. The caretaker was complaining about the welfare reform program and some of the proposed reductions. He felt that the reductions were unfair and that they would hurt his brother. He told the Governor that he had been saving up his money to buy his brother a rocking chair for Christmas because rocking seemed to be the only thing that the impaired brother enjoyed. He feared that with the changes he wouldn't be able to afford the rocker. The Governor wrote back to him and assured him that there would be no impact on the brother. As he looked across the office at a rocking chair sitting there he said, "I don't use that one. Let's send it to this man." Somewhere out there, there is a gubernatorial rocker being enjoyed by a man who probably doesn't know from where it came.

Reagan was a great pen pal. He regularly wrote to people for years, many of whom he had never met. Perhaps it started in Hollywood when he was in movies and members of his fan club would write to him. However he got into the habit, it was deeply ingrained and sometimes caused people to wonder about his choice of priorities. As Governor, he always liked to look at his mail and draft his own responses. Even as

---

* A few days later the story hit the local papers. It wasn't as a result of any leak from the Governor's Office. Reagan had just walked up to the door and rung the doorbell. When the lady answered, he said, "Hello, I'm Ronald Reagan. Your husband asked me to get these flowers for you." The story got around the neighborhood and someone called the local paper. I am sure he never cashed the serviceman's check.

President he spent an awful lot of time reading and responding to letters that complete strangers had written to him. And all of his personal responses were hand-written and then given to his assistant for typing.

I once got a letter from a distant relative of mine in the state of Washington. She found out that I was working in the White House and wrote to me to tell me that as an elementary school principal she supported the President's call for bringing discipline back into schools. She included a package of material outlining what she was doing at her school to achieve the goal. I sent the package in to the President just to show him that the National Education Association (NEA, the teachers' union) didn't speak for all educators. He sent me back a note that said, "I just dropped your new found cousin a note. I hope you don't mind. I just wanted to commend her for what she's doing. …" Attached to the note was a copy of his handwritten draft to the principal.

Sometimes after reading someone's hard luck story, Reagan would take out his personal checkbook and write the individual a check. In one incident after he became President, he wrote a check to a woman who had written him with a hard luck story. She did not cash the check thinking that someday it would be worth a lot more than the face value. When Reagan found out that she hadn't cashed the check, he called her to urge her to do so. She told him that she wanted to save the check and he responded that if she would cash the check, he would send her another as a souvenir.

He was so interested in the mail at the White House, that Anne Higgins who headed up the Presidential Correspondence unit had to be careful which letters she selected for his review because she knew that some could elicit an over-caring response. Despite the nasty things his opponents would say about him being hard hearted or mean, Ronald Reagan was really a big softie.

He also liked to make phone calls to people. He really liked to call people and just cheer them up. When I learned that Paul Beck, one of his press secretaries in Sacramento was terminally ill, I mentioned it to the President one afternoon and he reached right over and placed a call to Paul. Similarly, when I found out that the Nobel Prize winning economist and a member of our President's Economic Policy Advisory Board, Milton Freidman, faced heart surgery, I alerted the President. Freidman had long been a favorite of his and Reagan promptly called him to wish a speedy recovery.

He always loved a good joke. He liked telling them and hearing them. He had friends in Hollywood, professionals who had professional joke writers, who would call or write and give him new material and he used it frequently. He would almost always open a formal meeting by telling some sort of a story. He liked good clean funny jokes but not "dirty" jokes. You could tell that he was uncomfortable when some staff member or visitor would tell a really off color joke to him. He might laugh a little, but only to be polite.

Reagan really loved jokes about the Soviet Union and communists. On one occasion, I think it was one of the Issue Lunches, he walked in and in a serious tone spoke to the Vice President, George H. W. Bush. He said, "George, I just got off the phone with Gorbachev. He said they have a problem and need our help." The Veep said, "Well what is it?" And with a straight face that would have made Bob Hope proud, the President said, "They have a serious shortage of condoms. I told him we would help. I told the fellas to order up ten thousand gross and send them to Moscow." Reagan paused while the Vice President's brow furrowed. "But I also told them I want each one 3 inches in diameter and 14 inches long. And I want them marked 'Medium.'"

Sometimes he would just surprise you with his down to earth common sense. During a lunch meeting with space scientists, the President listened intently. The briefing was about the probe that we had sent to Uranus several years earlier. Data was just now being collected. We heard sounds from outer space. It was fascinating. At the end of the presentation, the President thought for a moment and then asked: "In the past, growing up and in schools, we always pronounced it 'urAnus'

11

with a long A. Now you are pronouncing it 'UrInus.' Why?" A sheepish spokesman for the group admitted that the scientific community didn't think the network anchors would give it as much coverage if it was pronounced the old way! We got right to the crux of that issue.

He liked starting meetings with a little fun. One time my mother, Esther, the long-time Reagan political worker, sent me a little cloth doll with legs that were disproportionately long. It had been made by a friend of hers and was called a "Dammit Doll." The instructions said that when things weren't going your way, you take the doll by the legs and slam it on the table while yelling, "Dammit!" I gave one to Reagan just before we went into a Cabinet Meeting. He laughed at it and stuck it into a large file and we headed into the meeting. Without any prompting or preparation (other than reading the four lines of instruction attached to the doll) he started the meeting by asking a question of one of the Cabinet members. It was a question that he knew would elicit a disappointing negative answer. When he got the answer that he expected, he pulled out the doll by the ankles and started hammering it on the Cabinet table all the while yelling, "Dammit! Dammit! Dammit!"

I might add here that it was very unusual to hear Ronald Reagan swear and you almost never heard him utter a profanity. We used a lot of profanity at times around the White House but it did not come from Ronald Reagan. I have read some of my colleagues' accounts of discussions with Reagan in which they attribute certain epithets or foul language to the President; the accounts always sound more like the language used by the colleague rather than that used by Reagan. Even when writing notes in margins of correspondence, staff reports, or as we later learned in his own diary, Reagan would abbreviate what he felt were strong words rather than spell them out. We're not talking trash words here; we're talking "h- -l" for "hell" and "d- -n" for damn.

And I never heard him take the Lord's name in vain. Someone once told Nancy Reagan that the President had said "God Damn." She replied, "Ronnie never says God Damn." And when the pressure was on for him to get rid of Don Regan, it was reported in the media that he had told Nancy, "Get off my back, Goddamnit!" I would put a lot of money on that never having happened. It is just another occasion of someone trying to put words in his mouth.

He did have a temper, however. When he got really mad in a meeting, he might take his glasses off, toss them on the table and say, "Damn it." When he threw the glasses down, you knew he was mad. Or if someone really ticked him off, he might refer to them as "those bastards" or "SOBs," but that was about the extent of it. And even when he did say something he considered strong, you almost got the impression that he did it deliberately just so that you would understand that he really meant what he was saying.

I never heard him use the "F" word in any conversation. But I did hear him use it in telling a particular story. The first time I heard him tell the story was many years ago in California, but the second time he told me the story, it scared the hell out of me. We were standing together on West Executive Boulevard between the Old Executive Office Building (OEOB) and the West Wing of the White House. We had been in the OEOB to speak to a group in the beautiful Indian Treaty Room. The President and I were walking back to the Oval Office with the ever-present Secret Service detail. By this time, I was the only West Wing inhabitant who had been with him in California and he started reminiscing about those days. The story was about an encounter with a young woman on the street when he was Governor. It was a time of protest and as Governor he had had to order some very unpopular things for the University of California system.

As we stepped onto West Executive (which is really the parking lot for senior staff) he grabbed my arm and stopped. He started to retell the story; I knew what was coming and I tried to interrupt him, but he was into it and not about to stop. It was a story about a group of students who were demonstrating outside a Board of Regents meeting at one of the UC campuses. He said that one pretty young woman approached him "and she just stood there and screamed 'Fuck You! Fuck You! Fuck You!'" And I saw my whole life pass in front of me.

We were in public out in the open. The nasty White House press corps was usually set up on the North Lawn, no more than a hundred feet away. I visualized one of them with a directional microphone picking up the President as he stood there shouting, "Fuck you." The best headline I could hope for was "Reagan chews out staff guy." On the other hand, I could see a very big embarrassing episode on the horizon. Thankfully, it didn't happen. He finished the story. We continued on into the building and I accompanied him into the Oval Office. As I left the Oval, I said a little prayer to make that the last time I would hear that particular story.*

After I left the White House, I wrote him a note in 1987 after Nancy had cancer surgery. Among other things, I told him how much I missed the jokes. He wrote back and after thanking me for my thoughts, he wrote:

> "So you haven't heard a joke lately? Here's one the Russians are telling between themselves: A citizen in Moscow is walking down the street one evening. A Russian soldier calls, "Halt!" The man starts running. The soldier shoots him. Another man says, "Why did you do that?" The soldier, looking at his watch, says, "Curfew." The man says: "But it isn't curfew yet." The soldier says: "I know, but he's a friend of mine. I know where he lives; he couldn't have made it."

On another occasion, Jill and our two children, Kirsten and John, were visiting me in my office in the West Wing. It was Christmas time and the Residence was all decorated with the big tree in the Blue Room

---

* I know that in his autobiography, *An American Life*, Reagan related a similar story where a young woman came up to him during a demonstration outside the University of California at San Diego. He said the girl left the crowd of demonstrators and came over to him and told him that she liked everything that he was doing as Governor. And he said that he thought of her often but had never gotten her name. I don't know about that story. I only know the one he told me. Twice.

as was the practice. Congress was out of town and it was a Friday afternoon. Late in the day, after we had dropped by the Oval Office to have the kids' pictures taken with the President, I took them over to the Residence to see the tree and the rest of the decorations. As we were walking up the colonnade past the Rose Garden on our way back to the West Wing, the President came out of the Oval Office and headed toward the residence. He was by himself with just a small personal detail of Secret Service. As he approached, he was smiling. He had a rather large disk-shaped object in his hands and proffered it to Jill. There was a button on top of the disk and he said to her, "Push it! Go ahead push it!" Jill did as directed and tried to push the button. It turned out that the "button" was really a hologram and did not exist. The President howled with laughter at Jill's mistake. Jill, on the other hand said something like, "Oh you!" and hauled off and hit him on the bicep. The President, still laughing at having fooled her, continued on his way to the residence. I told Jill that she was very brave; to hit the President of the United States in full view of two armed secret service agents.

I think that one of the most telling traits that separated Ronald Reagan from all the politicians that I have known over the years was his judicious use of the pronoun "I." When talking about accomplishments he always uses "we" or "our" never "I" did this. The only time that he used "I" was when he was accepting responsibility for something unfortunate having happened. Most politicians do it the other way around, taking credit for anything good and quickly passing responsibility for anything bad to "they."

Much has been said and written about when Reagan actually contracted Alzheimer's disease and whether it affected him during his presidency. I never saw it. In a recent book, his son Ron wrote that he felt that it did and used the first debate with Walter Mondale as the example of Reagan's illness. He didn't do well in that debate, but it wasn't because of Alzheimer's. It was because he had been overtrained.

Today when I hear dyed-in-the-wool Reagan haters spitting venom as his reputation steadily becomes greater and greater, I just smile. Ronald Reagan fooled the Washington establishment and they resented it. He was a much different, deeper person than the conventional wisdom portrayed him. Because his detractors felt they were right, they consistently underestimated him. That was the key to his success. That and his determination to bring the country back and to provide opportunity to all Americans has made him one of the country's most beloved figures.

Chapter 2

The Beginning

I grew up in government. I was born in New London Connecticut during World War II. I am not a baby boomer. I got a three-year head start on that crowd. My father, Albert Russell Svahn, was a submariner in the United States Navy. He spent several years out in China on submarines in the Asiatic Fleet before the war. They didn't get to come home on leave in those days. When, at twenty-three, he did return home to Spokane Washington in 1941, he married my mother, Esther Marilou Caferro, an eighteen-year-old first generation Italian American. Two years later, on May 13, 1943, John A. Svahn was born. In 1946 my brother Robert Russell (Bob) was born and six years later, Richard Gustaf (Gus) rounded out our family.

I was named after my grandfather, John A. (Jack) Svahn who emigrated from Sweden in 1901. My grandfather had been a member of the Swedish King's guard when he left there to find his fortune and fame in Montana. In 1908, he moved to Washington state having found farming a better prospect than bumming around western Montana.

Our family moved a lot when I was growing up. By the time I got out of high school, I had attended eight schools—and I skipped the second grade. I graduated from Radford High School in Hawaii. Hawaii was a great place to be at that time. Most people still came there by ship. Jet airplanes were just beginning to transport people to the islands. It was a laid back idyllic place. Nothing to do but go to school, go surfing, go sailing, or go camping. We didn't drink, smoke, or do drugs. The islands were nothing like they are today. Even on Oahu, where I lived, most of the island was either sugar cane or pineapple fields. Today, most of the island is condominiums.

We left Hawaii in the summer of 1960 on the Matson Lines ship, *Matsonia*. I had selected the University of Washington as my school and when we got to San Diego, I got on a bus and headed north to Seattle. What a shock for a pigeon-speaking hapa-hoale from Hawaii. I had long hair, aloha shirts, and bell-bottom pants. All of the male students at the UW had short hair, pegged pants, and button-down shirts.

That fall John F. Kennedy was elected President. He went by the nickname, Jack. I had been called Jack by my parents up until I was nine years old. Just back from Africa and attending a U.S. school for the first time, I found myself in a class with four "Jacks." Now four jacks is a good poker hand, but the teacher didn't want that many and I volunteered that my "real" name was John. For the next fourteen years, I was John. I don't think that my mother ever forgave me for the change. For the last forty-four years I have been Jack Svahn. As a sign of the times, it seems that most people today have forgotten that Jack is a nickname for John. People seem to know Bob is for Robert and Bill is for William, but Jack for John is slowly being lost.

In 1983, President Reagan nominated me as Under Secretary of the U.S. Department of Health and Human Services. (Much more about this later.) At the time, the Under Secretary was the sole deputy of the Department and the position required Senate confirmation. I had been through the conformation process in 1981 so I wasn't concerned. As part of the process, a nominee is expected to make "courtesy calls" on Senators who are members of the confirming committee. Courtesy calls are on the surface an opportunity for you to meet one on one with the Senators and get to know them and them to know you. In reality, they are an opportunity for Senators to quiz you on their pet projects and extract promises from you for the future without going through the process in public session.

I was going up before the Committee on Finance. I was currently the Commissioner of Social Security and had been before Finance on many occasions. I knew the members quite well. During my courtesy call with Max Baucus, the Democrat from Montana, Max told me that he was having a series of town hall meetings in Montana on Social Security. He asked me if I could send a senior SSA person out to Montana to do them with him. I sent my Deputy Commissioner, Paul Simmons. I have forgotten how many town halls Paul did with Max but I know there were several.

After my confirmation hearing, the Senate Finance committee voted to move my nomination to the floor. Max voted against me. I called him up and asked why he had done that. He said he hadn't. But I said that I'd been told that he did. After checking, he called me back and apologized; he said another Senator had asked him to vote no on John Svahn and he didn't realize that this John was Jack Svahn. He voted for me on the floor. I learned a lesson: now I use "John A. (Jack) Svahn."

It took me six years to get an undergraduate degree. Some of the delay was caused by my working and going to night school for a while. Much of it was caused by partying, growing up, skiing, and the 1962 World's Fair in Seattle. During those years, the Vietnam war developed into almost a full-time obsession with a lot of people on campus. I had a 1Y student deferment and didn't really get concerned about it.

In 1964 the Selective Service Administration announced that married men would be exempted from the draft. I was engaged to Jo Marie Burns, a naturalized U.S. citizen from England whose father had been a Czech RAF pilot killed in World War II, and my mother wanted us to elope to Reno and get married immediately. We didn't. We got married in 1965, my last "senior year."

As graduation approached I got a letter from the Selective Service Administration telling me to show up for a draft physical. I was going to be drafted, and being drafted in 1966 was a sure ticket to Vietnam. I didn't take the letter personally; a lot of people were getting draft notices at the time. I lost my student deferment when I graduated. I was now 1A, a classification that made you immediately eligible for the draft.

I did what every red blooded American student facing the draft did: I looked for an alternative way to do my service. I wasn't going to go to Canada or England but I really wasn't interested in going to Vietnam. I have always believed that if the government gives you a legitimate option, you are perfectly justified in exercising that option. If the government tells you that fingernail clippers are tax deductible, take the deduction; don't avoid it just because you don't think it is right. Later when I was with the state of California, Governor Ronald Reagan would give speeches railing against the excesses of federal government spending. But when he came back to Sacramento he would always say, "Make sure we get our fair share fellas!"

Approaching graduation, I looked for a position with the National Guard or the reserves or some other entity. I didn't want to go in the Army and I knew what the Navy was like since I grew up in it. And I knew that Navy service at the time almost assuredly meant six-month tours in Westpac on a ship standing watch around the clock. No, I decided that if I had to go to war I was going to do it day by day. Get up, fly a mission, come home, go over to the Officers Club for a few beers, sleep between sheets and then get up and do it all over again. I was going to join the Air Force. At the time the Air Force was only accepting volunteers who could fly either as pilots or navigators. I took all the tests and the powers that be decided that I should become a navigator.

In 1966 I graduated with a Bachelor of Arts degree in political science in June, door belled for Ronald Reagan in the fall, and was sworn into the United States Air Force in November as an Airman

Basic headed for Officer Training School (OTS) in San Antonio, Texas. Ninety some days later I was a Distinguished Graduate of OTS and commissioned a Second Lieutenant. I had orders to Navigator School at Mather AFB in Sacramento California.

My military career was short. It wasn't because I wasn't doing well, it was because I had flat feet. I got grounded, or, as the USAF calls it, Duties Not Involving Flying (DNIF). The flight surgeon explained to me that the USAF had a regulation that required flight personnel to be able to fly anywhere in the world. Another regulation said that if you flew in South East Asia, you had to wear a particular type of flight boot. It had a steel shank in it to protect you from pungi stakes in the event you were shot down and had to walk out. And since I was headed for Southeast Asia, this regulation was definitely relevant. I appealed the decision and after a lengthy appeals process, I was permanently grounded and offered a choice of non-flying assignments or discharge. It wasn't a tough choice for me and shortly thereafter, I was honorably discharged from the Air Force with a disability—EPTS (Existed Prior to Service).

It was 1968 and I was unemployed in Sacramento as a civilian for the first time. Married, but with no children, my first priority was to find a job. Now in 1968, Sacramento had just undergone the melt-down of the aerospace industry and the biggest employer in the rather sleepy valley town was the state of California. I went downtown to the State Personnel Board to see what jobs might be available. The staff told me that the entry level professional level was classified "Administrative Trainee" and that there were very few positions and that the competition was ferocious. They did not encourage me but allowed me to take the written examination to see if I might be qualified. I took the test and apparently scored pretty high because the staff started setting up appointments for me that afternoon.

You didn't make much as a Second Lieutenant in the sixties, but with a quarters allowance, subsistence, and flight pay I was able to pay all the bills. Without any of it, I was going into debt pretty quickly so finding a job was priority number one. The first interview that I had was with James D. Lothrop, the training officer for the Division of Highways. Jim and I hit it off pretty well and he offered me a job in the training department. I knew nothing about training but figured that I could learn.

The training office was fairly small, with about six or eight professionals. I was getting some instruction from one of the more senior trainers, Carl B. Williams. Carl was a very bright guy, originally from New York but definitely into the California lifestyle at this time. Unfortunately, shortly after we began working together, Carl left Highways to take a temporary assignment on a USAID project in East Pakistan.

I was then assigned to another training officer and that is when the trouble began. My new supervisor was a bureaucrat. You could set your watch by the time he reached for his coat to leave for the day. Official quitting time was 4:15 PM. This guy hit the crossbar on the door to the street at 4:14 and 30 seconds. I also noticed that productivity on my supervisor's part was, to put it mildly, minimal. I couldn't figure out what he did. I sometimes didn't leave the office right on time. I'm not talking all-nighters or the hours I later kept when working in the White House. But if I hadn't finished the tasks that I was working on, I would stay a few minutes, rarely more than a half an hour, to finish up. My supervisor did not like this and told me so. He said that it was bad for office morale for me not to leave on time. Needless to say, we did not get along.

This went on for several months. I was still an Administrative Trainee, but was scheduled for promotion at the end of my six-month probationary period to become a Junior Staff Analyst. One day one of the ladies in the small typing pool (we're talking manual typewriters here) stuck her head into my area and said that she was going to lunch and she hadn't finished an assignment. She suggested that I might be interested in what she was working on; it was in her typewriter. I don't remember her name, but I guess the credit for my entire career in government both with the state of California and with the federal government goes to that lady. Many thanks.

In her typewriter was a notice of termination. My termination. Since I was still on probation, I could be terminated without cause and that was what my supervisor had in mind. What he didn't count on was that I wasn't going to take it sitting down. By the time he returned from lunch and before he had a chance to finalize his letter I had filed a bunch of grievances against him with his supervisor, Jim Lothrop. That stopped the termination right in its tracks. But it caused some other problems—for Lothrop. He recognized that I was probably correct in many of my allegations but trying to fire someone in the government is difficult under any circumstances and impossible at the level that Jim held. There were just too many people above him who would try to "solve" the problem.

Jim did what any good bureaucrat would do; he bucked it upstairs to his boss, Richard T. Soderberg. Dick called me in and tried to calm things down. I was having none of it. I told him in no uncertain terms that there was a lot of goofing off going on; that productivity was way down and that we were wasting a lot of taxpayers' money. Dick said that I sounded like a member of the Reagan Administration. Waste, fraud, and abuse. Dick said that he was being promoted to Assistant Director of our parent agency, the Department of Public Works. And he suggested that when that happened he would like me to move to the Director's office as a Special Assistant doing "special projects." It sounded good to me.

For the next year, I worked in the Director's office doing all kinds of things that Dick and Deputy Director John F. (Jack) Maloney dreamed up for me. In the meantime, Carl Williams came back from Pakistan and was assigned to the Director's office to work with me.

One of the reasons that my wife and I decided to stay in Sacramento after I was discharged from the Air Force was that I wanted to go to law school and Sacramento had a well-respected part-time night law school. I thought that I could work during the day and study law at McGeorge School of Law in the evening. In March of 1969, I entered law school. I found law school to be challenging while at the same time it seemed to fit like an old shoe. At the end of the first quarter, I found that I was number one in my class. I was offered an academic scholarship. I was already on the GI Bill, so the combination of the two eased the economic situation substantially. Going to law school at night and with a fun day job, life was pretty good. But I was still learning about bureaucracy.

Like most states, California had an employee suggestion program. You see something that would improve government and save money; you submit it as a suggestion and if it is accepted and saves money, you get a monetary award. California had such a program and I frequently submitted suggestions to save money.

At that time, all state cars had a large circular seal on the two front doors. The purpose of the seal was to identify the vehicle as an official vehicle and hopefully deter state employees from using the vehicle for personal purposes. When the cars were sold the seal had to be removed, leaving a large round circle of discoloration on the doors. The cost of removing the seal was fairly substantial in those days, but the real cost was in the decrease in car value due to the discoloration. I made the simple suggestion that they use a decal on the windows. The theory being that the combination of the decal and the state license plate would serve the purpose of identifying the vehicle as a state vehicle and removal of the decal would be a lot more efficacious than removing the seals on the doors.

Usually, my suggestions were summarily dismissed but this time there was a delay. Eventually, I received a notice, suitably cloaked in bureaucratic jargon, that the suggestion was not accepted. I couldn't understand it and tried to appeal to the department's common sense. No dice.

Now, it turned out that the suggestion program had a "statute of limitations" associated with it. Two years. Yup, after two years, the Department came up with a great way to save money—decals. Today every car in the state of California inventory has decals on the windows identifying it as a state vehicle and not for personal use. And I didn't get a dime out of it.

I have done a lot of things without making a dime. Ronald Reagan always had a plaque on his desk. We called it Reagan's law: "There is no limit to what a man can do or where he can go if he doesn't mind who gets the credit." Through the years I developed Svahn's Corollary to Reagan's Law: "There is **absolutely** no limit to what a man can do or where he can go as long as he's not worried about getting paid for it."

As an example, about the time I left the White House, the California voters passed Proposition 65. Prop 65, as it is called, requires the Governor of California to assess the levels of carcinogens in all products sold in California and, where cancer-causing agents are found to exist, notify the public that such and such is present and is a known carcinogen.

Proposition 65 caused quite a bit of confusion when it first passed. I had done a few speeches for the Grocery Manufacturers Association and its President, George Koch, asked me to come over to talk with their senior staff regarding Prop 65. The GMA's concern was the broad nature of the requirement and the fact that their members, unlike the auto industry, didn't make product solely for sale in the state of California. Added to their concern was that many products that their Association members sell contained known carcinogens naturally. As a specific example, they cited broccoli, which in its natural state, contains arsenic, a known carcinogen. (This may explain why George H. W. Bush dislikes it so.) The GMA was concerned about having to label all kinds of products as California declared them to contain known carcinogens.

I had reviewed Proposition 65 and had talked to a former colleague of mine, Dave Swoap, who was then California's Secretary of Health and Welfare and charged with the implementing Prop 65. I concluded that it was such a complex mess that GMA ought to comply with the letter of the law. My suggestion was that they advise grocery stores to place a sign on their doors that read something like, "The state of California has determined that some products sold or consumed in this establishment have been known to cause cancer."

The staff of the GMA was not impressed and of course the lawyers weren't sure that a notice like that would meet the requirement, etc. I was politely thanked and escorted to the door. I could tell they didn't think much of my solution even though it literally met the requirements of the law. They were certain that Proposition 65 was going to require that each piece of broccoli was going to have to be individually labeled. And these were highly paid, well-educated Washington, D.C., executives.

Today, you can go into most any grocery, corner store, bar, or restaurant in California and see a little sign very similar to the one I recommended. Sometimes you have to look for it, but it's there. Proposition 65 requires it.

Meanwhile, I was happily working on special projects for Deputy Director Jack Maloney in the California Department of Public Works, learning how the bureaucracy works, and going to law school at night. That is up until August of 1970. That is when my world began to change.

Chapter 3

Welfare? I think that I know how to spell it.

By the summer of 1970, I had been with the state for over two years. The attempt to terminate me during probation was a dim memory. I had received several promotions, liked the people that I was working with, and was feeling pretty good about myself. I was on vacation in August of that year when I got a call from my office. I was told that I had to come in the next day for an important meeting. I asked what it was all about and the secretary in the office, Barbara Hartsfield, said she didn't know but that I was needed. Now, normally people on vacation would balk about breaking it up, particularly relatively low-level bureaucrats. But I was painting the outside of the house and figured that I could use a day off of that job even if it entailed putting on a suit and going into the office.

When I got to work I was summoned to the office of Robert B. Carleson, the Chief Deputy Director of Public Works. Bob Carleson had been a city manager in a number of cities in Southern California before joining the Department of Public Works. He was a graduate of the University of Southern California and had done a stint in the U.S. Navy after college. His father had been Mayor of Long Beach and once he was out of the service, Bob just gravitated to public service naturally.

I didn't know Bob other than to say hello to him in the hall. He had done a lot of the legislative work for the department and that was an area to which I had not been exposed. The third person in the office that day was a young lawyer from the Division of Highways Right of Way Department, Ronald Zumbrun. I had never met Ron before, but was quickly intrigued by his wit and obvious intelligence. Bob asked us what we knew about welfare and in my usual engage-mouth-before-thinking, I said, "I think I can spell it." What a dumb beginning to a chapter in my life that would last almost two decades and would be the issue that would catapult Ronald Reagan onto the national stage and into the White House.

Now welfare was not a new topic for Ronald Reagan. In fact, many times over the years I heard him talk of the welfare problem. With Reagan, whether he was talking about taxes, education, trade, or welfare, he often used his own experiences as a framework for discussion. When welfare was the subject, he would tell about the Depression when his father, Jack Reagan, was running a WPA project in Illinois. In the case of welfare, Reagan felt that most people didn't want to rely on it. He based this conclusion on the fact that during the depression, men would seek out his father to get WPA work rather than rely on the dole. Ronald Reagan believed that it was government's failure that caused the welfare problem in this country.

In "The Speech," Reagan went after welfare saying, "Federal welfare spending is today ten times greater than it was in the dark depths of the Depression." He went on to say that the 20 percent of American families that were below the government defined poverty level could be raised out of poverty just by prorating the amount of government welfare spending. The poverty level in 1964 was $3,000 per year per family. Reagan said, "If this present welfare spending was prorated equally among these poverty-stricken families, we could give each family more than $4,500 a year." Noting that welfare averaged less than

$600 per family, Reagan in a classic understatement said, "There must be some administrative overhead somewhere."*

And when he was running for Governor, he spoke out against the welfare system, even when his advisors were cautioning that the subject was taboo. In his Inaugural speech on January 5, 1967, Governor Reagan referred to welfare as "another of our major problems" and directed his new health and welfare chief to see how much public sector work could be done by welfare recipients. His goal he said was simply to substitute a paycheck for a dole check.

One of the things that dogged Reagan throughout his public career was a myth that he did not work hard. Nothing could be further from the truth. But one of the contributing factors to that myth was the "issue paper" that was used in California. When I joined the Public Works Director's office, I worked on some issue papers. Essentially, anything that went to the Governor had to be condensed to a one-page paper with the issue properly formed, a discussion stating the pros and cons, and a recommendation made.

Most first drafts of an issue paper would be sent back from the Agency Secretary's Office for rewriting, either for format or because it was not an objective piece. Department Directors tried to use the issue papers as advocacy documents. The Governor's Office didn't like that. But it was darned difficult to reduce a complex public policy issue to one page. In drafting an issue paper for the Governor, you used all kinds of tricks—margins, punctuation, and grammar. But they would get returned to you if they weren't in the proper format and if they weren't on *one* page. The bureaucrats in Sacramento used the is-

---

* Dave Stockman, Reagan's first Director of OMB, must have heard the speech also, because frequently during budget debates in the White House, Dave would bring a complex economic and political issue down to terms that a common man could understand. For example, in arguing for an end to Amtrak subsidies in late 1984, Stockman cited statistics that showed that for what the government spent on subsidizing the Chicago to Florida route, it could buy every passenger a first class airline ticket and still save money.

sue paper as an example of Reagan's perceived limited grasp of issues. I don't know who dreamed up the one page issue memo for the Reagan administration but I am fairly certain that it wasn't Ronald Reagan. He was a voracious reader.

During 1970, a reporter for the Reagan administration-friendly *Sacramento Union*, K. W. Lee, was doing a series of stories in the paper about the abuses and failures of the welfare system in California. K. W., as he was known, was of Korean ancestry, and he once told me that toward the end of World War II, he had been trained by the Japanese as a kamikaze pilot. I don't know whether he was pulling my leg or not, but I can tell you that when he got on a story he drove it like a kamikaze. And that is what he was doing with the welfare story in 1970. The welfare stories that Lee wrote were factual but with a flair that would have made the *National Enquirer* envious. They told of abuses in the system and of the failure of governments, both state and local to clean up the system.

The major welfare program in California was Aid to Families with Dependent Children (AFDC). AFDC had its origins in the Social Security Act of 1935 when it was a program designed to keep widows and orphans from becoming destitute. By 1970 it had come a long way from its original design. AFDC was primarily for single parent families, the vast majority of which were female-headed households. There was an ancillary program entitled Aid to Families with Children—Unemployed Parent (AFDC-U). This was for two parent families where one or both parents were unemployed or underemployed. The Aged, Blind and Disabled programs made up the rest of the welfare system. In 1970 over 15 percent of the population of California was on welfare.

The real problems were in the AFDC and AFDC-U programs. The caseloads were rising at a dramatic rate. During Reagan's first term the AFDC caseload went from approximately 770,000 to 1,550,000. And by the time he was re-elected in 1970 it was growing by an astounding

20,000 to 40,000 cases a month. And the amount that California was paying to welfare recipients was woefully inadequate. The grants had been set in the late '50s and hadn't been increased during Governor Pat Brown's tenure or during Reagan's first term.

In all the years that I knew Reagan, he was always clipping articles out of news media and storing them away for future use. He had files full. He clipped *Fortune*, *Forbes*, and the *Reader's Digest*, almost anything he read. One of his favorites was *Human Events*. In the White House, he had two copies of *Human Events* delivered each week, one for reading and one for clipping. He could remember stuff that he had in those files years later. And he would use them. In 1970, he was clipping the welfare articles by K. W. Lee.

On August 4, 1970, after finally becoming fed up with his administration's inability to get its hands around the welfare problem, Ronald Reagan sent a memo to his cabinet and senior staff with the subject line entitled "The Number One Priority." In that memo, he directed a major team effort of the administration to study the welfare and education programs for the state. Turning to the successful "Businessman's Task Force" model that he used in 1967, Reagan said in the memo that he would "ask proven leaders in business, labor, industry, local government and state government to volunteer" to conduct the study. He said, "This study will place heavy emphasis on the taxpayer as opposed to the taxtaker; on the truly needy as opposed to the lazy employable; on the student as opposed to educational frills; on basic needs as opposed to unmanageable enrichment programs; on measurable results …"

He directed that the Task Force make recommendations by January 1971 and that they include actions that could be taken by the Executive Branch, the Legislative branch, the federal government, and local government. He summed up his directive by saying:

"I am determined to reduce these programs to essential services at a cost the taxpayers can afford to pay. This is our NUMBER ONE priority. We must bring all our resources to bear on this endeavor. Therefore, I am asking you to make available your best employees including directors (department directors) for this all-out war on the taxtaker. If we fail, no one again will be able to try. We must succeed." He signed it "Ron."

As Governor, he often signed letters and photos to senior people and friends as Ron. He didn't do it as often when he was President. In the twenty years that I worked with him, I never heard any of the cabinet or senior staff call him Ron. It was always Governor or Mr. President. Of course, Nancy Reagan always referred to him Ronnie and it was sometimes a shock to hear some old friend from Hollywood call him Ron or Ronnie. I recall one time in June of 1985 I was taking Armand Hammer, the chairman of Occidental Petroleum into an Oval Office meeting with the President. Hammer was Chairman of the President's Cancer Panel and had been personally funding some cancer research through the National Cancer Institute.

The meeting was ostensibly to report on the panel and to tell the President about some new research. It was a little touchy because Hammer had been to the Soviet Union and met with the new leader Mikhail Gorbachev. Bud McFarlane, the National Security Advisor, cautioned me to keep the meeting about cancer research not foreign policy. I talked to Armand in a pre-meeting and he assured me that he would stick to the domestic agenda. When I opened the door to escort him into the Oval Office, Armand hit the carpet running: "Ronnie, I met the new guy Gorbachev …" I don't know whether I was more shocked that Hammer immediately broke our agreement not to discuss Gorbachev or by the fact that he called the President "Ronnie."

I don't know what happened to the education study that the Governor wanted in 1970, but over the next three years, I played a role in implementing the initiative that he laid out in that August 4 memo.

In those three years, we were engaged in Reagan's "all-out war" with the media, the Legislature, the welfare industry, and the liberal poverty lawyers. In the end, the effort resulted in what became known as "welfare reform."

During the original meeting with Carleson, he explained to Zumbrun and me that the Governor was setting up a Task Force on welfare reform and that he wanted us to be on it. Our group of three, Carleson, Zumbrun and me, was to study the state aspects of the program and make recommendations to clean up the system. Because it was an election year and the Governor was running for re-election, the study was to be done as quietly as possible—that meant no leaks. Further, Reagan specifically wanted people who knew nothing about welfare to take a fresh look at it. I knew that we fit that bill. Carleson told us that he saw no upside in participating. He called it a "suicide mission." Ron and I said, "we're in."

The group's official designation was the Governor's Task Force on Public Assistance. It was headed by Ned Hutchinson, the Governor's Appointments Secretary. Ned had been one of the "loaned executives" who worked on the Governor's original Businessman's Task Force. After the recommendations were made, Hutchinson stayed on in Sacramento to monitor implementation statewide. I had met him in this capacity since I was doing the monitoring for the Department of Public Works. There were three other members of the Task Force that were named by the Governor: Bob Carleson, Chief Deputy Director of Public Works, Jerry Fielder, Director of Agriculture, and John Mayfield, Deputy Director of the Department of Conservation. Since the welfare program in California is a state supervised, county administered system, the Task Force decided to split up the work, with Carleson taking the state aspects (which presumably the Governor would have some control over) Fielder would review the federal aspects of the program and Mayfield would look at county administration. Hutchinson decided that we needed a legal component to the group and he recruited Los Angeles super lawyer to the stars, Neil Papiano, for that effort.

Each of the principals in the Task Force was to recruit a staff person or two to assist them. That's how Zumbrun and I wound up working with Carleson. The other principals went outside state government with Mayfield getting M. E. "Gene" Youngreen, a management consultant from Southern California and Fielder recruiting Walter Rountree a Los Angeles attorney. For his legal review, Papiano drafted Jules Markowitz and Jerry Salzman both from Los Angeles as well as Richard Moore, another LA attorney.

I once asked Bob Carleson why I was singled out for the Task Force. I was only twenty-seven, had limited professional experience, and neither he nor the Governor knew me. He said that I had been highly recommended by Jack Maloney, the Deputy Director of Public Works, as a guy who could get things done in the bureaucracy and besides, he said, I met the primary qualification: I had already proved that I knew nothing about welfare.

Ron and I left our respective offices and set up shop in a little room on the first floor of the Public Works building. We had locks installed on the door and file cabinets. We weren't going to be the source of any leaks. We began to collect material on welfare in California. We got copies of the Welfare and Institutions Code and copies of the state regulations. We set up meetings with people in the State Department of Social Welfare (SDSW) and related agencies. At SDSW, the then Director, Robert Martin was not overly cooperative. I don't think that he liked the Governor's idea of having people with no experience looking at why his programs were in such a mess. One individual who was very helpful was Charles D. Hobbs, the Chief Deputy Director of Social Welfare.

Chuck Hobbs had been recruited for that job out of the aerospace industry. I never did understand why Reagan reached out and brought an ex Air Force officer from Alabama to Sacramento to help run welfare but Chuck was able to quickly orient Ron and me and point out some of the more egregious results of the states' administration of AFDC.

Bob, Ron, and I concluded early on that we needed to see what actually happened at the working level. California's AFDC program was administered at the local level by the fifty-eight counties. Each county had its own welfare department, the director of which reported to the County Board of Supervisors. Each Board was comprised of five Supervisors elected by the people.

Mayfield's group was conducting extensive interviews at the county level but their interviews were designed to get input from the counties (usually in the form of complaints about what the state was or was not doing) and build a little good will with county employees. Mayfield, Hutchinson, and Youngreen conducted 768 interviews of county employees.

The survey consisted of forty questions asked of each employee. Interestingly enough, the higher the level of county employee interviewed, the more likely he or she was to say that the state caused the problem and that SDSW needed streamlining and reorganizing. One astounding fact came out in response to the question "In your opinion, what should be the objective of the public assistance program?" Only 3.4 percent of the respondents answered, "Break the welfare cycle."

Carleson asked me to attend a meeting of the county welfare directors to just observe. He figured that a baby-faced twenty-seven-year-old wouldn't draw too much attention and he wanted to gauge the tenor of the county directors. Bob Martin, SDSW Director made an appearance and the audience tore him apart. There didn't seem to be anyone at that meeting who supported the State. It was close to anarchy.

At the same time, as a result of questions that we were asking around SDSW, the Department decided that they needed to get in front of this parade and they requested that an audit of the eligibility process be undertaken at the county level. Essentially, our interviews had raised enough questions that Hobbs and Martin felt that they needed to see if what we said could be happening actually was.

Hutchinson and Carleson discussed the request and it was decided that the audit would be conducted by the Department of Finance Audit Division rather than by the Governor's Public Assistance Task Force. It was rightly assumed that the Audit Division would raise fewer hackles wandering around the county offices than would a Governor's Task Force. But to ensure that we got the information that we needed we decided that I should join the audit team, "undercover" so to speak. Fortunately, the fellow assigned to head the audit, Ken Wagstaff, was amenable to having me tag along and was willing to give me the cover needed if he was asked.

The few days I spent in the counties with the Finance audit team were a real eye opener. I concluded really quickly that none of us on this project knew anything about how the welfare program was being run in California. The offices were crowded beyond belief; necessary paperwork was left undone; workers didn't seem to care about doing their jobs and management blamed it all on the State. The majority of county directors, most of the state bureaucracy and for that matter, most states were looking for the federal government to step in and run the whole system. Nixon, at the urging of his domestic policy advisor, Daniel Patrick Moynihan had been pushing the Family Assistance Plan. FAP as it was known was to be the be-all-end all for the welfare system, a guaranteed annual income for all Americans. As a consequence, the county personnel were less than enthusiastic about Governor Reagan looking to reform welfare. I had a lot to report when I returned to Sacramento.

Our next thrust was to review the regulations issued by the SDSW. Being the junior guys on the team, that task fell to Ron and me. We spent weeks cooped up in that little room looking at the mish-mash that SDSW used to manage the counties. That review became another eye opener. Everywhere we turned we were amazed at the complexity and the absurdity of the program in California. Years later, when someone asked how we made the big dent in the program that we did, Bob Carleson allowed that it was easy (in retrospect) because California's program was so far out of control that we couldn't have failed. And it was.

In November, it became apparent to us that if we were ever going to get a unified direction out of the Task Force that some more changes had to be made. Like so many "volunteer" efforts, there has to be some nucleus around which the rest of the group's ideas can attach. In layman's terms, someone has to do the work. Carleson talked to Hutchinson and it was decided that Zumbrun and I under Carleson's direction should re-focus on reforms in legislation, administrative matters and regulatory acts that could be done at the state level. They wanted us to start coming up with recommendations.

In late November the entire Task Force met in Los Angeles at a hotel. The purpose of the meeting was to review what had been done and to formulate recommendations for the Governor. Unfortunately, the welfare rolls were continuing to skyrocket and the Director of Finance, Verne Orr, desperately needed initiatives to put in the Governor's Budget to be sent to the Legislature. Verne was looking to this group to come up with the solution. There was quite a bit of posturing during this meeting as the egos in the room were formidable. Being by far the youngest and lowest level person in the room, I kept my head down. I did learn one lesson from that meeting however. It was a working session and when it came time for lunch, someone suggested ordering from room service. Well, I was a low level state bureaucrat on $25 per diem and when it came time for me to order, I ordered a tuna sandwich. I remember that Neil Papiano ordered the steak sandwich and wine was ordered by several attendees. When the bill came, Papiano offered to pay but Chairman Ned Hutchinson said that since he and the others had volunteered their time that lunch was on the State people. It was the most expensive tuna sandwich I ever had.

The election was over and the Governor was reelected. But around the Capitol, politics with a small "p" was still in play. The Human Relations Agency and the SDSW were concerned about what our Task Force was going to recommend. In an effort to get on the train before it left town, the SDSW had formed an intradepartmental group to review their regulations to make recommendations for change. They came up with their recommendations just as the Task Force was completing its work. The Department of Finance wanted immediate recommendations to put in the Governor's budget and there was a lot of hum going around in the State Capitol about welfare reform

It was time for the Governor's Task Force on Public Assistance to complete its work and issue a report. The job of drafting the report fell to a Special Assistant in the Governor's office. His name was Thomas P. McMurray.

Tom was a really hard working and bright individual. He was an early Reagan supporter from Illinois. In fact, on the wall in his office, he had a handwritten letter from Ronald Reagan. As a young man in Illinois, Tom had seen "The Speech" and had heard later that Reagan was going to run for Governor. Tom wrote him and told him that if he did run, Tom would come to California to help. The letter on Tom's wall from Reagan thanked him for his offer and said that he had no intentions of running for political office, but that if he ever did, he would contact Tom for help. When Reagan decided to run, he contacted Tom.

McMurray had not been a part of the Task Force but he had been following the situation closely. Bob, Ron, and I brought him up to speed quickly. Ron and I were designated to work with Tom on the drafting of the report. The three of us worked day and night during December to get the report finished. Since he was from the Governor's Office, Tom was looked at as an honest broker because by this time, there were a lot of folks in Sacramento who were concerned about having their ox gored. Little did they know that Tom was working with Jim Hall, the Secretary of Business and Transportation, and the three of us. He was another "true believer." The final report was dated December 1970.* The report was given to the Governor and the Cabinet on January 1, 1971. We weren't sure where we would go from here. We thought maybe that our job was done.

---

* Tom McMurray died on September 11, 1980, after heart surgery at Johns Hopkins University Hospital in Baltimore, Maryland. He was forty years old. He did not live to see Ronald Reagan elected President.

Chapter 4

The Blue Book

Governor Reagan liked the report of the Governor's Task Force on Public Assistance. But even more, he liked the guys who put it together. So much so that he decided that they should be the ones to implement the findings.

At the end of the year, Reagan appointed the sitting Secretary of Business and Transportation, James M. Hall to be the new Secretary of Human Relations. Hall was an attorney from San Diego.[*] Jim kept the Secretary's office small, believing that the Department Director and his team was the pointy end of the spear. He proved to be an excellent strategist, sounding board, and coach for our team. But just as important, Jim was an effective "expediter" and "protector" for us within the administration and with the Governor.

For staff, Jim recruited Tom McMurray, our Task Force editor from the Governor's Office. With press officer Alex Cunningham, a career Highways employee from San Diego, the office started with just three

---

[*] Jim had originally been recruited to the administration as the Superintendent of Banks. He later moved to be Secretary of Business and Transportation. He said he was referred to in both positions as the SOB. When he became the Secretary of Human Relations, he thought that he would lose the moniker. Then he found out that his new office address was State Office Building One—and he became the No. 1 SOB.

principals. Later Hall added Clyde Walthall to the staff to do legislative liaison.

The Governor at the same time appointed Bob Carleson to be the Director of the Department of Social Welfare, Ron Zumbrun to be the Deputy Director, and me to be the Assistant Director.

Bob decided to keep Chuck Hobbs on as a Deputy Director as he had been quite helpful to the Task Force, and he had a very good grasp of the department and its budget. We recruited our assistants from the Department of Public Works also. Marilyn Caruthers was Bob's and Barbara Hartsfield, who had worked in Jack Maloney's office, came over as mine. Our last recruit from Public Works was Carl Williams. Carl had been in Highways with me when I started in state service. Carl was always looking for a project and he and I worked well together.

When I talked to Bob about bringing Carl with us he was a little concerned. He said that he didn't know Carl very well but his impression was that if you told Carl to get rid of someone, he might. He was joking of course, but Carl was a very focused guy. I assured him that Carl would be fine and we brought Carl with us to work with me. There we were—six people from Public Works—charged with "fixing" California's 2.3 billion dollar welfare problem. There was a lot of snickering going on in Sacramento and throughout the whole welfare industry about the "highways" people running welfare.

Our initial task was to develop a reform program. The Task Force study was a good start, but it was not a detailed blueprint for how to proceed. We knew that we needed to change regulations, get legislation, recruit, and reorganize; but we didn't have the full coherent plan for doing so. So our first major task was to put together a comprehensive program that would accomplish true welfare reform.

Carleson sent Zumbrun and me over to SDSW as an advance team. Hobbs cleared out the director's office suite of its current occupants and we began to change the culture of the department. Someone once said when taking over a large operation that the order of action was "first do no damage." In most cases I have found this to be good advice, but at SDSW, doing nothing would have allowed the damage to continue. So while we started developing a formalized blueprint for reform, we also took immediate actions to prevent the agency from creating more problems. Among the actions that we took in the first thirty days:

- Froze all proposed regulations
- Revised the regulations processing system
- Froze all hiring in the Department
- Requested a lay off list from the State Personnel Board
- Eliminated all mailing of draft reports, data, and regulations to HEW
- Canceled all media appearances of Department staff
- Relieved all of the career executives in the Department of their responsibilities
- Began the process of moving all professional social workers into social work positions as opposed to other management positions
- Prepared a list of management personnel who were near retirement so that we could plan for vacancies
- Arranged for the Department of Finance Audit Division to do an Administrative Cost Review
- Began plans for a reorganization of the Department
- Conducted a security sweep of the Director's Suite and telephones

I was assigned the responsibility for revising the regulatory issuance process and reviewing all regulations that were already scheduled to go out. Bob gave this assignment to me because I had spent the most time on reviewing the current regulations during the Task Force Study. I got Carl Williams working on the issuance process and we concluded that we needed a special group to handle regulations writing and began to recruit people for this task.

Carl had worked with a fellow at the Department of Water Resources during his Pakistan assignment. His name was Bill Montgomery. We brought Bill over and tried to convince him that coming to SDSW was a good deal and would be good for his career. It was a hard sell. SDSW was looked upon in state government as a less than desirable assignment. I don't know how we did it, but we convinced Montgomery to take on the role as Chief of our regulations writing group. As Carleson reported to Jim Hall on February 4:

> "A regulations writing group has been established to provide technical expertise in the development of regulations. The group consists of administrators, technical writers and engineers, and includes three people on loan from the Department of Water Resources."

At the same time I reported to Carleson that the group was re-writing regulations that we had frozen and that I had reviewed their work product and it looked like it would meet our requirements. I recommended "beefing up the unit."

Ron Zumbrun was not idle during that period. Ron was working on the legal aspects of the Department and strategizing the legal aspects of our as yet undocumented proposed reform. Ron rightly assumed that we were going to be hit hard with lawsuits as a result of our initiatives. I don't know if even Ron at the time envisioned the ferocious legal battle that was to come. But he knew that he needed lawyers.

When we arrived at SDSW, the Department had only one lawyer. Ron had the incumbent transferred out of the Department and recruited a new chief counsel from the Office of Administrative Procedure. Zumbrun begged borrowed and cajoled so that at the end of the first month Carleson could report to Hall:

> "Have arranged for a staff of hand-picked attorneys to be loaned to this Department for six months. They total up to a maximum of seven in number and are from Public Works, General Services and the Attorney General's Office."

This was a period of trench warfare in the Department. This was an agency that was run by social workers. We immediately began to move all of the social workers out of management positions and replaced them with administrators, fiscal types, and other professions that more nearly fit the job descriptions. We put social workers in social work jobs. This did not sit well with the Department's elite. We had a lot of grievances and complaints to the State Personnel Board, but I think that the speed with which we moved and the momentum that we had when we arrived at the Department just overwhelmed the opposition and allowed us to take over the operation.

While we were securing a hold on the Department, Bob was doing advance work for the program that we were developing. He met with just about every player in the Capitol and many leaders, not just in the welfare industry, but throughout the State. We knew that if we were going to be successful that it would require the assistance of a lot of people and entities that normally wouldn't get involved with welfare. Our strategy was to overcome the traditional welfare momentum by making it irrelevant. We wanted the public to understand the failures of the program and demand that they be changed to be more effective and equitable.

Welfare in California was at a turning point. The caseload was growing at an alarming rate and expenditures were doing the same. The caseload when Reagan became Governor was about 750,000. By the time that we moved over to SDSW, there were 1.6 million on AFDC and projections showed that an additional 550,000 would go on the rolls that fiscal year. California had 10 percent of the nation's population and 16 percent of the nation's welfare recipients. Without doing something, a massive tax increase was going to be needed in 1972 in order to balance the budget. We had found that the program was riddled with abuse, some of it on the part of recipients, but much of it built into the system by the welfare bureaucracy. On the other side of the equation, California had not increased benefits in thirteen years and what had been considered an appropriate grant level in the late 1950s was now universally recognized as not meeting the needs of the poor.

The major conclusions that we reached were:

- There were a lot of people on AFDC who had sufficient outside income that they shouldn't have been eligible
- The state regulations had been drafted to assure that the maximum number of Californians were eligible
- The system was designed to keep people on welfare, not to make them self-sufficient
- Citizens who were really in need—the truly needy* as we called them—were not having their needs met
- The fifty-eight California counties charged with operating the program were doing so in a non-standardized manner

By the end of February, we had completed work on the plan and had drafted a lengthy blueprint for implementation. The entire package was presented to the Governor and the Cabinet at a meeting in the Governor's office. The Cabinet consisted of the four Secretaries, Earl Coke at Agriculture, Frank Walton at Business and Transportation, Ike Livermore at Resources, and Jim Hall at Human Relations. Ed Meese, the Executive Secretary was there sort of as the first among equals in the Cabinet. In addition to the Cabinet those in attendance included Jim Crumpacker, the Cabinet Secretary, Paul Beck, the Press Secretary; Ed Gray, the Deputy Press Secretary, George Steffes, the Legislative Liaison, Mike Deaver, ostensibly Meese's Deputy, but already at this time developing into the first lady's liaison and keeper of the body, and James E. Jenkins, a key strategist in the Governor's Office. Bob Carleson, Ron Zumbrun and I were there also. The meeting was lively with participation by the Cabinet and the Governor's staff.

Our goals for the program were simple:

---

* Truly Needy was the term we used to denote those who through no fault of their own have nowhere else to turn to meet basic needs.

- We must strengthen the role of the family as the basic element in society.
- We must require those who are able to work, to be productive, and to meet their own responsibilities.
- We must assist the truly needy who have nowhere else to turn to meet their basic needs.

To implement this in the fairest way possible, we had recommended that there be no net cost shift between levels of government and that the government level closest to the people was most responsive to individual needs.

California had developed a program that was so liberal that schoolteachers were eligible for welfare during the summer months. It paid welfare to union members who were on strike, to illegal aliens, and to persons who took a leave of absence from a job. For purposes of the AFDC-U program, California's regulations defined unemployment as working thirty-five hours or less in a week. All of these issues were addressed in the proposal. The presentation included almost forty pages of detailed recommendations and cost/savings estimates for "fixing" the AFDC program. Reaction by the Cabinet was quite favorable with several people wanting to go further than we had recommended in some areas.

Jim Jenkins, who had come back to Sacramento from the California State office in Washington, D.C., tried to sum up the presentation and develop the public themes for the program. He suggested that it was not to reduce the welfare rolls but he said the "real selling point" was to take the limited money that the State had and "divert it from the non-needy and give it to the truly needy." He said the best points of the program were that welfare grants would go up for the truly needy, loopholes in the regulations would be closed and the proposed closed end appropriation for welfare would make the bureaucracy try to keep non-needy persons off welfare.

Some areas where we thought we might have some opposition were also reviewed at that meeting. Several of our proposals were sure to cause uproar and we figured it best to understand them. Four major areas of concern were identified.

The first was the work requirement for women. There was no concern about a work requirement for the fathers in the AFDC-U program, but several people at the meeting expressed concern about making single mothers in the AFDC program subject to a work requirement. But we felt that a lot of women were in the workforce and the mere fact that the welfare mother had children should not be the reason for keeping them in dependency.

The second area involved several proposed provisions regarding financial responsibility for persons on welfare. Everyone agreed that absent parents had a responsibility to provide for their offspring. Even though the state had a weak child support program, there was universal agreement on that fact. But, we were proposing that other relatives assume some of the responsibility for care.

We proposed that adult children who could afford it be mandated to contribute some amount to care for their parents who were on welfare. We also proposed that a lien be placed against the estate of welfare recipients (mostly the elderly) so that after they died the state could recoup some of the cost of caring for them. And we proposed that parents with means whose children were placed in foster care due to neglect or abuse be required to reimburse the county for the cost of care. We could see no reason that the taxpayer should have to pay to care for these individuals.

Finally, we had proposed that step-parents be financially responsible for some measure of their stepchildren's care. Several people at the meeting expressed concern that these proposals were going to be controversial and would generate a lot of criticism.

The final area of concern dealt not with policy but instead with the mechanics of the reform. We didn't know how good our estimates of the fiscal impact of each of the provisions were. For the past two months, we had been pushing Chuck Hobbs and Bill Price in the Department for cost estimates on every proposal and every permutation of every proposal. They unfortunately had very little detailed data to rely on for estimating purposes so the quality of their estimates was questionable. We knew that the Legislature and the counties would question every estimate and construe them for their own purposes. The only saving fact was that they would have no better data than we had.

I might add that within the administration, this project, even though it was the Governor's number one priority, was not universally endorsed. Welfare reform was wanted by everyone, but some people felt it was best left to the other guy to do. We knew that some of the staff in the Governor's office felt that way and felt that welfare was a subject better left untouched. Fortunately for us, in addition to Jim Hall, there was another guy at the table who was all for it, Ronald Reagan.

The Governor had a number of questions and raised several issues. This was a project within which he was completely immersed. A major concern of his was whether the people that we loped off the state AFDC rolls would just end up on the county's General Relief rolls and thereby be a bigger burden to the counties. Bob Carleson assured him that the people that we were going after had other income and assets and would not be a burden on the General Relief programs in the counties. The Governor ended the meeting in a pretty good mood. He said it was a "damn good plan."

The wordsmiths in the Governor's Office went to work on the package. Jerry Martin, the Governor's Director of Research, and Ed Gray, the Deputy Press Secretary, led the effort. Tom McMurray, Ron and I once again became foot soldiers for this effort. We monitored the writing and made sure that all of the technical material matched our findings. It was a day and night job again. When we finished, Jerry Martin sent me a letter expressing his appreciation for my contribution.

"The fact that we made the deadline is largely a result of your excellent work. Believe me, I know and appreciate the long hours you put into the project. When these reforms are adopted, it will be because of your tremendous effort."

In the end, we developed a 180 page legislative message. It was the longest legislative message ever prepared by a California Governor. It laid out the need for welfare reform, gave specific examples of the inequities and abuses of the current system, and included almost all of the proposals that we had developed. The finished product, titled **Meeting the Challenge: A Responsible Program for Welfare and Medi-Cal Reform**, had a blue cover. Thus, it became known as "The Blue Book."

Chapter 5

All Out War

In his August 4, 1970, memo, Governor Reagan had said this was an "all out war on the taxtaker." He never defined "taxtaker" and over the next two years, the identity of the taxtakers changed from time to time, but one thing was certain. It was all out guerilla war. And it started with the Blue Book. The Governor requested a joint session of the Legislature to present his welfare message. The Democrat Legislative leadership denied his request. That was their first mistake.

After the Legislature refused the Governor's request, the decision was made to announce the program through a gubernatorial speech at the Town Hall of California in Los Angeles. The Town Hall is a prestigious forum and was more than happy to accommodate the Governor after the Legislature denied him the opportunity to speak. The speech was delivered at 1:00 PM on March 3, 1971. The speech was preceded by the delivery of the Blue Book to the Senate and Assembly. The Governor joked with the audience that he had planned on a personal delivery to the Legislature, "but a funny thing happened to me on the way upstairs." He wasn't invited. Ironically that day, at about the same time as the Governor was making the Town Hall speech and laying out his plan for welfare reform, the California Assembly was being addressed by the Maid of Japan.

Ronald Reagan was always a very misunderstood man. Whether in Sacramento or in Washington, people were always trying to figure out what his "angle" was in a particular situation. Most of the time others, the pundits, the legislators, and the media, would draw their own conclusions and then attribute their conclusions to Ronald Reagan. "This" is what Reagan means they would say. They were almost always wrong. With Ronald Reagan, what you saw and heard was what you got. I don't think that he had a disingenuous bone in his body.

In his Town Hall speech he pointed to a key element in our reform package, the need to help the truly needy. He said:

> "Reform is needed not only because welfare is an administrative disaster leading us to bankruptcy, but because it is a tragic failure for those who are destitute and have nowhere else to turn for the most basic requirements of living. Let me emphasize this latter point because anytime changes are proposed in welfare there are those who will raise the cry that we are lacking in compassion for the poor. The very opposite is true. Welfare today is spread so thin it is incapable of properly caring for the truly needy and destitute. It is spread thin in attempting to provide for too many who are not needy but who through loopholes are legally eligible to claim welfare benefits, and to many who are receiving aid illegally because there is just no way to prevent their cheating and because there is a gigantic extravagant administrative overhead bound in endless miles of red tape and born of overlapping and duplicating agencies."

In addition to closing loopholes and removing abuse, our program was designed to increase assistance to a large part of the welfare population—the truly needy. This aspect caught a lot of the non-believers by surprise. And in fact it was an underlying factor in our eventual success.

After laying out his seventy-point program in general and citing specific evidence of waste and abuse in the system, Reagan again referenced his request to the Legislature for time and their refusal to grant it:

"I asked for the opportunity to address the joint session of our legislature precisely because of the news coverage that would follow. It is absolutely imperative that the people of California understand what we are trying to accomplish."

The legislature's refusal was a mistake. If they had allowed the Governor to give a joint address, it would have hit the news and been a dead story in a day or so. But the fact that they denied him the opportunity and he went to Town Hall upped the ante. Every reporter in the state smelled a good fight brewing. The speech got a lot of press coverage.* The second mistake that the legislature made was in underestimating the Governor. They hadn't been around him for the past nine months while he developed this welfare reform program. They weren't listening to his speeches on the subject starting with his first inaugural. They didn't connect the dots. The Governor was personally committed to finishing the job. The train was leaving the station and you either got aboard or you were left behind or, in the case of some who made the mistake of thinking they could stop the train, you got run over. Most of Sacramento fell into one of the three categories. I was on the train.

A schedule of briefings was set up to coincide with the Governor's speech. Press packets were put together along with Q and A's and a fact sheet on welfare reform. And the show went on the road. The Governor personally did a group of editors from Northern California on the third, covered the middle of the state on the fourth with an editorial board in Fresno and one in San Francisco. On the fifth he

---

* Interestingly, although this speech made a lot of news after it was delivered and it was the kickoff for the welfare reform campaign that became the signature campaign of his governorship, it has received very little coverage in the ensuing years. In fact, it is not even listed in *A Time for Choosing – The Speeches of Ronald Reagan 1961-1982*, the 1983 book found in every Reaganite's library. And when President Reagan wrote *Speaking My Mind*, a book of speeches he had made during his career, he did not include that one either. It should be noted that in his book, he only included two speeches from his time as Governor and neither speech was about government.

traveled to San Diego and Los Angeles to do editorial boards in both of those cities. Most of the other briefings during that first two weeks were done by Jim Hall, Bob Carleson, and because we had a strong work component built into the package, Gilbert Sheffield, the Director of the Department of Human Resources Development (HRD), the state manpower agency.

The initial reaction to the release of the program was interesting. We had an early advantage with the media due to the Governor's travel to the different markets and due to the fact that some of the papers and television stations didn't like the legislature denying a joint session to allow the Governor to present his message. This had never been done before and the moralists in the Fourth Estate were taking umbrage.

The federal government, HEW and the White House didn't like it because they were sure that they were going to take over the welfare program from the states under Nixon's Family Assistance Plan (FAP). They didn't like the fact that Reagan was going it alone. HEW under Bob Finch and Elliot Richardson had been pushing California to raise its grant levels for the prior two years. It had gotten to the point where Richardson, the Secretary, had notified California that in April of 1971, he was going to withhold federal funds for AFDC (the feds paid 50 percent of the cost) if we didn't raise the grants.

Now grant increases were in our package but needed legislative approval. Richardson felt that California had taken too long to implement the increases and he wasn't interested in waiting any longer. He did nothing to endear himself to Ronald Reagan. Elliot forgot that Nixon's western White House was in California. Reagan went to San Clemente to visit with the President. Out of that meeting, we got a reprieve from the onerous sanction and a mild encouragement from Nixon to proceed with our program.

What the White House and HEW put out was that Reagan, in return for Nixon's acquiescence, had agreed to tone down his criticism of FAP. I never asked Reagan about what he did or didn't agree to in that first meeting (there were two) with Nixon, but he did not tone down his criticism of FAP. If he had told President Nixon that he would tone it down, then he would have. One thing you could bank on with Ronald Reagan, if he agreed to something he kept the agreement.

In the Governor's Office, there was a move about to set up a parallel operation in the private sector to push for welfare reform. The thinking was that if we couldn't get it through the legislature that we would use California's unique initiative process and take the issue "to the people." It was accurately dubbed "Operation Crossfire" and coordinated by Bob Walker, one of the Governor's top advisors and later a Washington representative for Joe Coors of Coors beer.

Key to Operation Crossfire was Roy Green with the California State Chamber of Commerce and Al McCandless, a county supervisor in Riverside County who chaired a citizens group for welfare reform. They set up over 120 local groups and printed up thousands of post card brochures addressed to the Legislature demanding welfare reform.

On March 15, 1971, Senator Claire Burgner, a Republican from San Diego, introduced our package in three Senate Bills, SB 544, SB545, and SB 546. Claire had "volunteered" to carry the legislation. On that same day, our first child, Kirsten Marie Svahn, was born.

Bob Carleson and I were making a lot of appearances around the State pushing for welfare reform and Operation Crossfire was cranking up the post cards to the legislature demanding the same. At the department, Ron Zumbrun had the regulation writing group drafting up regulations to implement the reforms in the Blue Book. Those that we could do without legislation or federal approval, we issued as quickly as possible. Those that required legislative changes or federal waivers were prepared well in advance of legislation passing. Incredibly, this action, anticipation of legislation and advance preparation of regulations, proved quite controversial after the legislation actually passed.

Also, at about that time, we completed our reorganization of the department and on May 28, 1971, Bob announced the new organization to the Department. Bob always said he felt the need for some maturity in the group and he recruited one of his mentors in the city manager business, Richard Malcom, to be sort of his chief deputy with the title of Deputy Director of Social Welfare. Bob originally stationed Dick in Los Angeles (which had 40 percent of the state's welfare caseload) and looked to him to be the "chief contact" with county organizations involved in the administration of the welfare program.* Ron stayed as Deputy Director, Legal Affairs and Chuck Hobbs stayed as Deputy Director, Operations. I got promoted to Deputy Director, Administration with responsibility for Planning, Management Information Systems, Personnel, Training, Licensing, Communications, Public Information, and the Press Office. While this new organization radically changed the character of the department, nothing changed at the top management level. We were a team—just a little larger than when we started. Within the department there was much uncertainty as to where all the social workers would end up, but we avoided layoffs through attrition and personnel freezes.

It was in 1971 that I made my first trip to Washington, D.C., to meet with HEW regarding funding for our yet to be designed data processing system. The HEW people were very pleasant. They talked in acronyms and we parted on good terms. On the plane going back to Sacramento, with a warm feeling about the job I had done in Washington, I realized that I had gotten nothing from HEW to further our project.

Several years later when I was in HEW, an Illinois state legislator I knew called and told me he was bringing his committee to Washington for their annual trip and wondered if I could meet with them. I said

---

* This little phrase was typical of Bob Carleson's methodical strategizing. Heretofore, there was only one county agency involved in the administration of welfare—the county welfare department. Bob, however, envisioned the County Supervisors, the District Attorney, and the County Administrative Officer being involved. This was a shot across the bow of the County Welfare Directors and they knew it.

sure and arranged a conference room. When I entered the meeting there must have been twenty-five legislators there and my friend banged a gavel and called the "hearing" to order. Feeling that I had been sandbagged into being the "witness," I asked the Chairman if it was customary in Illinois for the witness to be allowed an opening statement. He said sure, and I told them the story of my first visit to Washington ending with "and that's my job today. To make you feel good but send you home with nothing." They all laughed. Later at lunch, the dean of the Senate in Illinois started to laugh. He said, "He told us what he was going to do and here we are laughing and smiling and we are buying *his* lunch."

A funny thing happened in California during early 1971. The AFDC caseload decreased. It actually went down in April—there were 26,000 fewer people on welfare than there were in March. This was the first time the caseload had decreased in years. In all of our material we never predicted that the caseload would actually decrease; we just projected less of an increase than was being projected by everyone else. The actual decrease was a surprise. And it went down again in May, by about another 20,000 people. Carleson and I sat in his office actually giggling about it. That month we crossed our fingers and Bob announced that he felt a trend was developing. We hoped so, because we were on a roll. The opposition hadn't jelled yet.

We kept the pressure on through a major media effort. Each month we would announce the caseload statistics and nudge the legislature about the need for legislation. A major component that we couldn't do by administrative action was to increase the grants to the truly needy. That required legislation. As Bob Carleson said announcing the decrease in June, "If the trend should continue, and legislative reforms such as equitable apportionment are adopted it will allow us to actually increase grants to those recipients with no other source of income."

By the time we got the numbers for July, Governor Reagan was so pleased that he announced them himself. The caseload for July was down 12,000, over 105,000 fewer than were on the rolls in March. The Governor said:

> "These latest figures constitute dramatic proof that the actions we have taken are grabbing hold and really work. They bear out the effectiveness of the overall approach we have taken to bring welfare back under control in California."

The specific reasons for the downturn were not able to be documented and most of the opposition attributed it to an improved economy, "draconian" actions taken by us or just sunspots. But it was clear that the administrative and regulatory reforms that we started instituting in March were having an effect. Jawboning was changing the culture of the welfare program and the change was being felt at the local level where individual decisions were made regarding eligibility. Just making the counties use the state regulations rather than make up their own had brought a small modicum of standardization to the process. And new regulations were tightening up on the eligibility rules.

This was a great learning experience for me. Bob Carleson was an accomplished student of human nature. He was always analyzing and figuring out what the reaction of different parties would be to the actions that we took. And Bob was constantly testing theories and proposed actions just to see if the reaction was as he predicted. He poked the bear a lot, but always with an underlying purpose. It was good that it always had a purpose, because as we found out early on, every time you poked that bear, it poked back.

One evening Bob and I were attending a county welfare director's function in Southern California. As usual, there were a few county directors who were very vocal in their opposition to what the Governor was doing. One of them accosted Carleson and me and called us "a bunch of reactionaries." Bob looked at him and said, "We're proposing reforms; you're reacting to them. That makes us the reformers and you the reactionary." It shut the guy up.

In California, the caseload continued to decline during 1971 and postcards were flooding the legislator's offices demanding that the legislature enact the reforms proposed by Governor Reagan.

Our strategy was fairly simple; keep the pressure on and keep moving. Our day would start early and end late. Frequently, we would have dinner together with Jim Hall. Jim was single at the time and enjoyed having dinner with us. Carleson was married with family, as was I. And I was supposed to be going to law school at night. At those dinners we would go over strategy, where the problems were and who was with us and who was against.

Jim's counsel was definitely beneficial. He provided a reality check for our wildest schemes and for our ever-present paranoia. He also ran interference for us within the Administration. He had a seat at the cabinet table and was able to deflect some of the negativism that occasionally popped up from the Governor's staff. Not that there was a lot of it, but other than the Governor, I don't think that any of the staff came to Sacramento thinking that they would be working on welfare.

At the end of a strategy dinner, we would frequently walk over to the Capitol Building and as Bob put it "just wander around." But our wanderings always took us up to the third floor of the Capitol, to the press room. Another of Bob's little lessons: "Newspapers have deadlines in the evening. If you get there before they file their stories you will have a chance to tell your side of the story. "

This was in the days when the print media still had considerable say in how the public viewed an issue. People got their news from the paper and from the local TV news. There were two papers in Sacramento, Copley's *Sacramento Union* and McClatchy's *Sacramento Bee*. McClatchy also owned two other central valley papers and several television stations. Copley owned the San Diego papers. The other major players were the *Los Angeles Times* and *San Francisco Chronicle*. Generally speaking, Copley was favorable to us and McClatchy was not.

In the early seventies, there were over two hundred newspapers being published in California but only eleven papers had a Capitol bureau. Most of the other papers in the state got their Sacramento news from the wire services. There were two wire services, United Press International (UPI) and The Associated Press (AP), with offices in the Capitol. The wire services necessarily took on an important role. A nightly story (and there was a nightly story on welfare) on the state wire of either service guaranteed that it would run in a lot of the local papers in California. That reached a lot of people.

I don't know why, but everywhere I have been (with the exception of Helen Thomas in the White House Press Corps) UPI has been easier to work with than has AP. The UPI Bureau Manager in the Capitol was George Skelton. He was assisted by a reporter, Carl Ingram. George later followed Reagan to Washington as a White House correspondent for the *LA Times*. They were both friendly and receptive to our visits and we were able to make some stories and more importantly, spin some stories on these late night trips. We did nothing to threaten their journalistic ethics but instead tried to explain the events of the day and put the best light on the story.

Throughout the year, a monthly press release came out announcing that the caseload had decreased the previous month and urging the legislature to enact the legislation that we had requested. And the cards kept coming into their offices.

In addition to not voting, a lot of Americans don't think that their opinion expressed in writing or orally makes a difference. But it most certainly does to a legislator. A lot of them that I have known continuously have a figurative finger up in the air to see which way the public's wind is blowing. It's those calls and letters that tell them. Even in the White House, after a major Presidential announcement or press conference, they keep track of the calls to the switchboard. All elected politicians are interested in how many people care enough to contact them and voice an opinion on a current topic.

I recall one occasion several years after I had left the government, that I was in Mississippi trying to convince the State Legislature there to allow my company to improve the State's record on collection of Child Support. The Governor, Kirk Fordice, a Reagan delegate in 1976 was all in favor of it. It was a tough battle with the Democrats, the state employee's union, and the AFL-CIO heavyweights from Washington trying to bludgeon the Legislature into prohibiting the contract. We thought that a few calls and letters would help explain our side.

The public was so fed up with the state's failure to get the support owed to the children that the calls came in fast and furious. For several days, the Capitol switchboard was jammed with only the child support incoming calls getting through. Finally, Dick Hall, the Chairman of the Senate Health and Welfare Committee came over to me in the hall of the Capitol building and quietly said, "Jack, Kendra (the committee's staff assistant) has asked me to tell you that I am definitely on your side. You don't have to worry about my vote. And if you have anything to do with those calls coming into the office, we wish that they would stop." So those calls and letters can have a real impact. I encourage everyone to make them. And in the summer of 1971, those post cards in California had a big impact. Operation Crossfire was working.

I don't know exactly how it finally came to be that the Democrats in the Legislature decided to negotiate welfare reform, but they did. There are at least two versions of how this played out. Ronald Reagan's and the one reported by Lou Cannon in his book *Reagan*.

Over the years, I heard Reagan tell his story many times usually prefaced by a favorite comment of his: "When legislators feel the heat, they frequently see the light." The Reagan story is spelled out in his autobiography. "One day the liberal Democrat who succeeded Jesse Unruh, Speaker of the Assembly Bob Moretti, came into my office holding his hands in the air as if I had a gun on him and said, 'Stop those cards and letters!'"

Cannon's version is a bit more complex. To start with, he gives credit for "leadership" to Moretti, saying that it was Moretti that recognized the need for some movement and that it was Moretti's aide and George Steffes, the legislative assistant in the Governor's office who actually put the meeting together. I have no doubt that both aides were trying to get the problem "fixed." That is the mentality of the majority of the legislative staffers that I have met. But I can assure you that Moretti wouldn't have written a letter suggesting compromise, wouldn't have walked in with his hands up or anything else but for the tremendous pressure that we had put him under.

As a practical matter, both stories are probably somewhat correct. Moretti and Reagan did not like each other and it is highly unlikely that Moretti would have walked into the Governor's office uninvited. In fact, it would have been damned near impossible. There was pushing and pulling between the staffs and there was a letter sent from Moretti to Reagan suggesting getting together. Reagan may have been speaking metaphorically when describing his version. On the other hand, once the meeting was arranged, Moretti being young and brash, might well have tossed his hands up in the air because any way you look at it, he was surrendering. I am not sure I would call that leadership unless it's like the guy being run out of town getting in front of the crowd and calling it a parade.

Whatever the genesis, the meeting actually was arranged, it did happen. In Lou Cannon's *Reagan*, he describes Moretti's version of the first one-on-one meeting that Moretti "vividly recalled." Cannon quotes Moretti as saying that the Governor started the meeting with, "Yeah, what do you want to talk to me about?" In twenty years of working for Ronald Reagan and watching him meet and talk to dozens and dozens of adversaries, I never heard him say, "Yeah." And I doubt that he would ever start a conversation the way that Moretti says. He was too polite.

Unfortunately, by the time I got around to writing this, both individuals in that meeting had passed away so we will never know what happened except that the Governor and the Speaker agreed to face to face negotiations.

This was it. Hand to hand combat. And the guy most excited about it was Governor Reagan. He wanted to roll up his sleeves and get into the fracas. In fact, every time an occasion came up over the years where there was an opportunity for him to get in and personally negotiate an issue, Reagan seemed to relish it. He wanted to negotiate Social Security with Tip O'Neill, the Speaker of the House and he did negotiate many issues with General Secretary Gorbachev of the Soviet Union. He liked to negotiate. In preparatory meetings with staff, he would always bring up the fact that he had been President of the Screen Actors Guild and that he had personally negotiated the deals with the studios when he was an actor. And he, and I guess others at the time, felt that he had done a heck of a job in that role. So when the negotiations were agreed to, the Governor was really up for it.

What followed was a week of intense negotiations in a small conference room in the Governor's Office complex. Governor Reagan personally headed up his own team. Bob Carleson was point man on welfare with Ed Meese as the Governor's top staff man in the room. Ron Zumbrun was the key to the legal aspects of what we wanted done. The rest of us continued with administrative changes and cheered from the sidelines.

On the legislature's side, Moretti handled the top negotiator's position and he had Assemblyman Leo McCarthy, Senator Anthony Beilenson the chairman of the Senate Health and Welfare Committee, and Assemblyman John Burton, all Democrats on his side. The legislative negotiating team also included Republican Assemblyman Bill Bagley.

Bagley had been appointed Chairman of the Assembly Welfare Committee by Moretti so he had mixed loyalty. He was also working with his friend and former colleague, John (Jack) Veneman, the Under Secretary of HEW, to get Nixon's FAP program approved. Bill, although a good old boy Republican, was opposed to Reagan's welfare reform program.

The negotiations between the Governor and Moretti lasted for about five days. Carleson again strategized that we would have an advantage if we worked off of our bills that had been introduced by Claire Burgner. The Burgner bills had been killed in Belienson's Senate Health and Welfare Committee. Beilenson had instead sponsored his own bill, SB796, which had passed the Senate and was sitting in the Assembly.

Bob's theory was that we had drafted them to our specifications; they were what we wanted and the other side should have to explain why it didn't want them. So it wasn't a negotiation from ground zero. Bob did one other thing with the bills. He secretly annotated each section of the Governor's copy of the bills with a code explaining how important the section was to our program. The theory was that this allowed the Governor to deal on each area without having to turn to someone and ask, "How important is this to us." So the Governor knew which sections he could give on and which ones he couldn't.

It was clear that Moretti was not very familiar with the welfare issues involved and when Reagan would go over each one in our bill, Moretti said that it sounded fine. After the first day, Bob was ecstatic. He said, "We got everything." The second day Moretti was not so happy. When he had returned to his office, the legislative staff raised all kinds of objections to what he had agreed to with Reagan. The other side had time to regroup after our initial breakthrough and began to raise objections.

Each day the negotiating sessions would go on for a while and then there would be a break. Each side would caucus. On our side, there was not unanimity. Several of the Governor's staff felt that there was a need to compromise and to get an agreement and a bill through. Then we could claim victory. Carleson and Meese were willing to compromise, but not on the key elements of our package.

Bob kept using the Public Works analogy of bridge building: "You can't just stop with a bridge 90 percent done," he would say. "It doesn't accomplish your objective." In one meeting George Steffes, the Governor's legislative guy said to the Governor, "We need to get a bill through the legislature" and Carleson retorted, "No George, we need to get welfare reform through the legislature." Reagan agreed.

There was a lot of heated discussion and charges back and forth between the Governor's team and Moretti's team over the next four days until finally on Friday the two principals reached an agreement. Reagan and Moretti, along with the rest of the participants in the room went to the Governor's outer office and shook hands in front of the media gathered there. We had a deal. The only thing left to do was to clean up the writings that the two had negotiated and draft them into the bills. This was a technical task that was to be left to the Legislative Counsel's Office.

The next day, Saturday, July 31, we were all in the office going over what had happened. Bill Bagley had arranged to have the Legislative Counsel deliver the final legislative draft to the Governor's Office first thing that morning. When it didn't arrive at the agreed upon time, Bob got nervous. Bob always had this "proximity" thing about hanging around where the action was or might be. He would wander around the Capitol or just drop by the Governor's Office to see what was going on there. It cost us a lot of nights and weekends. At about 10:30 he and Ron took "a walk," over to the Capitol.

The Capitol, except for the first floor, was closed to the public on weekends. Carleson wandered up to the Legislative Counsel's office and found the Moretti staff guy and a couple of outside poverty lawyers working with the Counsel's Office to plant land mines in the legislation. Since the negotiations were, by mutual agreement, very secret, and since the outside lawyers, led by Ralph Abascal of the San

Francisco Neighborhood Legal Foundation (SNLAF) who had been suing us at every turn, had no business drafting language, Carleson sounded the alarm.

The Reagan team accused the Moretti team of breaching the agreement. Moretti didn't want anyone to think that he was reneging on an agreement. The decision was made to try to keep the agreement together and negotiations were reinstated. This time Moretti and the Governor did not participate. Ed Meese took over for the Governor and Leo McCarthy did the same for Moretti. McCarthy had Beilenson and Burton there along with a staffer Bob Rosenberg. Rosenberg had been in the meetings the previous week and he was one of the ones that Carleson had found in the Counsel's office with Abascal.

These sessions, without the Governor and Moretti were even more confrontational. John Burton, who had had months of confrontation with Carleson in front of the Ways and Means Committee, exploded frequently. Ed Meese took the lead and finally, in his best prosecutorial fashion, accused Rosenberg of trying to sabotage the process and the bill. Rosenberg, after having been skewered by Ed, basically confessed and the wind was out of the sails of the Democrat's negotiating team. We had long believed that the legislative staff and some of the legislators were using the SNLAF and the California Rural Legal Assistance (CRLA) lawyers to assist their efforts.

The reason being that when the Democrats came to the conclusion that Reagan was going to get a welfare reform package, either through the legislature or by executing the Operation Crossfire initiative, they enlisted the help of the so called poverty lawyers who were suing us. Their purpose was to create flaws in the legislation that would finally pass so that it would be subject to invalidation in the courts by the very lawyers who helped draft it.

The next ten days of negotiation were an acrimonious attempt to bring the language back to what was agreed to by Reagan and Moretti. Beilenson's staff guy sitting on the side of the table made it clear that they were "passing all drafts through Abascal" and his associates. On the evening of August 3, it looked like it was all over when McCarthy and staff admitted that they were not going to abide by the original agreed to language. Late at night on August 5, the Reagan team, in order to get a deal, agreed to the new language that the legislative team demanded. The final draft of the language was done right in the conference room and the bill was done.* The deal was finally agreed to and drafted. The parties no longer needed the small conference room that had been the locus of the negotiations. Rumor had it that the Governor said, "I never want to see that room again." Whatever the reason, the conference room was dismantled and no longer exists.

Since the Beilenson bill was sitting in the Assembly, having already passed the Senate, Moretti stripped of all of the provisions enacted by the Senate out of the bill. That left a shell to which he substituted the agreed upon language. It no longer had any of Belienson's provisions in it. The bill, SB 796 (Beilenson) passed both houses in three days. The Welfare Reform Act of 1971 was signed by the Governor on August 13, 1971.

I use this episode in Ronald Reagan's political career to comment on his official biography. Ronald Reagan and Bob Moretti did not like each other and they made no bones about it. They were a generation apart in age, and more than that in custom and manners. Years later, when he was President, Reagan granted unprecedented access to Pulitzer Prize winning author Edmund Morris in order that Morris could do an authorized biography. No other staff person in the White House had the access that Edmund had to the President. His biography of Reagan,

---

* Jim Hall, our boss, was not among the negotiating participants at the end. His philosophy was to let us do the job. We were the nuts and bolts experts. So early on he voluntarily withdrew from the negotiating room figuring that there were already too many cooks. As he had done all along, and as he would continue to do over the next thirteen months, Jim gave sage counsel and ran interference for us within the administration. At one point, he had serious words with Ed Meese about reining in the Governor's staff and getting the staff "off my guys' backs."

Dutch, A Memoir of Ronald Reagan, drew much criticism because of the way Edmund chose to narrate it. During the time he was hanging around the West Wing, I liked Edmund and I eagerly awaited the publication of his biography. After I read his book, I was disappointed at the opportunity that Edmund had wasted. It seemed that even with all that access, that he still didn't understand Reagan. He, like so many others, kept trying to find out what Reagan was "really" about rather than accepting him for who he was. When he was commenting on this period in Reagan's governorship, Morris fantasized "hot Friday lunch hours while he (Reagan) and Bob Moretti chewed over policy at Wing Fat's." Ronald Reagan rarely went out for lunch unless it was to an appearance or function. And Ronald Reagan sitting in a Chinese restaurant with Bob Moretti is unthinkable. I doubt that either one of them would have agreed to do that. How Morris could have gotten it so wrong is baffling. By the way, the restaurant in Sacramento was Frank Fat's, not Wing Fat's. There was a lot of fiction in *Dutch*.

Chapter 6

Be Careful What You Wish For

Be careful what you wish for, it may come true. We would have been better advised to heed that old Chinese proverb. The Governor was very happy. The signing ceremony went very well and most of the parties were pleased. All except Beilenson. Beilenson recognized that the Governor had won. He was particularly upset with the fact that Moretti had stripped his original bill and substituted our program for what he had introduced. This meant that his name was on the bill even though, other than the number of the bill, SB796, nothing remained of what he originally introduced. Moretti, along with the other legislators on both sides of the aisle, was just happy that the fight was over.

We had a signing ceremony to celebrate the passage of the legislation. As was the practice, the Governor signed the original and a copy for Jim Mills, the President of the Senate, and one for Speaker Moretti. At the conclusion of the ceremony, a defeated and disgusted Moretti tossed his copy of the signed bill down on the Cabinet Room table and left the room. I picked it up.

We had all wished that we could get welfare reform and now we had it. The legislation was signed. Now we had to implement it. The effective date was October 1, 1971. That gave us forty-eight days.

Forty-eight days to write regulations, get them issued, train the counties, and fight off the lawsuits designed to stop us from implementing.

Amid the celebration surrounding the signing of the Welfare Reform Act of 1971 was the sobering reality of what was ahead of us. We came out of the blocks running. Ron Zumbrun already had his regulation writers working on regulations for things that were in the legislation that were also in our package. As soon as the Bill was signed we began issuing those regulations on an emergency basis.

Immediately, we were accused by the legislators who were involved in the negotiations of only implementing the sections of the bill that we supported. They had added some new programs and different twists to certain sections that we had not anticipated so we had to start on those regulations from scratch. And they enlisted their co-conspirators, the poverty lawyers, to file suit against us alleging that we were only implementing sections that we liked.

We were pushing hard to implement the whole thing by October 1, but still had to spend valuable time explaining to the legislature and the court that the sections that they were interested in were in development; that they hadn't been anticipated and therefore we hadn't "pre-drafted" them. The fact of the matter was that Beilenson and Burton and the Democrat staff just weren't interested in seeing the thing implemented at all.

Sometimes reform was serendipity. During the weekend of June 19, 1971, the Department of Social Welfare (SDSW) was implementing a new data processing program for the MediCal program. MediCal is California's name for the federal Medicaid program, the health program for the poor. SDSW didn't run MediCal but it did do the data processing for it. Our data processing manager, Gene Reich, worked for me and I was concerned that the new cards got out correctly and in a timely manner. This was part of the Governor's MediCal reform and I wanted to make sure that we did our part. Consequently, I spent the weekend in the office, most of it in the data center. Earl W. Brian, MD was the Director of MediCal and he was there with me for much of the time. We were like expectant fathers hovering over the machines.

The project involved the issuance of a new Central ID card for MediCal recipients. On the card were a bunch of sticky labels that were to be detached by the healthcare provider and affixed to the claim presented to the state for payment. And the cards proved very difficult to print because of the sticky labels. The labels would peel a little bit and the high-speed printers would jam causing a big pile up and delay. At one point, completely frustrated by the continual delay caused by the jams, I looked into the printer box at the mangled cards. The one staring me in the face had an address in Guatemala on it. Guatemala! Now we were printing off our master list of welfare recipients so that meant that the person to whom this card was going to also was getting a check each month. A California welfare recipient with a home address in Guatemala!

I called Earl over to the printer and asked him about the card going to Guatemala. He said, "We send cards to the address of record, could be anywhere." I asked where they got their medical care and he said it could be they would come back to California or in case of "emergencies" they could get it where they were. In the case of recipients in other states, we had reciprocal agreements to pay providers in those states. One of our proposals on the table in the Legislature was to limit the time a recipient could be out of state and still receive benefits from California. Anyone out of the state for sixty days or more was presumed to have moved and dropped from the rolls.

As soon as we were done with the MediCal project, I had Gene Reich run a list of recipients whose addresses were out of state. Then just as the legislature was in the final throws of negotiation we put out a press release. Actually, we put the press release out a day after K.W. Lee of the *Sacramento Union* "learned" that 6,425 California welfare recipients were living outside the state of California. Front page, banner:

"WELFARE EXPORTED." Four columns, front page: "California Exporting Welfare to 6,500."

We found over 200 people living in foreign countries. Not just Mexico and Canada as one might assume, but in Argentina, Central America, England, Greece, Ireland, and Sweden, a total of twenty-three countries. And over 6,000 living in other states. A quick check with Nevada, our close ally in welfare reform (Nevada's Governor Paul Laxalt and Reagan were good friends), showed that six out of ninety-five of our recipients living in Nevada were also on the welfare rolls in Nevada. This news caused quite a stir statewide and put more pressure on the legislature for reform.

While six thousand plus out of state recipients was not a huge number, it did cost California about $550,000 per month. We sent the names and addresses of our recipients who got their checks in another state to each of those states and requested them to match the names with their rolls. Some states did it but most of them ignored our request.

It seemed odd that up until this time, no one had ever bothered to inquire if checks were being mailed out of state, let alone why. It seems like a pretty simple precaution, but in 1971, checks were mailed to welfare recipients by the counties and computers were not nearly as sophisticated as they are today. Besides, the counties were run, just as the State Department of Social Welfare had been until Reagan changed it in January of 1971, by professional social workers. The social workers operated under the mantra of "of course they are eligible; they wouldn't have applied unless they were needy."*

---

* Ten years later, when I was at Social Security, I asked the same question preparing for confirmation hearings. I was told that yes, we did send Social Security checks to retirees who live in foreign countries. They had the right to live wherever they chose. In fact, Social Security has "treaty" type arrangements with a number of countries to try to make it fair for everyone. So no big scandal. But the joke around the Social Security Administration was that if you wanted to live long in retirement, retire behind the iron curtain. On average, retirees who moved behind the iron curtain lived to be

That was typical of the mood in the welfare bureaucracy nationwide and certainly in California. What we were doing in California in terms of welfare reform under Ronald Reagan was becoming a threat to the national welfare industry. Other state's Governors were calling and writing us and asking for information on our reforms. They were finding out that their welfare departments looked just like ours did in 1970 and while their programs might not have been quite as liberal as ours; there was a feeling among elected officials around the country that perhaps a state could do something about the "welfare mess."

One fellow in San Jose who was so caught up in the need for welfare reform that he decided to apply himself. He was a businessman with a wife and two kids. He went in and applied for assistance and told the truth about his situation. He owned his own home valued at $50,000 at the time; he had an office and employed a secretary; he estimated his annual income at $35,000 to $50,000 (as a Deputy Director of Social Welfare at the time, a high paying government job, my salary was $28,000) and he said he owned $250,000 worth of real estate and other holdings. The Santa Clara Welfare Department, one of the more liberal in the state, qualified him for $106 in food stamps each month. He couldn't believe it. He went to the newspaper. We closed that loophole in a hurry. This kind of anomaly was not unusual in welfare in those days. When applicants used a simple declaration for eligibility and when welfare workers were trying to get everyone on assistance, rules were routinely expanded to make as many people eligible as possible. After all, they wouldn't apply unless they were needy, would they?

A few years later, while Secretary of HEW, Caspar Weinberger, was flabbergasted when I told him that because he and his wife, Jane, lived on Capitol Hill, if he had had children living with him, he would have qualified for free child care under the federal concept of group eligi-

---

117. Or at least that's how long we sent checks to the address where the government cashed them.

bility—living on Capitol Hill placed him in a geographic area where anyone living there was eligible. We closed that loophole too.

Things were going our way. In hindsight, it would have been hard for them to go otherwise. California was probably the most liberal of liberal programs. The system was so far out of whack that almost anything that we did would have had an impact.

We started off issuing a number of regulations and taking administrative actions to implement welfare reform. Those that we could, we implemented immediately. Some were pretty simple. The federal government said that a person could be considered unemployed and therefore eligible for welfare if they worked less than one hundred hours per month. In California, the state said that you could be considered unemployed for welfare purposes if you worked less than 140 hours per month (35 hours a week). We changed the definition of unemployed for AFDC-U purposes from 140 hours per month to the federal minimum standard of 100 hours.

One of the problems that led to so much waste and fraud was a concept developed by the welfare industry called the declaration method for determining eligibility for benefits. You declare you are eligible and we paid. This was implemented throughout most of California through the use of a two page application form. We felt that more information was needed to verify eligibility so we developed a new application form for welfare. It was nineteen pages long and required verification of all of the applicants stated facts.

Our new application form was designated "WR-2." The "WR" was for welfare reform and the "2" a play on the W-2 form you get at the end of each year for income taxes. The WR-2 was immediately and universally condemned by the county welfare departments. They said it was too long, too intrusive and would cause too much of a burden on workers. One county social worker was pictured in a San Francisco newspaper in a dress that she made out of the form. And in a very serious (at least for him) press release, John Burton nominated Bob

Carleson for the "Lewis Carroll Award of 1972" because Burton felt the form "had to be right out of Alice in Wonderland."

The WR-2 form as well as the reorganization that put administrators in administrative positions and social workers in social work positions did not sit well with the welfare industry. We were constantly appearing before the State Personnel Board to justify our personnel actions. People were resigning in protest of what we were doing.

Bob Fugina who handled administration and our personnel officer, Dave Dawson, were inundated with phony claims. Groups of social workers formed a committee and contributed thousands of dollars to hire lawyers and lobbyists to fight us. The national Service Employee International Union (SEIU) brought their brand of "advocacy" to Sacramento. And the poverty lawyers were filing lawsuits and requests for restraining orders and the judges were issuing them without restraint.

We almost lost the whole realignment, re-staffing, and reorganization effort in the budget battle the summer of 1971. As we proceeded to reclassify and recruit, the budget moved its cumbersome way through the legislative process. The legislature's conference committee worked into the wee hours one July night and finally reached agreement. Bob Carleson was on one of his "proximity" strolls in the Capitol when one of Willie Brown's staff people, Steve Thompson, gleefully let on that we'd been had. In checking out the language, we found that someone had added:

> "As of August 1, 1971, the department of social welfare could have no positions, or position classifications, which had not existed on December 1, 1970."

If this were to pass the next day, we would be stymied. No lawyers, no accountants, no fiscal types, the whole administrative welfare reform effort would be down the drain. Bob immediately started contacting the conferees and showing them the language that had been inserted in the conference version. Everyone, even Willie Brown, expressed surprise and chagrin at the added language. Most signed a statement saying that the language had never been agreed to by the conference committee. We were permitted to continue with the reorganization and the language was taken out in a trailer bill.

But here again, little legislative gremlins trying to thwart the program were found out just by Bob staying close to the situation at all hours of the day and night. By this time we were really living, breathing, and sleeping welfare reform. This was not the only time that the folks in the back room tried to thwart us by slipping a little language in a bill. I personally was the subject of a "language witch hunt."

When I went over to SDSW from the Department of Public Works, I was a career civil service employee. I went into a political appointment as Assistant Director. When I was appointed Deputy Director, we didn't have a position in the Department for me, nor authorization for another political appointee. This happened frequently in government. An authorized position was found and I was appointed by the Governor and sworn into the position by Ed Kirby. Ed had the position is his department and wanted to help the Governor in his welfare reform effort. The position was in the Department of Alcoholic Beverage Control. I was sworn in as the Assistant Director of the Department of Alcoholic Beverage Control. (It was great for getting tables in restaurants.) In reality, I worked in Social Welfare as Deputy Director.

By February of 1972, the legislative munchkins had found me and in a February 15 letter to Verne Orr, the Director of Finance, the Chairman of the Ways and Means Committee, Willie Brown deleted me from the budget. For the budget of the Department of Alcoholic Beverage Control he wrote:

> "An Assistant Director's position has been deleted. This position is presently occupied by a Deputy Director of the Department of Social Welfare, working in the Department of Social Welfare. Apparently, the position is

not needed in the Department of Alcoholic Beverage Control; therefore, it is being deleted."

I was very quietly moved out of that position and the Governor appointed me to the position of Chief Deputy Director of the Department of Rehabilitation. Willie's staff didn't find me there. Later, in 1972, Dick Malcom left the department to return to Southern California and the Governor appointed me to be Chief Deputy Director. The Chief Deputy position did exist in the department so I was able to stop "hiding" from Willie Brown.*

Somewhat more onerous and successful was an effort on the part of the California Welfare Rights Organization (CWRO) to grind our fair hearing process to a halt. Under federal law and a U.S. Supreme Court decision, prior to being removed from the welfare rolls or having a welfare check reduced, the state had to send the intended recipient a notice of intended action and provide an opportunity for the individual to have a hearing on the matter. One court case ruled that the recipient was entitled to continued welfare "pending" the decision of the fair hearing. Obviously this requirement was designed to protect an individual against an erroneous individual action. Upon notice, the affected recipient would file a request, come in and explain why the state action was mistaken, and continue on assistance.

But the welfare rights organizations figured that if they got everyone who might be affected to file for a fair hearing, we would not be able to keep up with the cases and the recipients would keep receiving assistance. These were not in response to individual actions; these were

---

* Brown was unique. When the legislature voted for each member to get a car leased by the state, most legislators went out and got Chevrolets or Fords. Not Willie, he leased a Cadillac. He said his constituents would expect him to have a car like that. Twenty-five years later, my wife and I were on a plane from San Diego to San Francisco. The last person to board the plane was Willie Brown. He sat on the aisle next to my wife. My wife and he had a conversation going up the coast. I never identified myself. When the plane landed and he got up, he pointed to me and said, "Reagan, right?" I had to laugh because I didn't look anything like the twenty-nine-year-old he tried to cut out of the budget.

in response to statewide changes in program rules that affected whole classes of people. So when we changed the AFDC-U unemployed definition to twenty-five hours per week from thirty-five hours, CWRO encouraged all to file a request for a fair hearing.

The same thing happened when the legislature changed the definition of a child from twenty-one to eighteen. There were approximately 29,000 cases affected by this change. We notified all eighteen- to twenty-one-year-olds of the termination of their welfare grants and got flooded with requests for fair hearings. And it was that way for almost all actions we took.

That fair hearing campaign by the California Welfare Rights Organization almost brought us to our knees. According to their signs: "THIS IS WAR." We had so many requests and so very few hearing officers. At my suggestion, we hired law students to do fair hearings. Many of those students became full-time employees when they graduated and augmented our growing legal staff.

The personal attacks were horrendous. Most of them were directed at Bob; he was the Director. As an example, the following appeared in the *San Francisco Examiner* on September 30, 1971:

> "Charging the California Welfare Rights Organization with deliberately jamming up appeal procedures, State Welfare Director Robert Carleson has asked Attorney General Evellel J.Younger for an investigation. Carleson told reporters yesterday that the CWRO had induced thousands of welfare recipients of Aid to Families with Dependent Children to appeal against reduced grants before the reductions had been made.... Assemblyman John Burton (D. San Francisco) called today for Carleson's firing for incompetence and for misinforming Governor Reagan on the welfare reform package. Burton also predicted Reagan eventually would make Carleson the "scapegoat" when, the San Francisco Democrat predicted, the courts throw out substantial parts of the welfare reform package…"

And John Burton was one of the primary legislative negotiators of the Welfare Reform Act. And he was already predicting that most of it would be struck down by the courts. He was certain of this because he had been assured by the poverty lawyers who help draft the legislation that the courts would void our program.

Burton wasn't the only one complaining and predicting utter failure. So was the nominal author of the Bill, Senator Anthony Beilenson. No sooner had the Act taken effect (on October 1, 1971), than Beilenson introduced Senate Concurrent Resolution No. 132 calling for each committee in each house that dealt with welfare policy to investigate the implementation of the Act to determine "the nature and source" of implementation problems.

Senator Beilenson didn't have to ask for a joint body investigation to determine "the nature and source" of implementation problems—he could have just asked me. I would have told him straight up. The problems were caused by Beilenson and Burton and by the poverty lawyers with whom they conspired.

Beilenson's call for a joint investigative committee to investigate the implementation got nowhere so he established a subcommittee of his Senate Health and Welfare Committee. The paper committee then held hearings or more to the point "kangaroo court hearings" on subjects they felt needed to be addressed. Bob Carleson offered all kind of assistance to this group but it was declined.

The poverty lawyers that the legislative staff worked with in drafting the bill filed lawsuit after lawsuit. They used every trick in the book to try to invalidate the Act.

With just forty-eight days to implement the Act, we were under the gun. Our greatest concern was for the fiscal disaster that would occur should the sections raising grants go into effect and the sections reducing payments be delayed. We brought in a group of people from the counties; people who felt that welfare reform was needed and who were willing to help out. They advised us and assisted with drafting regulations they felt could be implemented in the short time available.

Since we were required by law to give notice to recipients fifteen days in advance of any adverse action, we knew that the counties had to send out those notices on September 15. But there was absolutely no way in which individual calculations could be made in the remaining time so the notices could not be made case specific. There just wasn't any time. And it was the legislative negotiators who had insisted on the October 1 effective date.

On September 3 we sent a telegram to each county giving them instructions on how to implement on October 1 and including a lengthy and detailed proposed notice of adverse action to be sent to the recipients. We sent it as a telegram to give the counties an extra day for implementation.

The notice had been put together by Ron and his legal team with considerable input from the county advisory group. The notice included all information that we had and was designed to give the recipient as much notice as to what might occur on October 1. As we approached the deadline, the lawsuits came fast and furious.

The poverty lawyers had a simple approach: Shop for a liberal, sympathetic judge, file a motion for an ex-parte Temporary Restraining Order, get the order and stop us from implementing the provisions of the Act. It worked quite well for them but it caused us no end of administrative nightmare. We were getting restraining orders on the fly after having instructed counties on how to implement a particular provision of the Act. Then we would have to issue another emergency regulation telling them not to implement because of the court order. This confusion culminated in several decisions on September 28, 29, and 30 that stopped the implementation.

A federal judge in San Francisco ruled that recipients weren't given effective notice and he stopped any grant reductions until each county's notice could be reviewed. Counties which had followed the notice that we had prepared and sent them appeared to be in compliance whereas counties that devised their own notice did not.

On September 29, the California Supreme Court issued a stay of the key grant computation section of the Act. This was the section that was to increase the grants for the approximately two thirds of the welfare population who were without other income and decrease grants for recipients with other sources of income. This was the section that McCarthy and his associates insisted be drafted in the way that it was. On September 30, the Supreme Court tried to clarify its decision of the previous day.

The situation was dire. We found out that several counties sent NO checks out to welfare recipients for the October 1 payments. They were concerned that they would be sending the wrong amount so they sent nothing. After filing an emergency regulation the night of the first, we sent a night letter to all county departments directing them to send the already calculated October 1 checks and instructing them to correct any errors in the payment when they issued the October 15 check.

Things were a mess. And the detente that existed following the agreement between Reagan and Moretti evaporated. Reagan was hopping mad and not being a lawyer, he said so in plain English. On October 1, Governor Reagan came out blasting the courts that had issued the orders:

"Due to hasty and uninformed court decisions in the last few days (including a feeble 11th hour attempt by the state Supreme Court to correct its own error), the courts have succeeded in delaying welfare payments to thousands of needy recipients, preventing payments of deserved increases to thousands of others, and thoroughly confusing those responsible for administering the system at the state and county level, as well as the public in general. Further bungling interference by the courts regardless of intentions, or honest errors, regardless of how soon they are corrected, will simply prolong the discomfort of those they purport to be protecting and will add unnecessary costs to the program."

Moretti didn't hesitate either, saying on October 2, the day after the Act became effective, that he was "greatly disappointed that Governor

Reagan has once again blamed California's courts for what is obviously an administrative failure. It is clear that the State Department of Social Welfare under the direction of Robert Carleson has failed to properly implement the Welfare Reform Act of 1971."

Meanwhile, Beilenson was intent on finding mismanagement or illegality in our implementation of the Act. He had his personally created subcommittee hold a hearing and begin an investigation of the implementation. He also immediately began to work on his colleagues to enlist support for his interpretation of the program. Reagan wasn't sitting back and letting him get away with it without comment. On November 2, the Governor issued a release in which he called a group of so-called Democratic legislative leaders "disgraceful and cynically partisan" for contriving an ad hoc committee "for the sole purpose of harassing State Social Welfare Director Robert Carleson and undermining the administration's efforts to reform welfare. ... To blatantly exploit the legislative process in this way is thoroughly disgraceful and cynically partisan."

Beilenson was not always successful in convincing his colleagues of his point of view, but it was hard to enlist support of other legislators for our side. The subject was complex and lent itself to nuances which if not understood, could lead an individual to the wrong conclusion. I heard many a legislator say, "It's so confusing; I don't know what to think." I didn't realize it at the time, but this is a traditional fallback position for legislators at all levels of government. What it really means is "It's so controversial; I don't want to deal with it."

In fact, some of our proposals were extremely nuanced and confusing. And some of them weren't too bright. Oh they looked pretty good when we were sitting in the office, hashing them out between ourselves, but when they actually hit the street, the implementation led to some bizarre occurrences. This too, is not an unusual phenomenon in government. Too many decisions are made in ivory towers without regard to the realities of the world.

Two of the most onerous were our proposals to require stepfathers to support their stepchildren and to require adult working children to contribute to the care of their elderly parents. The latter, termed the Old Age Responsible Relatives provision drew a tremendous amount of fire from the public. This wasn't a new concept in California, but like the requirement for immigrant sponsors to support those they sponsor, it wasn't enforced. Once we started sending bills to adult children, it didn't take long for horror stories to surface: an abusive father on welfare and the abused child now an adult being hunted by the State to collect support or a convicted criminal who deserted his family decades before now on welfare and we were trying to make the children pay for his keep.

We also thought that it would be a good idea to have stepfathers take some responsibility for supporting the children in the home who were on welfare, but we were immediately attacked from all sides as being anti-marriage. The theory being that the guy wouldn't marry the mother if he thought that he would have to take care of her children from another man. But it made sense in the office. Unfortunately, not one of us thought to check to see how many members of the California legislature were stepfathers. "Dead on Arrival" as they say on Capitol Hill.

By the end of 1971, we had thirteen major lawsuits working their way through the courts. Several of them were headed for the United States Supreme Court. Eventually, twelve of the thirteen cases would be decided in our favor. Even though the poverty lawyers had tried to write the statute in their favor, they had failed. We had implemented the Act in a timely manner and were looking to a more peaceful 1972.

Chapter 7

Let's Wrap This Up

It was all implementation during 1972. Implementing the Act, administrative actions, and defending against the legislature, the poverty lawyers, the judges, and the federal government turned out to be more than a full-time job. We thought it might slow down now that we had won, but 1972 started out just as busy as 1971.

At a Governor's luncheon on March 7, 1972, we gave a progress report on the one-year anniversary of the Governor's welfare message to the legislature. We had raised grants to about two thirds of the recipients and we had reduced the caseload by almost 200,000 recipients. We had implemented 80 percent of the package. The major causes for delay and concern were the legislature and its staff, the courts and, unfortunately in some instances, elements of our own administration.

In the legislature, Beilenson continued his attacks. He was particularly mad about the fact that every time we sent out a notice to the counties or required the counties to send notices to recipients, we made sure that the citation read: "The Welfare Reform Act of 1971, SB796 (Beilenson)." Beilenson didn't like that. He didn't want his name on it. In a February press release, Carleson noted, "It is somewhat ironic that the nominal author of the Welfare Reform Act should be constantly attempting to belittle and disown it …" When Beilenson would express his frustration with the way the act was portrayed, we would always explain that it was a proper citation. In reality, we just liked sticking it to him.

In March, Beilenson held a press conference releasing the report of his trumped up *Subcommittee on Implementation of Welfare Reform*. He used terms like "inexcusable mismanagement," "incredible incompetence" and "clear violation of federal and state law." Capitol News Service quoted him as saying, "I don't know that a crime has been committed, I believe there have been violations of law ... whether that is a crime or not, I don't know." Beilenson called for an investigation of us by the Attorney General.

We came right back at him on the day of his press conference with a press conference of our own. Carleson was loaded for bear. He opened with, "I feel like a doctor performing an emergency tracheotomy with someone bumping my arm and telling me I'm doing a sloppy job." In a written statement, Bob said:

> "After a very quick review of the so-called report presented by Senator Beilenson, I find that it is nothing more than a rehash of the same charges made by Senator Beilenson as he started hearings of his personally created committee last November. ... I believe that Senator Beilenson and some other legislators who have been fighting real welfare reform from the start and who have done everything possible to obstruct this reform are now finding it impossible to explain to their supporters in welfare rights organizations and other groups why they were a party to the Welfare Reform Act."

You don't make a statement like that against the Chairman of a powerful committee unless you have given up on any possibility of civil discourse. We had.

Implementing welfare reform was difficult, but piece by piece, we were making headway. Most of our reforms had been run through the courts and Zumbrun's legal crew had been successful in eventually defending us. But there was trouble brewing within the administration. Too many people, in the Governor's Office and in other departments felt that we, "the welfare crowd," were getting too much attention from the Governor and that we were somehow getting by with things that other departments weren't allowed to do. Nowhere was that more apparent than with the Department of Finance. The bureaucrats in Finance were trying to kill us with a thousand cuts. Delay and study were their mantra.

It got so bad that, in frustration, Bob Carleson sent a stinging four page letter to Jim Hall on March 16, 1972, pointing out the Departments that were causing us trouble in implementing welfare reform.

> "I'm very pleased and most grateful for the strong backing I have received from the Governor at every critical point, when the opponents of welfare reform have thrown all their resources into trying to undermine and undercut the support. However, we are now entering an extremely dangerous and critical point. At a time when our opponents in the legislature, welfare rights organizations, OEO attorneys, and HR-1 supporters are intentionally attempting to spread our resources through a variety of attacks, hearings, etc., we are receiving an intensification of bureaucratic haggling from several agencies of state government from which we need the maximum support, cutting of red tape, and willingness to realize that we are in a unique situation. Increasingly, after my staff has butted its head against one of these bureaucratic walls and expended extremely valuable time and effort, the answer I get, although sympathetic, is that most other department heads believe they have similar problems and that my pleadings are really nothing new. Four agencies with which I am having the greatest problem are the Department of Finance, the Department of General Services, the State Personnel Board, and the Attorney General's Office."

Hall responded to the letter the next day with, "I think you and your staff have been patient under very frustrating circumstances, but I urge you and them not to become too discouraged. … While I counsel patience, I do not suggest relaxation. Stay sharp and keep the pressure on." And that is what we did.

The Governor, in limited trips outside the state, touted his welfare reform program. In fact he personally announced several monthly caseload decreases while on the road. He knew that what we were doing in California could be replicated by other Governors and he didn't mind telling them. Reagan was not one who went to a lot of out of state meetings, but he tried to attend the National Governor's Association and, when they had them, the Republican Governor's Association meetings. At one NGA meeting, Nelson Rockefeller, the Governor of New York, asked Reagan how it was that he was making so much progress in California cleaning up welfare. Rockefeller said that he found it impossible to do in New York.

Reagan was waiting for this one. He told Governor Rockefeller that one of his problems was that he had hired California's old welfare director, one of the guys who had gotten us into the mess in the first place. A few months after that discussion, New York had a new welfare director. The new New York director was Abe Lavine. His first assignment by Rockefeller was to get out to California and find out what to do to accomplish the same things in New York. Lavine and an assistant, Paul B. Simmons,* visited us in Sacramento and went back to New York with a full plate of initiatives.

Reagan was having a great time. He seemed to thrive on the moaning and groaning from the legislature and the press. He personally defended the actions that we were taking sometimes against the legislature in general, sometimes against individual legislators, and frequently against the judicial system and individual judges. One of those little outbursts resulted in an embarrassment for the Governor. And I am afraid that I had something to do with it.

---

* This was the first time that I had met Simmons. He had been a newspaper man for the Hearst organization before entering state government. Over the years Paul and I developed a close relationship and worked on a number of projects in various capacities. Paul was credited with coining the phrase Reagan used in the 1980 campaign for President: "Are you better off now than you were four years ago?" Paul passed away in April of 1994 at fifty-two years of age.

It was the tactic of choice for the California Welfare Rights Organization and their publicly funded lawyers to find a sympathetic judge and engage in an ex parte proceeding. These consistently resulted in the judge issuing a Temporary Restraining Order (TRO) that prevented us from implementing an administrative action or some part of the legislation with which they did not agree.

In the fall of 1971, we had developed a program to cross check what recipients of AFDC reported to us as income with the records that employers reported to a sister agency, the state labor agency, Human Resources Development (HRD), for purposes of unemployment compensation. The first run of the program sent a tape of the people on AFDC who reported earnings to us over to HRD one evening in October. The next morning, we found that 41 percent of the sample had more earnings than they reported. The headlines read: "41 Per Cent Fraud Rate Indicated in State AFDC."

The San Francisco Welfare Rights organization opposed our "Earnings Clearance System" and in late January of 1972, they appeared before a Sacramento Superior Court judge, William M. Gallagher asking him to enjoin us from doing any more checking. They alleged that what we were doing was against federal law. Gallagher issued an ex-parte TRO against us to prevent us from checking on outside income that welfare recipients might have without first getting the recipient's permission.

Reagan was outraged and so were the rest of us. He wanted to put out a statement denouncing the action. Bob and I sat down with Ed Gray, the press secretary, and drafted up some red meat. The Governor approved the statement and Ed sent it out. The statement used words like "unconscionable" and "a flagrant violation of public trust." But the part that went too far was where he said, "Such judicial misconduct certainly reinforces the public's low opinion of our court system." It was the use of "judicial misconduct" that caused the Governor to have to apologize the following week. "Judicial misconduct," it turned out, are words of art in the legal profession; it is an offense for which a judge can be removed from office.

Each month as the year went on, the welfare caseload would decline, the first time in the state's remembered history that this had happened. At the same time, caseloads in other states continued to skyrocket. The Governor loved this. We closely guarded the caseload numbers each month, much like the federal government guards economic news until its official release. As soon as the numbers were locked in, a press release was issued, usually by the Governor. By the end of the year the caseload had declined seventeen of the twenty months since we had announced the effort. The welfare caseload had a quarter million less people than it had at its peak in March of 1971.

On February 1, 1972, the Governor made his first and only ap-pearance before the United States Congress when he testified before the Senate Finance Committee about his welfare reform program and against the federal proposal known at the time as the Family Assistance Plan (FAP). FAP involved a national guarantee of income for low income persons and a federal takeover of the administration of the program. Most state agencies had given up on welfare and were sup-porting it strongly. It had passed the House in the previous Congress and was reintroduced by Nixon as HR-1 in the new Congress. It passed the House and was awaiting action in the Senate when Reagan testified against it.

Governor Reagan was critical of HR-1 and encouraged the Finance Committee to instead enact changes in federal law which would allow him to implement the rest of his welfare reform at the state level and would allow other states the latitude to follow. It was pretty powerful testimony and it impressed not only the Republicans on the Committee, but also the powerful chairman, Russell Long, the Democrat from Louisiana.

Later, several federal officials told me that those in HEW and at the White House who were committed to HR-1 felt that it was Reagan's testimony, backed up by his experience in California that killed HR-1 in the Senate. The testimony put the final nail in the coffin of the "guaranteed annual income." It died in 1972.

By the end of that year, much was happening. Jim Hall had resigned to accept a position running the big entertainment empire of MCA, Inc., the large California based conglomerate. The Governor appointed Carleson rival, Earl Brian, then head of MediCal to be the new Secretary. We didn't understand how Brian could be picked over Carleson for the job. It was Carleson who delivered the Governor's number one priority, not Brian. Earl was a young, brash physician who had earned a Silver Star in Vietnam before joining the Reagan administration. His appointment caused a great amount of concern for us. Brian's first actions were to reign in Carleson and crew. Earl let it be known that the times were changing and that he was going to be in charge.

Earlier in 1972, Jim Dwight left the Department of Finance and went to Washington to join his old Finance colleague, Caspar W.(Cap) Weinberger at the Office of Management and Budget. After Nixon's reelection in November, the President decided that he needed to shake up his Cabinet and one of the areas where he wanted to shake up the most was the Department of Health, Education, and Welfare. And he was going to do it by sending "Cap the Knife," his Deputy Director, Frank Carlucci, and the Associate Director, Jim Dwight over to HEW. Dwight was quite familiar with what we were doing in welfare reform and he was slated to take over the W in HEW. Nixon kept his plans close to the vest and very view people knew what was to happen after the inaugural.

Dwight briefed Weinberger on California's amazing welfare reform and convinced him that OMB needed to send a team out to Sacramento to document the success and develop plans for their soon to be stewardship of the nation's welfare programs. So late in 1972 and early in 1973 a joint team of state employees and feds from OMB studied the actions that we had taken and reported on the results. Never to be outdone, Carleson took the results of the study, co-opted the folks from OMB and published our second Blue Book, *California - Showing the Way.* Right after the report came out, Bob told me it was likely that he was going to Washington with Cap and that he wanted me to go also.

We all got invitations to Nixon's Inaugural Ball and headed to Washington, D.C., for the party. We watched the parade from Dwight's office in the Old Executive Office Building and attended the ball that evening. When we returned to Sacramento, Bob accepted a position with Cap at HEW and he announced his resignation. I was appointed Director when he left, but was still considering whether I wanted to go to Washington with him. Brian talked to me and asked me if I wanted the Director's job permanently. Given what I had seen of the operation of the Secretary's office to that point, I told Earl that I wasn't interested. I continued to serve in the Department, but in my mind I was already in Washington, D.C.

Chapter 8

Off to Washington

After I told Earl Brian that I did not want the Director's job permanently, things got very uncomfortable for me in the Agency. Earl's minions knew that I was not staying in the job and they felt that fact authorized increased involvement on their part in the management of the department and in continued implementation of welfare reform. Meanwhile, Bob, Ron, and I were still having discussions as to who was going to do what in Washington.

Welfare, at least AFDC, the part that we had the most experience reforming in California, was administered by the Social and Rehabilitation Service (SRS) in the U.S. Department of Health, Education, and Welfare (HEW). SRS was the W in HEW. In addition to AFDC, SRS administered the Medicaid, Rehabilitation, Child Support, and Social Services Programs. It had all Human Services except cash assistance to the Aged, Blind and Disabled, which had been taken over from the states by the Social Security Administration as the Supplemental Security Income program (SSI) in 1973. SSI was federally administered and paid with green U.S. government checks. All of the programs in SRS were federally supervised/state administered programs. This meant that the federal government authorized the programs and paid anywhere from 50 to 93 percent of the cost, but the states designed their own programs within federal guidelines and shared in the remaining cost.

Within SRS, there were four administrations, the Assistance Payments Administration (APA), the Medical Services Administration (MSA), the Rehabilitation Services Administration (RSA), and the Community Services Administration (CSA). These were the programmatic units. It also contained a well funded research operation, a systems unit, a quality control shop, and ten Regional Offices spread out across the country. During our two-year battle for welfare reform in California, the APA, responsible for AFDC, was the agency that caused us the most problem and therefore it was the agency that we felt we had to get our hands on quickly.

There were certain givens when we started discussions about roles. Cap Weinberger was the Secretary and he had brought his deputy from OMB, Frank Carlucci, to replace Jack Veneman as the Under Secretary. And Cap had designated Jim Dwight to be the Administrator of the Social and Rehabilitation Service. Bob Carleson was to be working for Cap in the Secretary's Office as a special assistant with a portfolio as a roving ambassador to Governors and state legislators to encourage and assist in welfare reform.

The problem as we saw it at that point was Jim. He had not been on our team in California and on many occasions we had butted heads with him over issues that we felt were in the best interest of the Governor's welfare reform program. On the other hand, Jim had been instrumental in getting the second blue book developed and, once he got to OMB, in getting HEW off our back. We solved this dilemma, quite simply. Ron was going to go to SRS to head up the Assistance Payments Administration (APA) and keep Dwight on the straight and narrow. The implication was that if Dwight started to stray, Ron would raise a red flag and we could fix the problem at the Secretary's level. Bob and I would be in the Secretary's Office to assure that it all ran smoothly.

That was all well and good until Ron decided that he wasn't going to Washington. Ron had lived in Sacramento for many years. His family was well established there and it was going to be difficult for him to uproot them. And there was another reason that Ron decided not to go to Washington.

It had all started during our legal battles with the poverty lawyers and legislative staff in California. One evening, sitting in Ron's office, we were lamenting the sad state of affairs where the liberals seemed to have all of the advantages in fighting against us. They had federally funded lawyers, legislators who were willing to shill for them, and legislative staff who collaborated with them in almost every endeavor. We vowed that evening that when "this" was over that we would each kick in some money and start a law firm that was going to combat this one-sided situation.

In early 1973, Ron was going to put his money where his mouth was. Ron co-founded the Pacific Legal Foundation (PLF), one of the earliest and most successful conservative non-profit legal groups in the country. Ron built and led PLF into a formidable force on behalf of business and conservative causes. It was just what we had talked about that evening in his office. But he never asked me for my contribution.

So, with Ron out of the equation, that left Jim Dwight in charge of SRS and welfare with no one on site to monitor him. Bob and I discussed the situation and Bob wanted me to take Ron's place as the head of APA. I was not enthusiastic about it; first, because I wanted to continue to work with Bob and second, I could see where it could cause a lot of internal conflict for me. We discussed it further and Bob convinced me that I had to do it. I finally agreed but I told Bob that I really had a problem going into it knowing that I might have to go behind Dwight's back to keep him on the straight and narrow. I told Bob that I couldn't start a deal on those terms and that if I went to work for Dwight, I would have to work for him. Bob was just going to have to trust me that I wouldn't let Jim get too far off the reservation.

93

Bob agreed but he didn't like it. This whole episode signaled a change in the relationship between Bob and me. Even though we worked together on a number of projects after that, both in and out of government, we never regained the really close relationship that we had during those two and a half years of welfare reform in California.

I left for Washington in April of 1973, flying across country and meeting up with Carl Williams. Carl and I got an apartment in southwest Washington, D.C., not too far from HEW. Carl was going to stay with Bob in the Secretary's Office as I had originally planned to do. I went to SRS with Jim Dwight.

Getting a federal job is no picnic. I soon found that one did not just waltz into town and start collecting a paycheck. Although once most people go through the process, the paychecks are permanent. This in itself can cause problems. But as a new political appointee, there are certain hoops that you have to go through. And it takes time. In the meantime, you are kind of in limbo. Management thinks that you are working hard but the personnel system prohibits you from doing anything until your appointment is official.

I was being appointed the Commissioner of the Assistance Payments Administration, running AFDC. It was a Schedule C position, a political appointment at the GS-18 level. GS-18 was the highest level of civil service at the time. But before I could be appointed, I had to be "cleared." Clearance was a two-step process, the first being political, which included financial disclosure, and the second being a top secret security clearance. Since I had only held a secret clearance in the Air Force, the top secret clearance required a full field investigation by the FBI.

Filling out the financial disclosure forms really wasn't a problem. As a twenty-nine year-old former state employee, I didn't have anything to disclose. The security forms were a little more difficult. Like many young adults in the '60s, I had had many addresses, not all of them remembered completely. The FBI, in its effort to assure itself that

I was not a sleeper Soviet agent and to make sure no one could compromise me for something in my past, wanted to visit every hovel and talk to every neighbor that I'd ever had.*

My clearance finally came through in July, three and a half months after we started the process. I went back to Sacramento and picked up my wife and daughter and brought them to Washington. I was sworn in as the Commissioner of Assistance Payments by Secretary Caspar W. Weinberger on July 29, 1973. It had been almost a four-month wait before I could do anything official. And I wasn't the only one in that fix. Dwight had been confirmed in March and he had been bringing on people to staff up our attempts to reform SRS and welfare as a whole. Those people were also hung up in the security clearance process. During the time we were waiting, we were put on the payroll as "consultants." Since none of us had any federal experience, this seemed a logical thing to do. And that in itself was part of the problem that was to hound us for the next two and a half years.

Jim Dwight hit SRS at full tilt. He had plans for reforming everything. And he wanted to start right away. Bob Carleson, on the other hand, had pretty focused plans for reforming AFDC along the lines of our California reforms. Bob felt that he should be in charge of welfare policy, but he didn't have the legal authority. But as the Administrator of SRS, welfare policy was an area that clearly fell under Dwight's legal responsibility.

The thing that allowed SRS to have a say in the way that the states ran their programs was money. Each of the programs had a large component of federal money involved. It ran from a minimum of 50 percent federal dollars up to 100 percent. The big programs of AFDC

---

* I took six years to get an undergraduate degree. I lived in a lot of places. At one point, I lived on a houseboat on Lake Union in Seattle. When I was there it was a lot more dingy than portrayed in *Sleepless in Seattle*. And the head of the Washington State Communist Party was a neighbor on the same dock. I guess I gave the FBI a run for their money.

95

and Medicaid ran from 50 percent to 93 percent at that time. Social Services were between 75 and 90 percent depending upon the type of service being delivered. SRS required states to submit a state plan for how they were going to spend money, what services were to be provided and to whom they were going to be provided. SRS approved the plans and then states could spend the federal money. There were only two constraints on the programs, the amount of money that the states could come up with to "match" the federal money, and the state plan approval process.

Prior to our arrival at SRS, the agency mission had been to expand the programs and fund everything. Dr. James A. Bax, then Commissioner of the Community Services Administration which administered the social services program was famous for his quote, "You hatch it, and we'll match it." There was no limit on the federal match—it was unlimited open-ended funding.

Jim had strong beliefs about what needed to be done in SRS but he really had no knowledge of the programs that were managed by the agency. He was a CPA by training and had a good grasp of numbers having been Chief Deputy Director of Finance in California and the Associate Director of OMB during 1972. He knew that SRS was spending money out of control and that the mantra of the organization was expand, expand, expand. He had seen the opposition to contraction and accountability that HEW/SRS had put up during the Reagan welfare reforms and he was determined to change the nature of the organization by instilling some discipline into the programs and by requiring the states to accept some responsibility for their actions in managing them.

Unfortunately, it wasn't a one man job. Dwight recognized this and in addition to bringing on me and a couple of other people from California, he began recruiting from a wide swath of sources in Washington and elsewhere. But the great majority of his recruitments, certainly all of them from the private sector or state governments, had to go through the same vetting process that had taken me four months. And in an attempt to get some input from his new recruits, Jim put them all on the payroll as consultants until they could be cleared and appointed to the positions for which they had been recruited.

Looking back on it, it is clear that Dwight had some clear objectives, although at the time it was hard to see them for all the raging fires that we were trying to put out. Essentially he had five goals:

• Reorganize the agency, staff it with professional managers, and devolve responsibility to the regional offices and the states
• Establish strong financial accountability for all SRS programs
• Stop the runaway growth in social services spending
• Change the goal of public welfare by instituting an effective work component
• Re-establish a degree of family responsibility

Although SRS's portfolio of programs was much larger than ours in California, Jim's strategy was based on what we had done there and it was all premised on the principle that there was a limited amount of resources available for the recipients of the agencies' programs and that those resources should be targeted to those people who truly need them. The "truly needy." In the end, we were successful in accomplishing all of his objectives to some degree but not without spilling a lot of blood along the way. We were constantly battling one constituency or another and it took its toll.

Reorganizing the agency would seem to have been the simplest thing. Government agencies are always being reorganized. The employees grow tired of it but they recognize it as a way of life and in fact they always expect it when a new agency head is appointed. SRS was an organization that had been in a constant state of flux since its inception in 1967. Up until the period when we showed up in early 1973, the philosophy of the agency had been that its job was to do "good." We agreed, but we just wanted it to do a good job.

When I was appointed the Commissioner of Social Security in 1981, I was advised that the Social Security Administration (SSA) had been through several reorganizations due to the number of Commissioners and Acting Commissioners who had passed through there in recent years. I had promised no reorganization when first appointed, but after a year in office, I decided that something needed to be done and announced not a reorganization, but a "realignment." By that time I was a known quantity to SSA and "realignment" became kind of a non-fearful buzzword for the reorganization I instituted.

In SRS however, there were no "non-fearful" euphemisms for reorganization. This along with the fact that Dwight was an unknown outsider and he and I were part of the "California Mafia" taking over the management of human services caused a tremendous uproar. Some people were just genuinely afraid of change, while others who had a career as professionals caring for people were completely opposed to a change in direction. We cared about people too, but we wanted to do it efficiently and effectively. So when you couple the expected paranoia about reorganization, the "mafia" designation, several key personnel recruited from private industry who were in a consultant status and a couple of high profile recruits from the Department of Defense, it resulted in a readymade classic "we versus they" confrontation. As Yogi Berra, the former New York Yankee catcher would say, "It's déjà vous all over again"—just like the highway guys taking over social welfare in California in 1971.

There were major differences between reforming welfare in California and doing it on the national level. First, in California we spent several months in planning our program and our approach. We studied the issues and learned the programs and the organization before the first shot was fired. The agency, SDSW didn't really have a methodology for formally opposing our changes. And we had, at least initially, the support of the entire government. We never lost the support of the Governor even as some of his appointees got a little tired of the "welfare crowd."

But in Washington it was different. We didn't know the programs, the personnel system, or the organization. We had Cap's support, but the rest of the Nixon Administration was still pushing for a federal takeover of the programs and they were constantly working on Cap to come over to their side. In SRS, there was a recognized employee union, a local of the American Federation of Government Employees (AFGE). And as a parting gift, the outgoing Administrator, John Twiname, had signed a contract with the local that basically gave them a management role in the running of the agency. It called for a lot of meetings, consultations, and notifications. The union used that agreement to harass us continually.

The union also fed the media. The syndicated columnist Jack Anderson got on our case as did the local trade paper, the *Federal Times*. The attacks in the press were unwarranted, one-sided, and in many cases personal. From a *Federal Times* story in mid 1974 about an appearance before the Senate Appropriations Committee:

> "James Dwight … He's a sad looking man with big, sad eyes, a round baby face with a thin mouth that belongs to an old man. … Jack Young, a nondescript man … and John Svahn, another baby-faced man who looks around with the air of a Rhodes Scholar."

And they also worked hard on union sympathetic members of Congress and were successful in getting one of them to rail hard against what we were doing. At one point, they succeeded in getting a rather obscure U.S. Senator from South Dakota, Abourezk, to spend almost eight pages of the Congressional Record castigating us under the title of "Operation Mangle Is Underway."

They also found an ally in the office of the Chairman of the Subcommittee on Labor-Health, Education, and Welfare of the Senate Appropriations Committee. The committee staff director, Harley

Dirks, did not like what we were doing and used any method he could to keep us from implementing reforms.

The Chairman, Warren G. Magnuson, a Democrat from the state of Washington went along with it, not out of any sense of commitment to the union but more than likely from a strong attachment to alcohol. Maggie, as he was called, had a problem that pronounced itself almost every day after lunch. I felt sorry for him but he made our life difficult. We would go to a hearing and Magnuson would be very late. When he appeared, his staff had to tell him who was testifying. On several occasions, I had to explain the difference between Medicaid (which SRS administered) and Medicare (which was administered at that time by the Social Security Administration).

At one point I was scheduled for an afternoon hearing before the Committee and I called Dirks and told him that I was not going to sit around in the witness chair while they looked in all of the bars on Capitol Hill for the Chairman. He assured me that the Chairman would be on time. He wasn't and I sat in the chair until his staff found him.

Today, with "gotcha" journalism, it would be much more difficult for any public official to function as Magnuson did. But in the early 1970s, there was almost an unwritten rule that precluded the media from exposing a member's personal weakness. Everyone in Washington, D.C., knew that Wilbur Mills, the Chairman of the powerful House Ways and Means Committee, had a drinking problem, but it wasn't until a thirty-eight-year-old stripper named Fanne Fox jumped out of the sixty-five-year-old Mills' car and into the Tidal Basin just below the South Lawn of the White House, that it was reported.

Magnuson and his staff continued to harass us at every step of the way. We were constantly barraged by requests to justify every move. The requests came into the office of the Assistant Secretary for Management in the Office of the Secretary. Charlie Miller, the Deputy Assistant Secretary and the initial recipient, called the missives "Harleygrams" because they inevitably came from Dirks. At one point, after having been repeatedly attacked by Magnuson for having gone to Hawaii "on a junket" to speak at a conference, I had to call on the good office of Senator Inouye to explain to the Chairman's staff that Hawaii was a state, just like Washington.

We occasionally got a little favorable press. The nationally syndicated columnist Victor Riesel wrote a column about the trouble Dwight, Carleson, and I had with Magnuson in 1975:

> "I have no doubt that these men … have been harassed because they were associated with Ronald Reagan. … [They] have brought in management experts, computer technology, lawyers and accountants. … Their thanks has been harassment by Sen. Magnuson's Appropriation Committee. … One might ask Sen. Scoop Jackson why he doesn't use his Government Operations Committee to question his fellow Washington state senator. It is in the public interest to determine who's covering up what and why Magnuson's committee is so antagonistic."

Mr. Riesel almost had it right. It really wasn't the whole committee that constantly went after us. It was just Magnuson acting primarily through his staff director that perpetrated the attacks. The rest of the Committee members were rarely heard from or seen.

Another difference between our effort at reform at the state level and the one at the federal level was that we made a lot more mistakes in Washington than we did in California. And when I say "we," I mean all of us. Some of them were serious and resulted in disciplinary action. Others were just plain dumb. But each time we made one, we could read about it in the newspaper or spend time on Capitol Hill trying to explain it.

A serious mistake, perhaps the most serious, involved the use of "consultancies" for the people Dwight brought in to run various components of the reorganized agency. I was one as well as M. Keith Weikel, a pharmacist, brought in to run the Medicaid program, and John C. (Jack) Young, a Naval Academy graduate recruited from Computer

Sciences Corporation, who was to set up and run an Information Technology shop. As the clearance process dragged on, each of us to one degree or another became more and more involved in SRS daily operations. Dwight and Weinberger were pushing for action, and it was only normal that people who were designated to take over operations found themselves responding. Making decisions. Directing people. Recruiting. And other actions necessary to move the agency in a new direction.

It turned out that what we were doing was also not legal, or at least not permissible under federal personnel rules. Consultants are not permitted to supervise government employees, nor are they permitted to make decisions. The union enlisted the support of several Democrat members of Congress and filed complaints with the Civil Service Commission (CSC) and tried to stop what we were doing. Eventually, we all received clearances and were appointed to valid positions. But the investigations continued for months and resulted in some very unkind things being said by the CSC about actions taken by us early in the process.

And unfortunately, the Commission came down hard on the SRS career personnel officer, Ladd Hamilton, handing him a suspension without pay as punishment for him allowing the rest of us to violate personnel rules. As if he could have done anything else. In fact, most of the agency career employees were doing their best to impress the new management and Hamilton was no different. The CSC took exception, saying that he should have known better. Ladd accepted the suspension. In government, we call that falling on your sword.

Looking back on it, some of the mistakes were just silly. Early on, one of Dwight's desires was to get his key Commissioners physically located close to him. To do this, he cleared out one wing of the fifth floor of the Mary E. Switzer building and redid the floor creating offices for the Commissioners of Assistance Payments, Medical Services, Community Services, and Rehabilitation, all his new appointees. Well, he got a lot of criticism for "expending money meant for the poor on redecorating" and the like, but the biggest symbolic flap was over the toilet seat in the washroom attached to his own office.

Both Jim Dwight and Bob Carleson had gone to the University of Southern California. I went to the University of Washington. Over the years a friendly rivalry had developed between us regarding the schools. Jim had rowed on the crew at SC as I had at Washington so we had that rivalry also. One day, I spotted a great looking toilet seat in SC red and gold, with a big USC decal on the cover. I bought it and installed it on his commode late one evening. We both got a big laugh out of it until we read all about it in the newspapers. It suddenly became the symbol of arrogance and waste of money at SRS. Dwight took a lot of heat for that toilet seat but he didn't remove it. I guess that it comes as no surprise that no one from the press ever asked where the seat came from or who had paid for it. The lesson that I learned was that our situation was no joking matter.

On the personal front, 1973 and particularly 1974 were extremely trying. When I left Sacramento, I was in the last year of law school at McGeorge School of Law. I had been on a scholarship and was at the top of my class and the Dean, Gordon Schaber, arranged with Georgetown Law School for me to take the last few class hours that I needed in order to graduate at Georgetown in their evening program. I had gotten along at McGeorge fairly well, but I had a reputation for not attending very many classes. McGeorge was known as a "bar school" (that is, it taught students how to pass the California Bar) and even though it had just recently become affiliated with the University of the Pacific, it still taught and graded like a bar school. I knew that now I was at a big time law school and the competition should have been a lot tougher.

I fully intended to be a conscientious student, attending classes and briefing cases, but like Sacramento, my more than full-time day job got in the way. One of the classes that I needed was Conflicts of Laws.

At McGeorge this was a senior year class, but at Georgetown it was a freshman class. And as such it was taught in a large amphitheater with a couple of hundred students. I attended the first couple of classes and then got caught up in SRS business. I ended up missing most of the classes. As the final examination approached, I decided it was time to learn Conflicts.

I didn't know what had been covered but I figured that somewhere in HEW there had to be someone who was also taking the class, so I put the word out. Sure enough, there was a young man right in SRS who was in the class. His name was Jack Sachetti. I asked him to meet me in my office and after introductions I told him that I was in the class. Jack looked at me and said, "I know you are." I asked him how he knew and he said, "Every night he calls on you, he's really mad that you aren't there." So much for Conflicts, I thought. I got what had been covered in the course from Jack and started cramming.

The night of the final exam, I sat in the big classroom, about twenty rows up and not calling attention to myself. The professor walked out on the stage and said, "Well, we will try one more time. Is Mr. Svahn here?" I put up my hand and answered. He said that they had missed me all semester and inquired as to whether or not I thought that I could pass the course. I told him I was going to try. He replied, "Good Luck" but his attitude and demeanor said anything but. I got a C+ in the course. I did not finish law school. I was taking the last courses that I needed for McGeorge to give me the degree in the spring of 1974 when tragedy struck.

My wife Jo gave birth to our son, John III, on March 16 of that year. We were very happy but things did not go right as soon as Jo came home from the hospital. She was in pain and her doctor said it was post partum depression. For a week, we kept going to the doctor and he continued to say it was unfortunate, but that nothing was wrong. Finally, the pain was so bad that we went to the emergency room in the middle of the night. They said it was a muscle spasm and sent us home. It got worse. Her doctor wouldn't talk to me; he would only talk to her. Finally, a nurse told me to take her to the doctor's office. About ten days after John's birth, I got a call at the office from the doctor and he said that Jo had been to see him and that he was sending her to the hospital by ambulance. Something was seriously wrong. The hospital diagnosed it as a perforated gastric ulcer that occurred during childbirth. They performed surgery shortly thereafter, but the surgeon said that it was all walled off with scar tissue and that there was nothing that could be done at this point. He said that it might be fine and then again, the scar tissue might cause some intestinal blockage in the future and have to be repaired. It all happened so fast and with a new baby that we fought through it and she came home in April.

Jo continued to be under the care of the doctors at the hospital in Virginia throughout the summer. Her mother and my mother visited and helped us with John and Kirsten. In September, Jo complained of pain and constant tiredness. The chief surgeon at the hospital said that it was adhesions from the ulcer in March that were causing the pain and that with some simple surgery, he would snip them off, remove the blockage and relieve the pain. Surgery was scheduled at the end of September and he promised that it would be routine. When he came into the waiting room after about an hour, he walked up to me and didn't pull any punches. "It's cancer throughout her whole body. She will die within two weeks." I was struck dumb. I tried to ask questions but there were no answers. He said he was sorry but that there was nothing that could be done. He suggested that we put her on chemotherapy but said that it would be more for research purposes than for any attempt to put the cancer in remission. Jo Marie died on October 2, 1974, just a little over the two weeks that the surgeon had promised. It was a bright sunny day with the trees in full fall colors. Everyone deals with death in the family in their own way. I locked that day away somewhere in the back of my mind. I rarely open it up.

Chapter 9

Transition

By the end of 1975, many things had happened. Cap had left HEW and was the general counsel at Bechtel, the huge contracting corporation in California. Frank Carlucci was off being U.S. Ambassador to Portugal, Jim Dwight was a partner with the Big Eight accounting firm of Haskins and Sells (later Deloitte), Bob Carleson was out consulting with states on how to reform welfare and I was winding up my federal career.*

I resigned from HEW in February of 1976. Secretary F. David Mathews, an academician appointed by President Gerald Ford, accepted my resignation "with regret" but it wasn't a very long letter. I think he was pretty happy to see me go. I had worked for the government ever since getting out of college, first in the military, then with the state of California, and finally with HEW at the federal level and now here I was starting out on a new career in the private sector. Jim Dwight had recruited me to join him at Haskins and Sells. They were a big eight accounting firm that had only rarely done business with government and they had just opened a Washington Office. Jim and I were going

---

* Caspar W. Weinberger, James S. Dwight, Jr., and Robert B. Carleson all died within a month of each other in the spring of 2006.

to be a nucleus with which to start a government consulting practice for the firm.

And there was something else. Several months before I left government, a cabal of friends and a lobbyist got together and invited me to a tennis match in Washington. Unknown to me was the fact that they also invited a young woman from Boston as my blind date. It was only eleven months after my wife had passed away and I really wasn't pleased that they had set me up without my knowledge. Keith Weikel and Jack Young convinced me that I should go ahead with it. "Why disappoint her?" was their common theme. It was on that night at a tennis match that I met Jill Weber. She was thirty-two, as was I, with red hair and freckles. We hit it off and "Boston Reds," as the folks in SRS thereafter referred to her, and I carried on a long distance courtship between Washington, D.C., and Boston. Jill eventually moved to Virginia and we were married on July 12, 1977. We moved from Virginia to Severna Park, Maryland, and my brother Gus brought Kirsten, now six, and John, now three, out from where they had been living with my parents in San Diego.

I only had occasion to deal with the Carter Administration twice, and both times were somewhat humorous, to me at least. In the first case, the same loose-knit confederation of intellectuals who convinced Nixon to sign on to the Family Assistance Plan and Weinberger to agree to push the Income Supplement Plan came back to the table again and in 1977 got Carter to buy into another guaranteed annual income plan, this time dubbed the Program for Better Jobs and Income (PBJI). When it looked like Carter might be getting some traction for his concept to scrap AFDC, SSI, and Food Stamps and replace them with a guaranteed cash income, conservatives on the hill became concerned.

Phil Crane, the Congressman from Illinois, was the chairman of the American Conservative Union at the time and he asked me if I would lead a small team of conservatives to develop an opposition response to the Carter proposal. I readily accepted. To kick it off we had a gathering on Capitol Hill for a strategy session. Included were Bob Carleson, myself, and Chuck Hobbs, all principals in the California welfare reform days. We were on the elevator in the Rayburn building when the door opened and who should be standing there but John Burton, now a member of Congress, but still smarting from the shellacking he took in the California welfare reform fight. Burton looked in and saw the three of us; exclaimed, "Shit!" and raced away down the hall. Guess we must have invoked some bad memories—either that or he may have thought he was hallucinating.

As a group opposing the Carter program, we wound up having only one meeting. There wasn't any need for more. Like Nixon's FAP and Ford's Income Supplement Plan (ISP), the Carter proposal failed to gain much momentum and our effort became unnecessary.

The second brush with the Carter Administration came while I was with Haskins (that was by this time Deloitte, Haskins, and Sells). Each week, the company published a newsletter for its clients and other interested people. It was entitled the *Week in Review* and because the economy was so bad and the government was doing so much to manage it, a lot of the material in it came out of Washington. To get the information to publish, Haskins was paying a large law firm in D.C. to report on activity. And they were paying a goodly sum each week for it. I asked the managing partner why they were paying this firm to read the *Washington Post* and the *Wall Street Journal* each morning and condense it into a report by the afternoon. He didn't understand so I decided to demonstrate.

I called the White House. When the courteous operator on the Administrative Board answered I asked for the Press Office. I introduced myself to an assistant press secretary as being from the *Week in Review*, a weekly financial publication, and inquired as to whether they had anything new on wage and price stability. He said that "they," the Council on Wage and Price Stability (COWPS), had their own press office now and he gave me the number.

I called COWPS and introduced myself to the press officer and indicated that the White House Press Office had directed me to him. I asked if he had anything new and he told me that they had a complete new program. He said it was embargoed until the next Monday and I told him that we didn't publish until Monday. I took the senior partner with me to the COWPS office to pick up the documents. I had to promise the guy that we wouldn't break the embargo, and then he gave us the package. On Monday, the *Week in Review* broke the story on the new COWPS program, right along with the *Washington Post* and the *Wall Street Journal.* But notwithstanding my initiatives, my career at Haskins and Sells did not last very long. They were very conservative and looked very much askance at "government work."

The next big transition came in November 1980. On election night in 1980, Jill and I threw a party at our home in Maryland to watch the returns. I had been over to campaign headquarters a few days before and knew that the numbers looked good. But when the networks called the election as soon as the polls closed, I was stunned with the victory. Ronald Reagan was going to be the fortieth President of the United States.

The first call came from Bob Carleson. Bob had been in the surrogate program during the campaign and he said he was going to head up the Transition Team for the Department of Health and Human Services. He wanted me to join him on the Transition Team. During the campaign, David Winston, another Californian, had asked me to do a piece on the Department for the Heritage Foundation publication "Mandate for Change" primarily on the Social Security Administration but including the Office of the Secretary.

Ever since my stint in SRS, I had been a strong critic of the Office of the Secretary (OS). At that time there were almost five thousand people in it and it hadn't gotten any smaller in the four years since. I could find no reason for that many people working there. Later as Commissioner of Social Security, when someone would call me and announce that he/she was from the Office of the Secretary and that the Secretary wanted me to do something, I would just say, "Well then just have him give me a call." I didn't get too many calls.

So I figured that Bob wanted me to do the transition for OS. He said no, he wanted me to do the Health Care Finance Administration (HCFA), the agency that ran Medicare and Medicaid after Carter had combined them in 1977. He said he was getting all the old crowd back together: he and Carl Williams would take care of OS, Dave Swoap would head up the team on Social Security and others would be brought in to handle the Public Health agencies. Now, transition teams are interesting phenomena. I have been on them coming in and going out and I can tell you it is a lot more fun coming in.

On most occasions, people who are appointed to transition teams come out of the campaign. That is how Bob was selected. But right after an election, the wannabes, all the usedtobes, the lobbyists, the industry people, and political hacks come out of the woodwork and want to get on the "transition team." It happened just that way with the Reagan HHS transition. We wound up with lots of help. As we moved closer to the end of the transition, the size of the "team" grew exponentially. And another thing about transition teams is that very few of the above really want to do any work. They just want to be able to say that they are on the transition team.

The HCFA transition team, for the most part, was me. Paul Wilging, the Acting Administrator assigned JoAnne Spalding to work with me. I knew both of them from my SRS days. It was long hours and lots of meetings with current HCFA staff, many of whom had worked for me in the SRS Medicaid program just four years before. Because of this and because I had some familiarity with the programs, I probably had an easier time of it than do some transition teams who truly are coming in from the outside. During most of November and all of December, I worked with HCFA in preparing an exhaustive study of issues facing the agency and programs that it administered.

We ended up with a three-inch book cataloging twenty-five areas to be addressed by the new administration. Issues ranged from those expected like the budget, the organization, and administrative problems to more detailed discussions of End Stage Renal Disease, long term care, primary care physicians, and a plethora of issues surrounding the state Medicaid programs.

I was also assigned to the SSA transition team, which was headed up by Dave Swoap. I did manage to get over to his office in the SSA complex late one night for a discussion with him. He, like me, seemed to be the only working member of his team. We talked about what he was finding out. He had major concerns about SSA's data processing capabilities, but he had no technical people to advise him and he, like me, was no IT guy. Having just been with a big eight accounting firm and knowing that they all had large systems consulting components, I suggested to him that he contact that American Institute of Certified Public Accountants and get them to put together a team to help him out. I thought nothing more about it but unfortunately that suggestion led to a personally trying time for me five years later.

Swoap was also assigned to my team at HCFA, but due to the size and scope of the problems at SSA, and his lack of familiarity with its programs, he was pretty much a no show at HCFA. Toward the end of the transition period, Bob got the whole team together at the Hubert Humphrey Building, HHS headquarters, to go over the plan and how we were to wrap it up. I was really surprised at the number of people who were there and "on the team."

Bob directed that our reports were to be delivered to him and that prior to the inauguration, he was going to brief incoming Secretary Richard Schweiker, the Republican Senator who had been Ronald Reagan's surprise choice as a running mate at the 1976 convention.

I am not sure what happened to those transition reports after we gave them to Bob. I know that he briefed Dick Schweiker. But I also know that the eventual Administrator of HCFA, Carolyn Davis, never saw the one that I put together and I did not receive the transition report for the Social Security Administration. After the transition and inaugural, an Administrative Law Judge (ALJ) wrote to Bob at the White House and asked for a copy of part of the report. Carleson wrote back to him and told him that the report was part of the transition materials and all of them had been turned over to Dick Schweiker. The ALJ then wrote to Schweiker, who by then was the Secretary of HHS, asking for the report. Schweiker responded that the report in question was part of the transition and therefore did not exist in the Department! When I asked what had happened to the transition reports at the time, I was told that the transition material was the property of the transition team and as soon as the President was sworn in, that material was no longer available. Go figure.

Real transition team members get a certificate and are paid one dollar for their time and effort. I spent two months of my own time on the transition. I got the certificate but never got the dollar. I jokingly asked Reagan about it once and, after I explained the process, he laughed and said I must not have earned it.

With my tasks completed at the transition, I turned my attention to a new task, finding a job in the new administration. I knew that I was not a candidate for Secretary of HHS, and I had initially thought that Bob Carleson was the logical choice for Ronald Reagan. Looking back on it, I guess that Bob didn't have any health experience and a massive part of HHS at the time dealt with health, either financing, public health, or research. Besides, he was setting up in the White House as the coordinator of all programs having to do with human services and I think that he figured that he would have more impact from that position. Since he had specialized in those areas as a Senator and probably being owed one by Reagan for the '76 campaign, Dick Schweiker certainly was a more logical choice. I did talk to Dave Swoap about what he was going to do and it turned out that he and I were both interested in becoming the Under Secretary of HHS.

The process of securing a Presidential appointment in the Reagan Administration seemed a little simplistic to me at the time. It was also mysterious. You filled out a form and were scheduled for an interview at the transition headquarters in downtown Washington, D.C. The transition personnel operation was headed up by E. Pendleton James, who later became the Director of Presidential Personnel for the first year or so of the Reagan Administration. I got a call and came in for my interview. I wandered around a bit and said hello to a few of the old California crowd and then was interviewed by a person that I did not know for a job that was not disclosed to me! I expressed my desire to be the Under Secretary of HHS, but said if that was not to be, I would like to take over HCFA. At the end of the interview, the transition official thanked me and told me that I would be hearing from someone.

The next time I heard, early in January, it was from Dick Schweiker's office and they asked me to come into to meet with the Secretary designate. Even though Dick had been in the Senate when I was at SRS, our paths had never crossed. He was a pleasant fellow in his mid-fifties and we had an interesting discussion. It seemed that as far as Dick was concerned, I was going to be the Commissioner of Social Security. He went through the ritual of asking me, but I got the definite impression that it had already been decided! By whom I know not.

I was pretty surprised by the whole thing. It was true that in the 1977 Carter reorganization that created HCFA and dissolved SRS, the welfare, child support, and refugee programs were given to the Social Security Administration, but the real behemoths in that agency were the Old Age, Survivors and Disability Insurance programs under Title II of the Social Security Act. I knew absolutely nothing about those programs or about the 83,000 people that administered them.

After meeting with Schweiker, I talked to David Winston, who was heading up Schweiker's transition. David had worked for Earl Brian in California and he had been on Schweiker's staff on the Hill. He told me that he was not going to join the administration, but that I was and that I was going to be the Commissioner of Social Security and the Swoap was going to be the Under Secretary. No discussion. I just wasn't ready for that. I was thirty-seven years old. Commissioners of Social Security were old guys. There was no market for used Commissioners of Social Security.

I went home and discussed it with my wife. The Social Security Administration (SSA) was big, with 83,000 people in 1350 offices around the United States. It paid benefits monthly to 51 million people. It was a big lumbering dinosaur left over from Roosevelt's New Deal and I couldn't see how getting involved with it was going to do anything for anybody. Furthermore, due to a quirk in legislative history, it was headquartered in Woodlawn, a suburban community on the west side of Baltimore, Maryland. I also knew that the agency had some very serious problems both from a financial standpoint and from a managerial standpoint.

A neighbor of mine, an associate from SRS days, Nelson Sabatini, worked at SSA and knew that I was on the transition team. Although he didn't know that I was slated to be the Commissioner, he kept bending my ear about the problems at SSA and the great potential there was in the organization. After a weekend of soul searching, I told Dick that I would accept the nomination.

The process to become a statutory Presidential appointee is quite a bit more complicated than most incoming new administration appointments. First off, you have to be formally nominated by the President. Before he does that, you have to be cleared, politically, financially, and for national security purposes. At the start of an administration, getting security clearances done by the Federal Bureau of Investigation can be a time consuming process. It is interesting to note that during the 2008 campaign, President George W. Bush authorized the security clearance process to begin during the campaign for a hundred or so people identified by both Obama's campaign and McCain's campaign so that no matter which one won, they would have a head start on the process. When Barack Obama became President, he was able to appoint many staff almost immediately, because they already had security clearances. President Jimmy Carter provided no such courtesy to the incoming Reagan administration.

I didn't have any problem passing the political test. Lyn Nofziger was the final word on that in the White House and by that time someone had already decided that Dave and I were going to be the Reagan hands at HHS. And I didn't have any trouble with the financial disclosure requirement. We didn't own much and I worked for a salary. In fact, in the 1982 Ralph Nader book, *Reagan's Ruling Class*, the authors barely mentioned any financial matters of mine, whereas with some other Reagan administration officials, they went on for pages.

But the security clearance was another matter. Even though I had held a top secret clearance and higher compartmentalized clearances in the Nixon and Ford Administrations, I still had to join the queue and wait for an FBI full field investigation. I filled out the forms and waited. In the meantime, just as had happened in 1973 when I first came to Washington, I was made a "consultant" at HHS for purposes of payroll while I learned about the Social Security Administration.

The word leaked out pretty quickly. Washington thrives on gossip and there is never more gossip floating around than during a presidential transition. Of course, a lot of it is self-generated. But in my case, I didn't leak anything and it didn't get to the newspapers or the trade publications.

The first inkling that I had that my name was being vetted for Commissioner of Social Security was from a phone call from J.J. Pickle, a Democrat congressman from Texas who happened to be the Chairman of the Subcommittee on Social Security of the House Ways and Means Committee. He introduced himself and then said, "Commissioner, you and I need to sit down and talk. I'm calling you to see when we can do that." I was pretty well surprised and sputtered something like, "Ahhh, Mr. Chairman, I am not the Commissioner of Social Security. Ahhh, the President hasn't nominated anyone to be Commissioner yet." Jake, as he was known, laughed a little and suggested that was OK, we could just talk then.

By the time the inauguration took place on January 20, 1981, I had still not been granted the necessary security clearance. But we were going to the inauguration and the Inaugural Ball knowing that shortly my name would be sent to the Senate for "advice and consent."

For the first time in history, the inauguration was to be held on the west steps of the U.S. Capitol. That allowed many more people to witness the event. It was chilly that morning, but not bitterly cold. In fact, by the time the swearing in actually occurred it was fairly warm and the frozen ground had thawed quite a bit. When President Reagan took the oath, the sun was shining brightly.

My mother, Esther, Jill and I were in "Preferred Standing – North Area" an apt description for a large grassy area off to the side of the Capitol building and pretty much out of sight of the actual event. But we were there. As the three of us stood in the crowd waiting for the President to take the oath, I recognized John Connelly, the former Governor of Texas, who was standing directly in front of us. I said hello to him and introduced Jill and my mother to him. He smiled and in a quick moment said, "You know, nine months ago I was running for President. And here I am, standing in the mud, waiting for my primary opponent's inauguration." I thought about the irony in it, but also thought that it pretty well summed up the political process in America.

After the event and the parade, we went back to the hotel to get ready for the "Ball." I had been to one Ball, Nixon's second, and knew that the term was somewhat of a misnomer. And this one was even more so. Everyone in Washington wanted to be at the White Tie California Ball at the Kennedy Center. It was so crowded that you could not move, let alone dance, drink, or converse. We did not see the President and First Lady during the time that they were in the Kennedy Center.

We were on a different floor and didn't even know that they had arrived until the crowd buzz got to us.

I have been to three Inaugural Balls and they have all been the same. And the noise, crowdedness, and confusion that occur cause a lot of otherwise polite establishment people to behave like street hoodlums. At the second inaugural ball for Ronald Reagan in 1985, the crowd at the D.C./Maryland/Virginia Ball became so upset at not being able to retrieve their coats and wraps, that they charged the coat room, climbing over the desk, and grabbed anything that looked familiar. Fur coats were a prime target.

The clearances finally were completed and the President announced his intention to nominate me to be the ninth Commissioner of Social Security on March 3, 1981. For over two months, I had been studying the Social Security Administration, the Social Security Act, and its programs. Now I was moving into the second phase of a Presidential appointment—Senate confirmation.

It should be no surprise, but the first task to be undertaken for Senate confirmation is to fill out *their* forms. The Senate has its own forms for conflict of interest and financial disclosure. Once I had done that I met with Robert Lighthizer, the Chief Counsel of the Senate Finance Committee to go over them. I had known Bob before so at least that went pretty smoothly. The next step in the process is to offer to pay a courtesy call on the members of the Committee. Finance at the time was chaired by Bob Dole of Kansas and the chair of the subcommittee on Social Security was Bill Armstrong from Colorado. Both were very congenial and the visits were short. Only one little blip occurred during my visit with Senator Dole. As I was leaving he reached out and grabbed my tie and said to a staff person, "Get a pair of scissors. We don't want any Carter/Mondale stuff here!" The tie I had on was a Countess Mara, a designer of the day, and had a stylized CM midway down the front of it. I never wore a Countess Mara tie again.

I did courtesy visits with Senators Grassley, Heinz, Long, Byrd, and Baucus. And all went smoothly. Another visit I made was quite memorable. Even though he wasn't on the Committee, Senator Goldwater wanted me to come by for a visit. Barry Goldwater was the first presidential candidate for whom I had voted. I had never met him before and I was very much impressed to be sitting in his office chatting with him. He told me that he really didn't have anything to tell me or ask me to do for him; he just wanted to meet the guy who was going to fix Social Security!

My confirmation hearing was on April 28, 1981. It was chaired by Senator Chuck Grassley, at that time number eleven in seniority out of eleven Republicans in the majority. Other than two housekeeping questions about the forms, the Senator had only one question. The Chairman of the committee, Dole had submitted four questions to be answered for the record. When the Chair turned the questioning over to Texas Senator Benson, the Democrat in attendance, he only had three questions for me.

Senator Benson may be best known and remembered for when he ran for Vice President on the Dukakis ticket against Senator Dan Quayle in 1988. Benson, known for some pretty good one-liners, said to Quayle after the Senator from Indiana had compared himself to John F. Kennedy in their debate, "Senator, I served with Jack Kennedy; Jack Kennedy was a friend of mine; Senator, you're no Jack Kennedy." His quip brought the house down.

After Benson finished with his three questions, Senator Grassley moved to vote on the nomination. Senator Benson seconded the motion. The vote was unanimous. I was approved. It was odd. The biggest financial problem looming on the horizon at the time, the program that members of Congress hear most about from their constituents, the focus of the very powerful elderly lobby and yet in the confirmation hearing for the person the President selected to run the program, only two Senators asked a couple of softball questions each.

As the hearing ended, Senator Benson took the microphone and looking straight at me said, "Mr. Svahn, this is your most popular moment." He brought the house down again. There was a lot of laughter in the Committee Room. My nomination came up before the full Senate on May 4, 1981, and I was confirmed "without objection." Benson was right—it was my most popular moment. The transition was over.

Chapter 10

The Third of Something

S ocial Security has always been called the "third" of something.
What that something is depends upon your perspective. Policy
makers, financial planners, and even the original designers of the
program have referred to the program over time as the third leg of the
three legged stool of retirement. The first leg is the pension plan gained
through a career of work; the second is private savings and the third leg
is social security. In today's world, with private pensions disappearing
and private savings at an all time low, and with its trust funds being
depleted, social security is looking like a really weak leg on a very wobbly three legged stool.

In Washington, Social Security is better known better as the "third
rail" of politics. The saying goes, "Social security is the third rail of
politics; touch it and you die." The metaphor of course refers to the
third rail of electrified train systems. There are the two rails of track
that the train runs on and then there is the exposed third rail which
is electrified with very high voltage to provide power to the trains' engines. Many people have died by falling, stumbling, or being pushed
onto this "third rail" both literally and figuratively.

In the political context, calling Social Security the third rail of politics was uttered by Thomas P. "Tip" O'Neill, who was the Speaker of

the House of Representatives during the first six years of the Reagan presidency. During the early years of Reagan's first term, social security was a volatile political issue, and O'Neill made the most of it.

These two metaphors speak volumes about what social security is and what it isn't. It is not a retirement program; and it is not sacrosanct. You have to go back to 1935 when it was first enacted during the Great Depression to find the seeds of confusion about the program.

Social security was not passed by acclamation in 1935. It was a tough sell by the Franklin Roosevelt administration. During the fight for passage, a lot of horse-trading took place; many promises were made and as a result many myths developed about the system. It wasn't by accident that confusion about the program has reigned for the ensuing seventy-five years. The Roosevelt administration deliberately hazed over the specifics of the program using language and words that misled generations of Americans as to what the program was and what it wasn't.

At its inception, it was promised that the amount each worker would pay would only be 1 percent of the employee's wages up to a maximum of $3,000. It was to be $30 per year, per employee. That was to be matched by an equal payment from the employer for a total maximum tax of $60 in a year. And there was to be a numerical identifier for each worker attached to those payments. This was the Social Security number (now called in the vernacular—"your Social"). The promise was that the Social Security number (SSN) would never be used for identification purposes. In fact, early social security cards bore the inscription, "Not for Identification" on them. Try to tell that to the cable TV provider or your power company today. Unfortunately, contrary to government's early promise, the SSN has become the national identifier it was never designed to be.

As the years went by, certain myths were allowed or encouraged by government managers during the growth of the program. Most of them have their genesis in the fight that Roosevelt had to get the legislation passed.

When I first became Commissioner of Social Security, I developed a stump speech about those myths. That speech has been published in several venues.[*] In it I described the beliefs of most Americans about what the system that they pay an ever increasing amount of taxes is and try to debunk some of the deliberate confusion that has developed over the years. To start with, even the statute itself contributes to the myths surrounding social security. For instance, the title, Federal Insurance Contribution Act (FICA) gives the impression that people make "contributions" to social security rather than pay taxes. The contributions that are made go into a "trust fund" and the trust fund is managed by a board of trustees. And it is dubbed "insurance." But it is "social insurance," a word of art coined by bureaucrats to describe a system that can be modified and manipulated to accomplish social goals held by those doing the modification. It does have some components of insurance as it is commonly understood, although most people don't know about them. Social security insures a covered worker with a family against premature death in that it pays survivor benefits. It also provides social insurance in the case of a disabled worker.

Another myth was that each person had an account in the Trust Fund and that the trustees managed the account for you until you were eligible to retire. The account was identified by your unique identifier, your Social Security Number. All of these things are true to a certain extent. You have an account, there is a "trust fund"; there are Trustees; but your taxes aren't put into your account or into a special account the way we all think of one. It isn't like a bank account.

---

[*] In fact, I once picked up a copy of *Parade Magazine* from the Sunday newspaper and saw my speech presented there as a column by none other than the muckraker Jack Anderson. I thought of suing him, but figured that I had given and published that speech so many times, that by then it must have been in the public domain.

The tax payments that you and your employer make go to the Department of the Treasury. Treasury borrows the money from Social Security. They do pay interest on the borrowing. At the end of the year, employers report to the Social Security Administration the amount of wages paid to each employee. The W-2s don't go to the Internal Revenue Service. They go to SSA. SSA makes a bookkeeping entry of the wages you made during the year against your SSN and that amount is the amount that is shown on your yearly estimate of benefits.

The Trustees are another well designed sham. The Managing Trustee is the Secretary of the Treasury* and the others are the Secretaries of HHS and Labor. Since 1984, there also have been positions for two public members and the Commissioner of Social Security on the Board of Trustees. In recent years, the public positions have remained vacant.

Myths continue to abound. Some have grown up in modern times. One such myth is "I'll never get back what I paid into Social Security." That may or may not be true in the future, but the fact is that most people who have reached retirement age and begin collecting social security get more from the system than they pay into it. Even today.

The U.S. government started to collect the payroll tax in 1937 and the first benefits were paid out during that year. From 1937 to 1940, all benefits were a one-time pay out. The first check was a one-time payment of $0.17 to a fellow from Ohio named Ernest Ackerman in January 1937. Mr. Ackerman retired one day after the program began. In that one day of participation, Mr. Ackerman paid $0.05 in Social Security "contributions." His investment was sound.

The first beneficiary who received monthly benefits has become some-what more famous. Her name was Ida Mae Fuller and she lived in a small town in Vermont. Ida Mae worked as a legal secretary for three

---

* It is interesting that President Obama's first choice for Secretary of the Treasury, Timothy Geithner, was roundly criticized for having not paid taxes. The media said he shouldn't have charge of the IRS because of this. The taxes he failed to pay were his payroll taxes, social security, and Medicare. No one in the media picked this up and said that he shouldn't be the managing trustee of the Social Security Trust Funds.

years under the Social Security system and retired at age sixty-five in 1940. During her three years, Ms. Fuller had $24.75 in Social Security tax withheld from her paychecks. Her first check from Social Security was for $22.54, just $2.21 short of what she had contributed. Ms. Fuller continued to collect monthly checks for the next thirty-five years—she passed away in 1975 at the ripe old age of a hundred.

So, for the first two beneficiaries of Social Security, the system proved to be a good investment if not an outright windfall. When I became Commissioner of Social Security, a person who had paid the maximum into the system and retired at the then full retirement age of sixty-five would have paid a little over $12,800 in payroll taxes. In 1981, the worker would have gotten that all back in about thirteen months. Not quite as good as Ida Mae Fuller, but still a good investment. Today, a maximum wage earner retiring at sixty-six would have paid in $119,865. It would take four years and three months to get it all back.

I was once invited to give a speech to the International Platform Association (IPA). I had never heard of them but my Deputy, Paul Simmons, insisted that I accept. It turns out that the IPA is an annual meeting of all of the people who book speakers for various meetings. The format was quite daunting; you have thirty minutes to speak; someone is before you and someone right after you. At thirty minutes, you get the hook.

I was scheduled to speak between Senator Bob Dole and the late singer John Denver. I gave my stock Social Security myth speech along with a description of the dire financial straits that the system was facing. The audience, used to non-stop speakers, didn't appear too interested. After my thirty minutes I went to the holding room for a reception for speakers that was already in progress. Apparently, after John Denver spoke, the speaker was James J. Kilpatrick, the conservative newspaper columnist. He tossed out his stock speech and instead commented favorably on mine. Jack Kilpatrick followed up with a nationally syndicated column that started out:

> "Washington – John A. Svahn, commissioner of Social Security, turned up
> the other day before the annual convention of the International Platform
> Association. He spoke to an audience of about 600. I wish he could have
> been heard by 60,000. For Svahn did a masterly job of laying out the facts.
> Simply, quietly, without histrionics or horror stories, he looked at the Social
> Security system past and present. He raised questions about the future –
> questions that must be raised and must be answered."

At least one person was listening and understood the significance of what I said. Unfortunately for me, there were a lot of listeners in 1981 and most of them didn't like what they heard.

Is Social Security a Ponzi scheme? Of course it is. Current workers pay for current retirees, just like current investors pay for previous investor's returns in an illegal Ponzi pyramid. The difference of course is that Mr. Ponzi didn't have the full faith and credit of the U.S. government behind his scheme.

After being confirmed as Commissioner, I was publicly sworn in by Secretary Richard Schweiker. I chose to have the ceremony done in the Altmeyer Building auditorium at Social Security headquarters in Baltimore. I did this because my orientation had shown me that the agency was flat; it had been run by absentee Commissioners for too long. I intended to remedy that.

My first commitment to the agency was that I would not reorganize it. Each of my predecessors had instituted a "reorganization." There was one in 1975, one in 1977, and one in 1979. The organization hadn't finished the first when the second and third were thrust upon it. My decision not to do a fourth reorganization was met with strong support within SSA. Second, my primary office was to be at the headquarters in Baltimore.

The Commissioner had a large office suite in Washington on the sixth floor of the Hubert Humphrey building. It was on the opposite side of the building from that of the Secretary of Health and Human Services.* The office suite was quite spacious and had its own bath and shower. It was so comfortable that the Deputy that I recruited from Illinois, Paul Simmons, lived in it for the first couple of months that he was house hunting in Washington. Paul commented that it had everything you needed, a great location, a bathroom, cable television, and a view of the Capitol that you couldn't buy. And the rent was free. I didn't use it much but the office was very convenient for those occasions when I had to be in Washington for appearances on Capitol Hill or for meetings with the Secretary or the White House. I felt that it was important for the people working in the SSA to have a leader who was visible to them. And they worked in the Baltimore headquarters.

I might add here, that when I was Commissioner of Social Security, SSA had very few political appointees. I can only think of two other than myself, Paul Simmons and an administrative assistant in my office. Early on, the White House recommended that I look at Robert J. Myers for a senior position in the agency. Bob had been a federal employee who was first employed by Social Security in 1936. He retired as Chief Actuary in a dispute with then Commissioner Robert Ball in the early '70s. Myers had always had his eye on becoming Commissioner himself. Bob was a Republican and had in retirement done a lot of consulting for Republicans on Capitol Hill.

As far as the White House was concerned, he was in effect a "must place" referral. But because he was a retired career civil servant when I hired him, he came back into the system, not as a political appointee but as a retired annuitant. Unfortunately for Bob, that meant that his salary was offset by the amount of his federal pension. No double

---

* The lore around HHS and SSA was that a lot of SS trust fund money went into the building of the Humphrey Building. As a result, the Commissioner of Social Security got prime office space, second only to the Secretary of HHS. My office was supposedly only one square foot less than that of the Secretary. I never measured it.

dipping then. He was without a doubt the best referral I ever got from the White House.

After being sworn in, I made a few remarks to those assembled. The live audience was made up of a few hundred employees in the SSA auditorium. What I said was intended to be heard by all 83,000 employees in 1350 offices around the country and around the world for that matter. "I'd like to restore public confidence in the system and restore the Social Security Administration's confidence in itself. What the Social Security Administration needs right now is a 100 percent fulltime manager."

I also spoke about the problems Social Security was having and about the challenge that lay ahead. In 1981 Social Security was paying monthly benefits directly and indirectly to 51 million people. One in five Americans was a recipient. When you couple that with working Americans who were paying the payroll taxes, Social Security was a fact of life for every adult in the country. If you weren't paying into or collecting Social Security, you knew a close relative who was. I used to say that it was the first federal agency you came in contact with during your lifetime and it is the last federal agency you come in contact with. It is a massive program affecting everyone. And it was a mess.

Actually it was several messes. The biggest mess was the financing situation. It was losing money. In 1981 Social Security Old Age and Survivors Insurance was paying out about $144 billion in benefits, about $12 billion a month. Billions are hard to understand, even in today's cachet of trillions. Put more simply, we were spending $275,000 per minute or about $4,585 per second. The financing dilemma was that we were only taking in about $4,372 per second. It didn't take a calculator or a whole office full of actuaries for me to figure out that it couldn't continue at that pace for very long.

Social Security is a simple system really. It works just like your checking account. It has money coming in, it has money going out, and it has a balance. We had over $12,000 per minute going out more than we had coming in. We were drawing down the balance. In fact, in April of 1981, we were projecting that the system would deplete its balance and would be unable to pay benefits in a timely manner in October of 1982. How do you fix it? Just like your checkbook, you either put in more money (in this case raise taxes) or you cut back your spending (reduce benefits/beneficiaries). Therein lies the problem. Elected politicians, the people charged with keeping the system balanced, don't like to do either. They don't like to raise taxes and they don't like to cut benefits. The reason that politicians don't like either of the two options is that senior citizens who pay taxes and receive benefits turn out in large percentage on Election Day.

The Social Security Administration had a long history of "can do" attitude. It was a proud organization which had accomplished much in the first four decades of its existence. It wasn't until the advent of the Supplemental Security Income (SSI) in the early 1970s that SSA suffered a humiliating defeat. The implementation of SSI, a welfare program for poor blind, aged, and disabled people, proved to take a lot of the luster off of the Social Security Administration. The district offices weren't used to a means tested program. The people on SSI were not folks who had worked all their lives. It was a welfare program. And most of the recipients had to be transferred from state welfare rolls to the federal program. SSI took the cover off of SSA and exposed some of the serious underlying problems confronting the agency. When I took over, those problems were very apparent.

Public confidence in the agency was at an all time low. A Roper poll at the time found that Americans believed that $52 out of every $100 collected in payroll taxes was spent on administrative costs for the bureaucracy. The truth of the matter was that administrative costs were only 1.3 percent of the amount collected.

My initial plan was to focus on four goals as Commissioner:

- Restore the public's confidence in Social Security
- Restore the Social Security Administration's confidence in itself
- Update and make functional the SSA's systems capabilities
- Reform the Disability Insurance program

Simple goals, shouldn't take too long. The public had lost confidence in Social Security. Even in 1981, most workers thought that they would never receive a dime from the program. The really ugly problem was that they didn't know the real state of the financial affairs of the Social Security system. SSA had not hidden it; they had just assumed that the powers that be understood the dire straits and that something would be done about it. During the ensuing debate over financing the program, there was a lot of blood spilled between problem recognition and problem solved. A goodly bit of it was mine.

The administration's recognition of the financing problem was immediate. At HHS, we put together a small working group in early February to develop options for restoring the financial integrity of the system. The Disability and Health Insurance Trust Funds were solvent but the Old Age and Survivors Trust fund was being depleted rapidly. Everyone wanted to solve the problem and there was pretty good support on the Hill for a bi-partisan solution.

With the Democrats holding the majority in the House, J.J. Pickle (D-Texas) was chairman of the Ways and Means Sub-Committee on Social Security. Another Texan, Bill Archer (R) was the ranking Republican. The full committee was chaired by Dan Rostenkowski (D-Ill.) with Barber Conable (R-NY) as the ranking Republican. The key staff people on the House side were well versed on Social Security. Pickle's person was Janice Gregory, a super competent staffer but also one who did not let you forget that she was a Democrat. On the Republican side, the line was a little thin; not because of any individual but because the majority Democrats just wouldn't give the Republicans any support. The Republican staff director was Pete Singleton, an affable senior staffer who was very helpful. On the Senate side, the Republicans had the majority with Bob Dole (R-KS) as Chairman of the Committee on Finance and Russell Long (D-LA) as the ranking Democrat. The Social Security Subcommittee was chaired by Bill Armstrong (R-CO) with Pat Moynihan (D-NY) as the ranking Democrat.

The financing issue was divided into two problems: a short term problem in that the OASI fund would be out of money, even by our most optimistic assumptions by October of 1982; and a long term problem that had the system substantially underfunded over the next seventy-five years. In the short term, we needed somewhere in the neighborhood of 150 to 200 billion dollars to be able to pay benefits on a timely basis. The long term problem was harder to estimate, but was predicted to be about $1.6 trillion in 1981 dollars.

With regard to the long term problem, some said that the very nature of Social Security caused it to be out of balance. Current workers pay taxes that are used to pay benefits to current retirees. In the long term, the cohort of baby boomers (those born between 1946 and 1964) would swell the roles of retirees, and those boomers hadn't done their task of providing new workers. Boomers had far fewer kids than did their parents. At the end of World War II, there were 42 workers paying into the system for every beneficiary. By 1950 the ratio was down to 16.5 to 1. By the time I got to Social Security there were only 3.2 workers paying taxes for each recipient of Social Security. Currently, the SSA projects that when the bulk of baby boomers are retired in 2030 the worker to beneficiary ratio will be down to 2.1 to 1.

The short term problem was less a problem of demographics and more a problem of politics. In 1972, when Richard Nixon was running for re-election, Congress passed and Nixon enthusiastically signed legislation to provide for an annual Cost of Living Adjustment (COLA) for Social Security beneficiaries. Soon after this went into effect in 1973 it became apparent that the politicians had overcorrected. The indexing formula overcompensated for inflation, essentially double-indexing the adjustment. The deteriorating economy coupled with the optimistic assumptions that were used in passing the COLA legislation caused the Carter administration to call for radical changes in 1977.

Carter understood the problem and proposed the only solution: raise taxes and cut benefits. The Congress responded by cutting future benefits for all beneficiaries born after 1916 by about 25 percent. About the 1977 amendments, President Carter announced that the changes would "guarantee that from 1980 to the year 2030, the Social Security funds will be sound."

The legislation increased the payroll tax in 1978 and scheduled more tax increases into the next decade. The change in the benefit formula also created a new problem—the troublesome "notch" issue. The "notch babies" born in 1917 and later received about 25 percent less in benefits than a baby born in 1916 or before. It didn't matter whether you were born in 1917, 27, or for that matter 1967, your benefit had been reduced by the 1977 amendments. By 1981, the notch babies were sixty-four and retiring at a fast pace. And they were finding out that their friend next door who was born a year earlier was getting a lot bigger check from Social Security than they were.*

---

* The notch babies mounted a concerted effort to reverse the 1977 amendments. Congress withstood the effort and did nothing, knowing that the problem would go away eventually. The notch babies who are still living are in their 90s and their number is dwindling fast. I guess Congress was right. Every time I referred to this action as a "25 percent cut in benefits" my good friend the late Pat Moynihan, the Senator from New York, would fume at me and scold that it wasn't a cut, it was a "correction" of a mistake made in 1972.

Jake Pickle was the first to make a move. He had an ally in Bill Archer. Both were fiscally conservative and both wanted to see the system fixed. Pickle in particular courted Schweiker and me from even before our nominations were announced by the President. Pickle said that he had a plan and was willing to introduce it in the House, but he wanted some assurances that the Administration would support it and he came to me to get those assurances.

At about the same time, somewhere in mid April, the working group that we had at HHS, chaired by Dave Swoap, the Under Secretary, was subsumed into a larger inter-departmental working group meeting under the auspices of the White House. Since the Administration had not yet developed its position on financing, I couldn't give Jake the assurances that he wanted.

Pickle introduced his bill in April. The key features were that it allowed inter-fund borrowing from the Disability and Health Insurance Trust Funds to shore up the short term problem in the Retirement and Survivors Fund, it financed 50 percent of the Health Insurance Fund with general revenues and in the long term, it raised the retirement age to sixty-eight. Sensing action on the hill, Dick Schweiker pushed within the Administration to get a position out.

Dave Stockman, in his book "The Triumph of Politics" says that as soon as he heard about the Pickle bill, he was determined to "derail" it. I wish that Dave had told us that because the rest of us, including the Republicans on the hill, were working to achieve a bi-partisan solution to a financial crisis in Social Security. Stockman made his desire for short term budget savings generally known to the working group, but I didn't realize the total duplicity in his actions during the deliberations until I read his 1986 revision of history. And I wasn't the only one. Even our mutual friend Jim Baker in his 2006 memoir, *Work Hard, Study … and Keep Out of Politics!,* in commenting on the Social Security reform proposal lamented, "Unbeknownst to those of us in the West Wing, Stockman had decided to squeeze billions of dollars of 'future savings to be proposed' out of the program."[*]

On May 1, a meeting was held in the Old Executive Office Building of the new high-powered Cabinet working group. The group included Dave Stockman, the Director of OMB, Martin Anderson, Assistant to the President for Policy Development, Bob Carleson, my old boss and now a Special Assistant to the President, Don Regan, then Secretary of the Treasury, Norm Ture, Under Secretary of the Treasury, Murray Weidenbaum, Chairman of the Council of Economic Advisors (CEA), Dick Schweiker, Dave Swoap, my new Deputy, Bob Myers and me. In addition, there were a few staff people from Treasury and CEA, and on occasion Don Devine from the Office of Personnel Management (OPM). The White House advance attendance list shows Craig Fuller and Dick Darman from the White House staff as attending the sessions the week of May 1 but I have no recollection of them being there.

During this working group meeting, options were reviewed and new "what if" scenarios were brought up. To the extent that we could, Myers and I tried to answer the groups' questions. When the group settled on a preliminary set of options, we took them back to the actuaries at SSA for costing.

Because the Carter 1977 package was doomed due to their reliance on rosy economic assumptions, we determined that our proposal would

---

[*] After Stockman's book came out, I was talking to friend of mine who had been one of Stockman's key lieutenants, having been with him on the Hill and at OMB. I asked him about all the vitriol in the book aimed at the President and Ed Meese. He smiled and said that there had been a lot more aimed at a lot more people. Dave had asked him to review a draft and he had asked Dave why all the trashing of former colleagues. I guess Stockman toned it down a little in his memoir because in Owen Ullmann's book *Stockman, The Man, The Myth, The Future* he references "Stockman's limited admiration for Donald Regan, Edwin Meese, Caspar Weinberger and at times the President, as well as certain White House staffers whom he considered 'assholes.'" I am pretty sure that I am one of those staffers.

be developed on the pessimistic set of economic assumptions.* All were in agreement that the pessimistic set was appropriate—Stockman because they yielded the greatest budget savings and us because they promised the most protection for the program. In fact, the pessimistic assumptions that we were using to predict the next five years were really a somewhat better case than what actually had happened to the economy over the previous five years.

As we got closer to a final package, the meetings became more rowdy. Stockman was fighting hard for immediate savings and Schweiker was pushing to get something out so that we could begin negotiating with the Congress. Bob Myers and I were really taxing the actuaries out at SSA. Harry Ballantyne, the short-range actuary, Frank Bayo, the long-range actuary and the rest of the staff were putting in long hours. After the May 1 meeting we put together a book with one page descriptions on each of the options being considered. On May 4, we sent the final set of one-pagers on the options being considered to Craig Fuller's office in the White House. Fuller was the Cabinet Secretary and responsible for distributing the material to participants. By this time, we had grouped the options under five basic areas for reform:

- Modification of the benefit rate to encourage people to work longer
- Reduce opportunities for Windfall Benefits
- Relate Disability Insurance closer to work history and medical condition
- Coverage of new Federal, State, and Local employees
- Reduce the welfare aspects of the system

At a May 5 meeting, we discussed coverage of new federal, state, and local employees and the reduction of opportunities for windfall benefits. Coverage of government employees meant quick relief for the

---

* Traditionally, the SSA develops three sets of economic assumptions: rosy, intermediate, and pessimistic. In most years, the Trustees use the intermediate set for projecting Trust Fund performance.

program because a lot of new revenue would come in while it would be decades before most employees retired and became a drain on the system. Several of us were wary of the option however because we couldn't see how adding more people to the problem solved anything. No one was opposed to reducing windfalls that primarily came from government employees retiring from government and then getting a short-time job in the private sector and becoming covered by Social Security. When they applied for Social Security they look like low wage earners and because of the way benefits are computed, they receive a higher benefit, a windfall.

Our final package was to be based on several assumptions. It had to:

- Solve the short term and long term crises
- Use pessimistic economic assumptions
- Use no general revenue financing
- Contain no unscheduled payroll tax increases
- Reduce already scheduled tax increases if possible
- Eliminate the retirement test if possible
- Lessen the welfare aspects of Old Age, Survivors and Disability Insurance
- Strengthen the social insurance concept

We met every day that week and on May 8, we had the last meeting of the group. During this session we discussed modifying the benefit rate to encourage people to work longer and including government employees in Social Security. Since this was supposed to be the final meeting of the group and we were supposed to present our recommendations to the President the following week, we included in the discussion book a draft memo from Schweiker to the President along with the latest estimates for the various options.

The meeting was a long one. We still had not been able to decide whether to include government employees and employees of non-profit entities. We had already spent a lot of time on the issue and after taking a vote decided to take it to the President as an option.

When we got to the options to encourage people to work longer the discussion became quite heated. The law at that time gave covered workers the option of retiring at age sixty-two. The full retirement age was sixty-five. A person who retired at sixty-two received a benefit that was equal to 80 percent of what they would have received at sixty-five. The trend was for people to retire earlier. When they retired before sixty-five, they stopped paying into the system and started taking out. It was exacerbating our financing problem. Most of us recognized that the age for full retirement should have been raised. After all, when the system was designed and the retirement age set at sixty-five in 1935, the average life expectancy for a male worker born that year was sixty-two. The federal government in 1935 never anticipated that most of us would make it to retirement!

Schweiker and I had proposed reducing the early retirement benefit and had early on presented two options—reducing it to 75 percent or 70 percent assuming that would encourage people to work longer. By the time we got to the May 8 meeting we had pretty well settled on 70 percent. In fact our working sheet for that meeting listed twelve "Agreed-Upon Options" and reducing the benefit rate to 70 percent for early retirees was Number 5. Our draft memorandum to the President read:

CHANGE BENEFIT RATES TO ENCOURAGE WORK BETWEEN 62-65

--Reduced Benefits for Early Retirements

Proposal would reduce early retirement benefits to 70 percent of the maximum, thus strongly encouraging workers to remain in the work force until age 65

The one page description of the reduction that accompanied the Memorandum clearly stated that the reduction was to be effective for all workers beginning in 1982:

> Early-retirement Benefit for Both Workers and Spouses at Rate of 70% of
> PIA for Retirement at Age 62 after 1981[*]

But Stockman wanted more. He saw that implementation of the proposal to reduce early retirement benefits in 1982 would help his budget saving agenda. He also knew that a bigger reduction than the 70 percent we had put forward would help more. And he was fighting for it. Dick Schweiker, the former Senator from Pennsylvania, argued that reducing early retirement benefits was a breach of the compact between workers/taxpayers and their government. We had had to work hard on Schweiker to get him to accept the reduction from 80 percent to 70 percent and he just didn't want to give any more.

The discussion became heated, multiple people talking at the same time, sidebar conversations and tempers and voices on the rise. Stockman wanted reductions and told Schweiker that if he "could get more from Social Security he wouldn't have to hit the National Institutes of Health," one of Schweiker's pets when he was in the Senate. Carleson wanted to go to 60 percent, CEA was somewhere between 70 and 80 percent but wanted to make sure that no current beneficiaries were penalized.

It was late in the day and everyone was tired. Norm Ture from Treasury summed up. "Why don't we randomly select one out of every ten people and harm them?' Stockman quickly replied, "We already have." We had been meeting almost continuously for six weeks and had read reams of paper on the problem and options to solve it. We had met every day of this week. Dick Schweiker and I just wanted to get to the President, get some decisions, and get something to take to Pickle and Archer so that we could begin to negotiate the solution to

---

[*] PIA stands for Primary Insurance Amount. The PIA is the benefit a person would receive if the beneficiary elects to retire at the full retirement age.

the financing problem. In the end Stockman and Marty Anderson won out. We gave in. It was agreed by all that we would propose a reduction of early retirement benefits to 55 percent of the full retirement benefit. The 55 percent was just something that was plucked out of the air. It was the number that Stockman needed in order to have his near term budget solution. As we were picking up the piles of paper, Marty Anderson said to me, "I think 50 percent would have been better."

Ed Meese, Jim Baker, and Mike Deaver (the "Troika" who managed the White House) did not attend any of the working group sessions so they were not familiar with the issues that we had struggled with for months. On Friday night I got word that Ed wanted to meet with Dave Swoap and me in his West Wing Office on Saturday morning, the ninth of May, to get briefed on the package. A meeting had been set for Monday May 11 with the President to go over the package that the working group had developed.

Dave and I went over to the White House on Saturday to meet with Ed before lunch. Ed had Craig Fuller, the Cabinet secretary and Dick Darman, the staff secretary sitting in on the meeting. Darman was Jim Baker's guy and it was the first time that I had seen him since the days when he was with Elliott Richardson at HEW. Dave and I went through the package with them for about an hour. Ed asked a few questions as did Fuller, but Darman didn't say a word. I knew that an hour wasn't enough time for them to grasp it fully, but Ed had guests coming in for lunch and was in a hurry. He laid out the way that he thought we ought to present the package to the President. He said we should review quickly the options that we considered but were not recommending. He wanted us to articulate the package as:

- Technical changes
- Elimination of abuses in the system
- Conforming the system more to private industry
- Providing employment incentives
- Preserve the integrity of the Trust Funds

- Continue benefits to the truly needy
- And a possible tax cut

We tried to impress on him that the package was a BIG change. He thanked us and said that we were meeting with the President for an hour on Monday morning, the eleventh. I told him that one hour was not enough time to understand what was being proposed but he said that was all that was scheduled. Ed told Darman to circulate the package around the White House staff and we were set to meet on Monday.

Dave Swoap and I stepped out on the northwest lawn to where the network TV anchors are usually set up. They weren't there this Saturday because the President was up at Camp David for Mothers Day weekend. I told Swoap that I was still very nervous that the powers that be didn't understand how momentous the package was. Bob Myers had been politely trying to tell me that what was being proposed was way too much. I felt that our underlying goals were justified; I just wasn't sure about the steps we were proposing to achieve them.

During our little standup discussion, I showed Dave a Gannett newspaper story in which a "high-level White House Source" was quoted commenting on a leaked "series of dramatic changes to the Social Security system." The source told the paper, "If they think we're being cruel to widows, orphans and babies now, wait until they see what we're going to do with Social Security." It was a very nasty article from an anonymous source who obviously knew all about what the task force was doing in Social Security. And the source chose to paint it in a very derogatory manner. We had our ideas about who the high-level source was. Paul Simmons, my deputy, had been in the newspaper business and had a lot of contacts in the working press. He found out who the leaker was. It was Dave Stockman, the Director of the Office of Management and Budget.

Swoap and I talked it over and decided that we had to show the story to Ed Meese and tell him about Stockman. I wanted to use it to slow down the movement of the package so that the President would have more time to understand it. We went back inside the White House and went downstairs to the Mess. Ron Jackson, the Navy officer in charge of the Mess, went into the senior staff dining room and got Ed for us. We briefed him on the situation. He seemed genuinely concerned, leaks were a real problem in the Reagan White House, but he told us that we were still on for Monday with the President.

Monday, May 11 came around. I had been scheduled to have a breakfast meeting with Senators Dole, Armstrong, and Heinz. Dole as chairman of Finance, Armstrong on that Committee as Chair of the Social Security Subcommittee, and Heinz as Chair of the Select Committee on Aging. The meeting was to be a discussion of the options we were looking at. At 7:00 PM on Friday the eighth, they cancelled the meeting. I think that they were already distancing themselves from the issue based on leaks like the one that appeared in the Gannett story.

I went over to the White House along with Schweiker and Swoap. We were meeting in the Roosevelt Room with the President. We had sixty minutes. It was the first time that I had seen the President since the assassination attempt on March 30. He looked really good and chipper but the staff said he was still recuperating. Schweiker took the lead going through our underlying assumptions and options that we had considered and the recommended package. Swoap and I chimed in as did Stockman when he felt it was to his advantage. For the most part he just sat quietly; if the President approved the recommendations, he had won. For the first thirty minutes, the President listened intently but then he seemed to be less interested. I think that the discussion was really just too complex to understand by someone who didn't have a background.

140

I gave it my one shot. I said to him, "Mr. President, there is nothing in this package that is good. There is nothing that will be popular. It is going to be attacked as soon as it comes out." He just looked at me and we moved on. At the end of the hour, he said he thought it was a pretty good package.[*]

We had left him the option of covering government employees and he said that he wanted to think on it. He said that he didn't think that adding people to the program was a solution. He did not say he approved or disapproved any of the package. Several colleagues of mine who have written about that meeting have said that Reagan approved the package on the spot. He didn't. Like so many other things, he wanted to consider the options. The minutes of that meeting of the Cabinet Council on Human Resources state:

> "Later that day the President decided to submit the proposals without the Federal/non-profit employee option and without the provision relating to eliminating eligibility for surviving spouse with children over twelve years of age."

Now that we had a package, what would we do with it? I guess that someone in the Roosevelt Room was listening when I cautioned about the package, because a Legislative Strategy Group (the LSG was a rump group held in Jim Baker's office to strategize tactics) meeting was called for that afternoon.

We—Schweiker, Swoap, and I—had always assumed that this was going to be the President's proposal to fix Social Security. And for once we had Stockman on our side; he wanted it to be the President's pack-

---

[*] The draft memorandum to the President had the sentence, "We have not included any of the controversial "big ticket" items." I do not recall whether that sentence survived in the final memo that went to him, but if it did, it was certainly proved to be misleading. Ronald Reagan's handwritten diary for May 11 reads: "Monday May 11, 1981 The big part of the morning was a meeting with the task force on Soc. Security. I believe they've come up with a plan to resolve the long term imbalance and without reducing any of the benefits for present recipients." The next comment on Social Security in his diary isn't until June 2.

age. At the LSG meeting, it became apparent that the Chief of Staff, Jim Baker didn't agree. He said, "It's Schweiker's package" and wondered aloud if we couldn't just take it up to Capitol Hill and "just slip it under the door." He said that it was to be a release from the Department "at the request of the Hill." He even went so far as to suggest that we do the release at SSA headquarters in Baltimore. Schweiker knew that he was being tossed under the bus and argued vehemently. But in the end he lost and we scheduled a press conference for the next day May 12, 1981, at 10:30 AM at the HHS Headquarters, the Humphrey Building.

Schweiker, Swoap and I were on the podium the next morning. I had finally been confirmed by the Senate and had been sworn in by a personnel clerk on May 6, in the middle of the package fight so I was legally the Commissioner of Social Security. I was (and still am) the youngest Commissioner in Social Security history. The day after the press conference I turned thirty-eight.

We started the Press Conference just as we had started the meeting with the President. Dick led off giving the background, explaining the situation, and talking about the system. He did not mince any words:

> "The crisis is inescapable. It is here. It is now. It is serious. And it must be faced. Today we move to face it head-on and solve it. If we do nothing, the system would go broke as early as Fall, 1982, breaking faith with the 36 million Americans depending on Social Security."

But the hundred or so media types wanted detail and they understood a lot more about the system than most people. Schweiker, figuring that he had given enough already, turned the microphone over to me to answer the barrage of questions about the mechanics and impact of the proposals. The press conference went on for an hour. Question after question. None of them easy to answer, all of them very hostile.

The media coverage was fast and sensational. By and large editorial pages were supportive of our effort to fix the system but the general reaction was negative and the politicians and the public picked up on it quickly. The big turkey was the reduction in early retirement benefits.

In those early days, I still had a telephone number that was listed in the telephone directory. As the news of the proposals spread quickly across the country, I got a call from a sixty-two-year-old man in San Diego, California, who was just getting ready to retire and felt that he would be caught in the proposed change to reduce early retirement benefits. He called me every name in the book. He called me a "God damn bureaucrat—just like the rest of them." And he said that he might even change his name. Then he said, "No. You change yours!" I replied, "But Dad …"

Unfortunately, Jim Baker was wrong. It didn't matter where we released it or what we said. It was the President's proposal. We had touched the third rail. Now it was a matter of whether or not we could survive.

Chapter 11

What a Mess!

The financing dilemma was the biggest problem that we faced in Social Security, but it was by no means the only one. The Social Security Administration in 1981 was a far cry from the can-do organization that I knew during my first stint in the federal government in the mid-1970s. It had been beaten up by constant re-organization, critical reports from the Government Accounting Office, and truly embarrassing reports in the media. Its data processing capabilities were almost non-existent. And the Disability Insurance program was sadly mismanaged and in complete disarray. In the three years that I was Commissioner, I made some progress in all of these areas. But today, two and a half decades later, the SSA is beat up, the Disability program is in disarray, and the agency's computer systems are archaic. As Yogi Berra said, "It's déjà vous all over again."

Morale at the agency was low. Staff was demoralized and the "malaise" that came to reflect President Jimmy Carter during the 1980 campaign was evident everywhere at SSA. I decided to try to turn that around. I started by having my formal oath taking at the Social Security Headquarters. No Commissioner had ever done that. I kept my primary office at the Baltimore headquarters rather that in Washington. It made for long days for me and my driver, Willie Falcon, shuttling back and forth, but it showed the staff that there really was a Commissioner.

Little things added up. I would eat lunch in the employee cafeteria. We had SSA night at the Baltimore Orioles baseball games a couple of times a year and Jill, the kids and I would be there, representing SSA by throwing out the first pitch. SSA has an annual awards ceremony where they bring in employees from around the country to present them with citations for outstanding service. There are a couple of hundred award-ees a year who travel with their families to headquarters to receive an award from the Commissioner. The ceremony takes about three hours. The first year, I said that before the formal ceremony, I would like for all the awardees and their families to visit the Commissioner's Office so that I could meet them and have a photograph taken. Nelson Sabatini, my assistant, cautioned against it. "You don't know what you're getting yourself in for Jack." But Jill joined me and we spent a morning standing in the office meeting and greeting over a hundred employees and their families. Word of the visit to the Commissioner's Office got around to the other 83,000 employees pretty quickly. It is a most popular event and is still going on today.

A critical problem for the Social Security Administration throughout its history has been its inability to admit failure and request assistance. SSA was a "can-do" organization. When it had a problem the first task was to deny the problem exists. Next the agency threw a couple of thousand people at it and worked around the clock until the problem was fixed or it went away. And problems could crop up in a variety of ways.

Early in my tenure in testimony before the Ways and Means Subcommittee I noted that I had read the 1980 testimony of the four most recent Commissioners of Social Security. All four of the former Commissioners testified that the data processing systems problem was the greatest problem administratively that Social Security faced. I also noted that Chairman Pickle commented in that hearing that none of the four had made those comments during their time in office. He was correct of course, because it wasn't in the culture of SSA to air problems in public. When I testified, I told the Committee, "I think in the past the problems of the Social Security Administration systems capacity have been swept under the rug."

In 1981, the problems were many. For instance, Social Security had almost no capability to tell when a beneficiary had died. If a family member didn't report the death SSA kept sending out the checks. The local SSA District offices would scan the local newspapers each morning for death notices and then report them to a central processing point. Without a way to formally receive a notice of death, stories were constantly appearing in the media about "dead people" on Social Security. We did a comparison of our file with that of Medicare and found thousands of people whose checks were still being cashed for almost three years after their death. And the reverse was true. We were routinely stopping checks for people we thought had died but who were in fact very much alive. Then the problem was how to make Social Security believe they were still alive.

Anything that could affect a beneficiary's check was trouble. A change of address could mean that the beneficiary got no check—or it could mean that they got two, one at the new address and one at the old. There was a similar situation involving prisoners in jail. We had no way to determine if a person was incarcerated. We didn't know the addresses of prisons and jails throughout the country. So we sent checks to them that generated stories about prisoners getting Social Security checks at the jailhouse.

We were slowly grinding to a halt. Social Security was a paper system. It started out as a paper driven program because there were no computers. When computers were developed, my predecessors had superimposed them on the paper system. Somewhere, in some office, there was a paper file of everyone who had ever had a Social Security number. Even people who were long dead. And we had backlogs. The first year I was there, we came within twenty hours of failing to get the checks out for the July 3, 1981, delivery. The reason we were late was that the July payment contained the annual Cost of Living Adjustment (COLA). It took us over 20,000 hours of programming and 2,500 hours of computer time to make the change. It was just one number! The system was so bogged down it took four to six weeks to issue a Social Security card! We had an 18,000-hour backlog in computer processing. There are only 720 hours in a thirty-day period; we were increasing the backlog by about 2,000 hours per month!

SSA posts annual earnings for each worker. Those earnings records are used to compute the worker's Social Security benefit when the worker retires. It is not how much you pay in taxes that determines your Social Security benefit; it is how much you earn over your working life. In 1981, the posting of earnings to an individual's account had a backlog of almost four years. That backlog caused more work for the local offices because they manually had to request the latest wage records for retiring workers.

In the '60s, SSA had been the darling of IBM. It had the most modern equipment and systems. It was the show house. By 1981 it was no longer in that position. It had been the victim of neglect and mismanagement. As a result the agency's capacity to perform the most basic functions was at the breaking point. As I stated on several occasions, "It is a miracle that we get the checks out each month."

Even by today's standards, SSA was then a very big operation. It kept records on over 200 million workers and got checks out to over 36 million SSA beneficiaries each month. It responded to over a half million inquiries each day. Social Security had started to keep records on wages in 1937 as a paper process and it still had all of those records, many of them on microfilm. There was a $100 billion dollars in unposted earnings because SSA was unable to identify the correct account in which to post them.

I used to conduct tours of SSA for members of Congress and the media as I tried to build support for our reforms and for funding a re-design of our data processing systems. The SSA complex in Woodlawn Maryland is a sprawling campus of many acres. I always started the tours in the Office of Disability Operations (ODO) mailroom. It was always in chaos. ODO's mailroom was where the Disability Insurance beneficiary's hard copy cases were shipped in and out of the build-ing—by the truckload. Some case files were a foot thick. My opening comment was "This is the ODO mailroom. In this building are the files of a little over 3 million beneficiaries of Disability Insurance. Today a third of those files are lost." And it was that way every day. We didn't have a foolproof method to keep track of all the paper.

Most members of the Ways and Means Subcommittee came out to Baltimore for the tour. Jake Pickle, Bill Archer, and John Rousselot, Republican from California made a visit along with staff and got the full effect of the mess at Social Security. I had tried to get the Chairman of the Committee on Ways and Means, Danny Rostenkowski out and had personally invited him during one of my visits to his office. One morning, I was in Washington and I got a call from John Salmon, Chief Counsel to the Ways and Means Committee. John said that the Chairman was flying into Baltimore Washington International Airport from Chicago and that he was going to come to my office. We got into the car and burned up the Baltimore Washington Parkway to get to Baltimore first.

When Danny arrived, I started him on the tour with the first stop in the Disability Mail Room. We left there and rode up the escalator to look at the acres of files in the building. At the top he stopped and said he would like to use the men's room. I thought that was a good idea also and he and I left the entourage and walked into the Men's room. It was a three urinal room and there was an employee standing at the middle unit. As we did our task, all of a sudden Danny said in his characteristic gravelly voice, "Commissioner, I need to ask you a question" to which I replied, "Yes Sir, Mr. Chairman." The poor guy in the middle looked one way and then the other and ran out of the room. I don't think he bothered to zip up his pants.

All of my tours of the Social Security complex ended in the new computer center. After looking at the computers and staring at the couple of acres of huge Exide batteries that provided immediate power should we lose power for some reason, I took the members to the back of the building. Our long-term emergency power was provided by two jet engines not unlike those on a Boeing 727. And I would let the member push the starter button and fire up one of the jets. I never had a person on the tour who didn't love that part—there is a little kid in all of us.

The problem in systems was threefold: Software, Hardware, and Personnel. All three were perplexing, but software was the key. The original claims processing system had been built in the heyday of the '60s. It had never been replaced but instead had been modified time after time as new requirements were adopted and newer generations of hardware added. The system for issuing Social Security numbers was even older and had received the same treatment.

Social Security had 76 software systems to run the basic operations of the agency. Contained within these 76 systems were 1,376 different programs and 13 million lines of mostly undocumented code. SSA's data processing operations had a few really big and complex files that it used. The Master Beneficiary Record had over 35 million active records that had to interact with hundreds of computer programs. So making simple changes like the annual COLA became extremely complex and costly.

Likewise, changing the maximum amount on the check was a Herculean task. When the payment system was originally designed, no one contemplated that a benefit would ever exceed $999.99 a month. When the maximum monthly benefit went over $1000 the whole operation was thrown into turmoil. It took us over 20,000 hours of programming time to change over 500 programs just to make it possible to make a payment of more than $999.99!

The situation was on life support and we truly held our breath each month. The career staff pretty much accepted poor performance as a way of life. I, on the other hand, was thinking about a system that could send each worker a statement each year telling them what their earnings were and estimating what their annual benefit would be at retirement. Everyone just looked at me like I was dreaming.

Our code was so complex and confusing that a programmer could only maintain about 22,000 lines of code. The industry standard at the time was 60,000 lines. Because so much of it was undocumented (in systems jargon that means that no one can figure out how it is supposed to work) we had to bring back retired programmers, the guys who had originally written it, to modify it. There had been no standardization over the years so programs were written in many different languages, some specific to some long gone employee.

The hardware on the other hand was simple. It was antique. We had eight mainframe machines and not one of them was still being manufactured. Two of the eight machines did not run; they were cannibalized for parts to keep the others running. All of our data was on magnetic tape. There were 600,000 tapes in the SSA tape library and a quarter of them were mislabeled. Tapes were slow and inefficient. The files were sequential so that if you wanted to find Mrs. Smith on the Master Beneficiary Record you had to start at the front of the file and go past every person before her. There was no random access to files. Tapes had to be handled by people. Over 150,000 of the tapes had to be moved, hung on tape drives and read each month. That is a lot of opportunity for mistakes.

When I got to SSA, I found that a new computer center had been built and that it was nearing completion. The old center was in the main building whereas the new center was to be in its own building with office space and state of the art security. The plan was to move all the old systems into it. I said that was crazy but something had to be done. The old center and hardware were falling apart. As I so often did in my stints in government, I turned to a known quantity to help solve a problem.

Marshall Mandell had been with me in the SRS days. He had come out of Computer Sciences Corporation at that time and he was still with the Office of Child Support Enforcement which was now part of SSA. Marshal had done an excellent job for me in setting up the Federal Parent Locator Service and I thought he was the guy to develop a plan to turn systems around. I called him in and gave him the job. It took awhile because it was a big task and I was only looking at it part-time due to the fight going on regarding financing. Meanwhile the move to the new computer center (NCC) was continuing.

To make the move, we had to get some "bridge" machines to put in the new center to use until we could configure the new systems. We bought the bridge machines from IBM. They were two surplus machines that IBM had in Europe—one from France and one from Germany. When the machines were installed the console markings and instructions were in French and German. When I noticed that, Marshall said that IBM was going to take the foreign language off and replace it with English. I told him to leave it as it was because on my now patented tours for members of Congress, I could point to them and comment how we were using machines that had been scrapped in Europe to service America's aged and disabled.

The 600,000-tape library posed a more difficult problem. How were we going to move it to the new center? The answer? Buy a lot of Coleman camp coolers; put a locking hasp on them and carry them two by two to the new center. Real high tech.

The personnel problem was not so easily addressed. Morale in the systems organization was terrible. Most of the staff was truly dedicated and hard working but years of toiling on systems that were steadily degrading had taken its toll—we had hundreds of vacancies in the systems shop. Recruiting for new people was very difficult because of the archaic software and the lack of documentation. College recruiting was even worse—new graduates didn't know the languages that our software was written in. It took an average of two years to train a new employee. But I felt that if we could show them a plan and make them part of a dynamic project that we would be able to fill the jobs with qualified people.

After a half day of testifying about the problems in data processing at Social Security, I was approached by long-time NBC television reporter Robert Hager. Bob had been at the hearing and was very interested in my testimony. He said, "Jack, it sounds like the real problem is the software." I replied that he had hit the nail right on the head, but his next comment floored me. He said, "Would you mind if I brought a camera crew out to Social Security and film some of it?" It was 1981 remember, and computers were mysterious big machines. I realized that I was going to have to do a lot of educating.

The problems were seemingly insurmountable. The *Washington Post* quoted me as saying about the system "You can't maintain it, you can't change it and you can't hire people to work on it." And that is how I felt about it.

Mandell and his team put together a five-year plan to get us from where we were to where we needed to be. We released the Systems Modernization Plan (SMP) on March 2, 1982. It was a comprehensive document that explained the problem in simple terms and laid out the path to recovery. Senator Bob Dole Chairman of the Committee on Finance put out a press release in which he "praised the Social Security Administration's decision to revamp its computer system." And on the House side, Chairman Pickle and Ranking Republican Bill Archer issued a joint statement stating, "Social Security Commissioner John Svahn took a courageous step today in putting forward a complex and far-reaching proposal to update the Social Security Administration's antiquated computer system. ... We endorse the concept and applaud the straightforward and open manner in which the Commissioner and the agency are addressing this critical problem."

Congress moved quickly and for the first time approved $475 million to fund the full five-year plan. It looked like we were starting with a winner. Unfortunately, not everyone was happy with it.

The Chairman of the House Government Operations Committee, Jack Brooks had hounded the SSA for years about their data processing. His whole thrust had to do with procurement. I don't recall him ever talking about service to the beneficiaries. Brooks had a reputation as mean-spirited and he used the General Accounting Office (GAO) to do his bidding. Brooks was a man of very modest means when first elected to Congress in 1952. By the time the House began forcing members to file financial disclosure statements twenty years later, Brooks had become a very wealthy man. And he made all his money while holding down a full-time job in Congress.

When I was being briefed for confirmation, I was told that Brooks had badgered GSA into suspending SSA's authority to procure information technology. I was told by our staff that before we could proceed with any system modernization, we had to get Brooks' permission. Apparently Brooks had gotten a commitment from my predecessor to pursue a particular path for SSA systems. The commitment was for a "partitioning strategy" of SSA's system. The partitioning strategy referred to breaking SSA systems capacity into several pieces and developing each piece separately. Any contracts for outside assistance in developing software or for hardware had to be competitively procured, of course.

I made an appointment and went up to the Hill to meet with Brooks. During our meeting he told me about his agreement and what he wanted done. I guess he didn't realize that his agreement was with a man who was no longer there who worked for a President who also had been retired. I told him that I was reviewing the current state of affairs and would be putting together an overall modernization plan and would certainly take his concerns and ideas into consideration. I could tell from the look on his hawk-like face when the meeting ended that he was not pleased.

All computers have operating systems that are written by programmers using a particular computer language. By design over the years since computers were invented, different manufacturers of hardware had developed different languages. The languages were so different that they were unable to communicate with each other. Brooks didn't care. He wanted us to let the contractors bid their particular equipment and if the current programs were written in an incompatible language, the software would have to be re-written. The problem with Brooks' strategy was that he wanted anyone to be able to bid *any* hardware on any procurement. As Renny DiPentima, Deputy Commissioner for Systems after I left the SSA, put it in an Oral History interview, "... even if the machine cost $5 million and converting the software to it cost $60 million, that's what he wanted us to do."

I talked it over for some time with Marshall Mandell and we decided that Brooks' plan was crazy and I made the decision that our plan would call for all systems, hardware and locations to be able to communicate with each other. Everything we did would be "code compatible" in systems jargon. I wasn't going to let Brooks run the agency anymore. His objectives were not the same as ours. He didn't like that I guess because he sic'd the GAO on me and several others.

Two years after I left SSA, Brooks held a committee hearing that resembled the proverbial kangaroo court and intimated that I might have steered the big systems modernization contract to Electronic Data Systems because one of their sub-contractors was a firm that I had worked for in the 1970s. And, according to Brooks' accusation, if I had done that and had accepted a few hamburgers in exchange for it, then I had committed a crime. He referred all his "facts" to the Department of Justice for an investigation of me and several other people at SSA.

At that point I didn't know where the thing was going. It was so preposterous on its face, but when I read about it in the newspapers; I figured I had better get a lawyer. I contacted Leonard Garment. Len was an old Washington hand having been in the Nixon White House and he had helped Ed Meese during the time that the mob was trying to lynch him.

Len was appropriately outraged by Brooks' action, but having been around Washington, he knew what direction the process would take from this point and he brought in a bright colleague of his, Ken Adams. Ken had a background in Washington white-collar crime and was very helpful to me in understanding the process. They both cautioned me that this process would take time and that I should cooperate fully with the investigation.

Because I was a very high ranking Presidential appointee, I came under the Independent Counsel Law. The Department of Justice asks the U.S. Attorney to get the FBI to do a preliminary review to see if the situation warranted the appointment of an Independent Counsel to conduct an investigation to see if criminal charges should be filed.

We cooperated fully with the FBI as they conducted their review. After over six months the U.S. Attorney in Baltimore, Breckinridge Wilcox sent Ken Adams a letter which read in part: "… we see no prosecutive merit in the matters raised in the GAO report, or any other information we are currently aware of." Normally, the U.S. Attorney doesn't publicly announce the disposition of an investigation but Ken had asked them to do so due to the circumstances and Mr. Breckinridge had agreed.

When we finally made the U.S. Attorney's decision public a couple of months later in response to a request, Spencer Rich of the *Washington Post* called me up for a comment. I told Spencer that the matter was closed and I didn't need another story raising the issue, nor did I need to comment. He responded by saying, " I wrote a story last year about you being accused of being a crook and now I am going to write one that says you aren't." That's the way Washington works.

One area of Social Security that very much interested me dealt with the Social Security Number and the use of it and the card. The original Social Security Act in 1935 did not mention the Social Security Number nor did it mention a card. The decision to issue a number and a card to workers was made administratively in order to have some way to track earnings. SSNs began being issued in 1936. Thirty million SSNs were issued in about a six month period. Since SSA (at the time it was the Social Security Board) didn't have many field offices, workers made their applications at the local post office.

The nine digit number was broken into three parts: three numbers, two numbers, and four numbers. A lot of concern has developed over the years about what the number means and whether each part means something sinister or smacks of big brother. The number is simple. It was designed in 1936 when there were no computers.

The first three digits are the Area Number. The area number represents the area where the card was issued. Up until 1972 it was the state in which the card was issued. In 1972 SSA began issuing SSNs centrally out of Baltimore and the Area Numbers are now assigned by Zip Code. The Area Number does not show where you live; it shows where you were when you applied for the number. The second two digits are the group number. Group numbers go from 1 to 99 within each area number. There is no significance to the group number. The last set of four digits is your Serial number. This is the number that identifies you specifically within a given group number. So contrary to the rumors about secret meanings in the number, the only thing that can be told by it is the geographic area that you were in when you applied for the number.

A lot of people never applied for the number. When the SSA first started issuing numbers, it was big news but people didn't know much about the process and public communication was slow. So people took advantage of a variety of ways to get a number. The most used number in the history of Social Security was 078-05-1120. This number was the SSN of Mrs. Hilda Schrader Whitcher, a secretary in New York. Hilda worked for a company that made wallets and the company had just come out with a wallet with a glassine slot in it. Hilda's boss thought it would be a good idea to promote the new product by putting one of the new Social Security cards behind the glassine. He used Hilda's card. Then he sold the wallets to the Woolworth nationwide chain of stores. People bought the wallet, saw the copy of the Social Security card in it and, even though the card was marked "Specimen," used the number as their Social Security number. Over 40,000 people used the "Woolworth" number over the years.

The use of the SSN grows every year with or without SSA's agreement. It has become the universal identifier. It seems like you can't get utilities, bank accounts, driver's licenses, student loans, or anything else in today's society without providing your Social Security number. And after you have provided it, then every time you call to inquire about something, you get: "What's the last four of your Social?" I always ask, "My Social what?"

Early on SSA recognized that overuse of the number might become a problem and in 1946 they annotated the card "Not For Identification." I guess that they realized it was a losing battle because in 1972 they removed the annotation. The problem with using the SSN for identification is that until 1978, SSA didn't verify any of the information that an applicant provided when getting a SSN. Verification is a lot of work and in the early days, you didn't need to do it until the person retired; it saved money because a lot of people never made it to retirement age. But when they did, you made them prove where they were born, and when, and that they were who they said they were. In 1978 SSA began verifying name, date, and place of birth and citizenship for applicants.

Aliens, legal and illegal have always been a problem. Through the years, there has always been a problem of counterfeit social security cards. It was a favorite topic of Senator Patrick Moynihan from New York. For a smart man, Pat irrationally believed that if you issued a counterfeit-proof Social Security card, you would eliminate fraud in the system and cut down on the number of illegal aliens. He pushed it sponsoring an amendment to the Social Security Act of 1983 that required the Social Security card to be issued on banknote paper (we had already decided to do it in 1982 but Pat wanted to make sure) and finally in 1996 requiring the SSA to develop a counterfeit-proof card.

I tried to explain to Pat that in 1982 that there was no reason for anyone to traffic in forged or phony Social Security cards; they could get a real one from us. And it was true. Over the years, Congress had mandated so many uses for the Social Security number that a non-citizen could legally get a number in order to use it for some Congressionally mandated function—like opening a bank account. In 1962, the IRS said that all taxpayers had to have a Taxpayer Identification Number (TIN). IRS doesn't care whether you are a citizen or even what business you are in; they want you to pay your taxes so they require a Taxpayer Identification Number. And where do you get a TIN? At SSA of course, it is your Social Security Number.

Miami is the U.S. gateway to Latin America. In 1982, we had many people from down south coming through Miami International Airport and stopping to get a SSN so that they could open a bank account in the United States. We had so many of them that we opened an office near the airport that did nothing but take applications for SSNs. Of course they could use those cards for other things like getting a job. Frustrated one day in May of 1982, I told the staff to buy a bunch of rubber stamps that said "NOT VALID FOR EMPLOYMENT" and stamp each one of those cards. Today the SSA prints the cards with that notation on them.

There are fifty or more variations of the Social Security card that have been issued over the years. All of them are still valid so it can be difficult to know whether you are dealing with a real card or a fake.

Since 1989 SSA has been issuing SSNs to newborns at birth and they put the parents SSNs on the birth certificate too. In 1996 Congress mandated that SSNs had to be placed on death certificates, so today you can't be born or die without a Social Security Number.

SSA urges people to protect their number. In 2004 SSA began annotating the front of the card with the legend "DO NOT CARRY IT WITH YOU." That is good advice. Unfortunately, the people who run Medicare don't know about it. They want you to carry your Medicare card with you in case you need medical care. And what number do they print on it for identification— it's your Medicare Claim Number. It is the same as your Social Security Number.

By the middle of 1981, I realized that we had another problem, and it turned out to be one that I never was able to get my hands around. It involved the Disability Insurance (DI) Program. Disability is the third major program administered by the Social Security Administration. It was enacted by Congress in 1956, during the Eisenhower administration. The law stated that the disability had to be a "medically determinable physical or mental impairment." It is basically a program to provide money to covered workers (those who are paying or have paid Social Security taxes) if they become disabled and are no longer able to work. But like a lot of things, and government actions, in particular, the devil is in the details.

To start, Social Security DI is not like private disability insurance. Private disability insurance pays you according to the terms of the contract between the insurer and the insured. Usually, if you have a condition that prohibits you from performing your job, the private insurance pays off either a lump sum or an annuity.

Social Security Disability Insurance is for the permanently disabled persons who can no longer work. Permanent disability is defined as a condition likely to last for more than a year. Disability is defined as being "unable to engage in Substantial Gainful Activity (SGA). Substantial Gainful Activity in the 1980s was defined as being able to make $300 per month. If you could be a parking lot attendant, you could engage in SGA. Of course no one but the bureaucrats understood the concept of SGA.* And like much of Social Security, the lack of understanding by the public and by most members of Congress was a big part of the problem. DI was not for people who, because of health reasons couldn't continue with their current job or profession. DI was and still is, for people who can do **no** job in the economy. So when an airline pilot has a heart condition and is grounded, even though he can no longer fly because of disability, he is not eligible for Social Security Disability Insurance.

In 1980, with the support of the Carter Administration and urging from the General Accounting Office (GAO), the Congress passed a requirement that the Social Security Administration conduct periodic reviews of the cases already receiving Social Security Disability Insurance. This review was titled a Continuing Disability Investigation (CDI) and was statutorily mandated to begin in January 1982 and be completed by January 1985. The mandate was quite popular on the Hill and in the Administration because several studies and audits had shown that there were many people on DI who were either no longer disabled or who had gotten on the rolls by mistake initially.

The DI program is somewhat confusing administratively. An applicant goes to a Social Security District Office and applies for DI. The claims representative interviews the applicant and determines what medical evidence there is and where it is located. In those days, all cases were hard copy. The case would then be sent to an agency, the Disability Determination Service (DDS), located in the state of the applicant's residence. The DDS was staffed with 100 percent federally funded state employees. These state employees would get the medical evidence, put together the case, evaluate it and make a decision as to whether the applicant was eligible or not. If the applicant was denied,

---

*Today, the amount is $1,000 per month and it is indexed to the cost of living so it rises in most years. In the '80s it wasn't indexed.

he could request a reconsideration which was done by a different DDS employee. If still denied, the applicant could appeal the decision to an Administrative Law Judge (ALJ) who worked for SSA but in reality was hired, paid, and (unlikely) fired by the federal Office of Personnel Management. If still denied, the applicant could request a further review by the SSA ALJ Appeals Council. The last step was to take the case to federal district court. The whole process was cumbersome, confusing and time consuming.

I never understood why a Governor would allow his state DDS agency to do DI determinations. It added state employees to his state work force and generated nothing but bad press for them. One evening I was in a bar in New Orleans. I was in that town to give a speech the next morning to the national association of health lawyers and a couple of the lawyers who were friends of mine had suggested that we go across the street from the hotel for a drink. After a few drinks Jack MacDonald, a long-time friend and lawyer for the nursing home industry, struck up a conversation with the man sitting next to him at the bar. The next thing I know my somewhat intoxicated friend was introducing this very large, very intoxicated neighbor of his to me.

He said, "Jack can fix it for you. He is the Commissioner of Social Security." Then to me, he said, "(This man) has been denied his Disability Insurance and he's real upset." I didn't know what to say. The guy was big and drunk. I asked him how he knew about it and he produced a letter from his coat pocket saying he was ineligible for DI. I looked at the letter and sure enough it was a denial letter from the Louisiana DDS. Right at the top was the state of Louisiana seal and "David C. Treen, Governor." I told the man that his problem was with the State. I pointed to the Governor's name and suggested to him that he call the Governor the next morning; tell him that he had talked to the Commissioner of Social Security and that I said it needed to be fixed. He seemed satisfied and I then made a quick exit.

In 1981 and 1982, this confusing Continuing Disability Investigation process resulted in a lot of anomalies. Rejection rates varied widely from state to state (as they do today). And the reversal rate at the ALJ level where denial appeals wound up was through the roof. State agencies denied about two thirds of the applications. Upon appeal to the "reconsideration" process, about 85 percent of the original decisions were upheld as correct. At the ALJ level, almost two thirds of the denials were overturned. A real mess.

The reasons for the wide discrepancy in decision making are many but they all boil down to the fact that determining disability can be very subjective. And there are a lot of people at different levels of government that get into the act. SSA, in trying to standardize the process, developed a "grid" of conditions and then dictated that the DDS's squeeze every applicant through the "grid." Also contributing to the problem, was the fact that the applicant didn't get an in person meeting with anyone in the process until they got before the ALJ. And in the ALJ hearing, no one represented the SSA and DDS. It was only the applicant, usually accompanied by an attorney and the ALJ and it was perfectly permissible to submit new medical evidence at any stage of the process.

In preparation for the beginning of the CDIs, SSA did a review of several thousand current beneficiary cases in the fall of 1980. The results were remarkable. They found that about 20 percent of the cases reviewed were no longer eligible for Disability Insurance. Since DI had about 3 million beneficiaries at the time, 20 percent ineligible was a lot of people and most importantly to Stockman at OMB; it represented almost $4billion in payments that shouldn't be made.

That was the status of the DI program when I was nominated to be Commissioner. After I was nominated, but before I was confirmed, as part of my orientation, I was briefed on the DI program and more particularly on the need to perform the CDIs. In discussions with Chairman Pickle and other members of the Ways and Means

Committee, I was reminded of the need to get the planning underway for the CDIs.

It was the opinion of career SSA staff, that the CDI workload was going to be substantial and that we should begin to implement CDIs as soon as was practicable in order to have more time to complete the task by the Congressionally mandated date. Not all agreed. The Operations people were concerned that the workload would be too great and that more time was needed to staff up, but the general consensus was that this could begin at most any time. OMB, on the other hand, wanted an early start. They figured that ineligible people getting kicked off earlier would result in earlier and larger savings to the budget. And finally, the GAO was criticizing SSA for not starting early.

Much has been written about the decision to begin the CDIs earlier than the date specified in the legislation. In hindsight, many have suggested that had we waited until January of 1982, the mess that later occurred would have been averted. They are wrong. We could have planned for five years and what happened would have still happened. And no one complained or cautioned against haste. Everyone thought that it was the thing to do.

I don't recall the specific decision to begin the CDIs before the statutory start date, but I am sure that I did not make it. I wasn't confirmed as Commissioner until May 6. The decision to begin the CDIs early and increase the number that was conducted was made before that date. I am sure that I was aware that they were going to begin and I supported that decision.

I won't go into the mess that ensued other than to say that many individuals were removed from the disability rolls and some of them were mistakenly done so. We did a study in 1982 and found that 97 percent of the decisions to remove were correct and that 3 percent were removed incorrectly. With three million people on disability, 3 percent was a pretty big number. And it seemed that each one of those that was incorrectly removed wound up on the front page of their local newspaper. Soon there were horror stories everywhere.

Contributing to the problem was that many of the DI cases were based on mental impairment. Evaluating mental impairment can be very difficult. Even though each beneficiary was sent to a contract physician for evaluation, it is tough to determine mental illness in a few minutes of face to face conversation. One minute the person could seem perfectly normal and the next do something totally irrational.

There were several very high profile cases that received national attention from the media in which the beneficiaries appeared on camera and said that they had physical disabilities when in fact they had been on the rolls due to mental problems. Unfortunately, due to privacy laws, we were never able to publically defend the agency decision. We had to grin and bear the criticism.

Some of the DI beneficiaries didn't go to the newspaper. They took matters into their own hands. A number of them committed suicide, some in or in front of our offices. We had an office shot up in Louisiana by a disgruntled beneficiary. Fortunately, no one was hit by the gunfire. In another incident an Army recruiter whose office was next door to one of ours in California was tragically shot and killed by a DI beneficiary when the staff in the Social Security office wouldn't unlock the door for the man. And many people who applied for Disability Insurance died of their ailments before they were found eligible or before their denial appeal was decided.

As a result of these and other incidents, including a lot of written threats, I was assigned "security." Security in my case came in the person of Robert Taylor, a U.S. Marshall and former Secret Service Agent. Bob changed the way I did business. He was always with me. If I was in the car, he was in the car. On a plane, he sat behind be on the opposite side aisle. In a hotel, he had the room across the hall.

Early on in our relationship I made an appearance at the American Bankers Association convention in Hilton Head Island. Late in the evening I decided to leave my room and have a nightcap in the bar. I opened the door and there was Taylor, in the room across the hall with the door open. I told him what I was doing and he grabbed his weapon and headed out with me.

I suggested that he was off duty and invited him for a drink. He established our relationship right away. He said, "No thank you. I am a professional working a security detail and you are the protectee. If something happens to you when I am supposed to be on duty, it's my fault and my career." He also told my wife, Jill, when she was trying to befriend him, that he didn't want to get to know the family. That his job was to protect me and that if he got to know everyone else, it might cause a problem in the future if he had to make a decision in a hurry.

Having security does have its benefits. Security details advance travel and you don't wait in security lines at airports. On a trip to a meeting in Mexico City, Bob went ahead and met with some counterparts in the Mexican Federal Police. When I arrived there were a bunch of them assigned to me. Walking down the street, I told Taylor that I wanted to go into a drug store to buy some cigars. He told the Federales and they said for us to wait a moment. They went into the drugstore and cleared it out before they would let me enter. Scary. But then Taylor had already told me that those fellows shoot first and then ask questions if necessary. He said it with a little smile but I was never sure he was kidding.

Having a bodyguard assigned to you is confining. I can't imagine what it would be to be the President and have a constant cocoon of security no matter where you were or what time of day it was. I know that the Reagan kids, Ron and Patti did not like it and constantly chafed at the Secret Service protection that they had due to the fact that they were the President's kids.

But about the Disability Insurance program I can say this unequivocally: I never did anything from the spring of 1981 to September of 1983 that tightened the CDI process. Every decision I made liberalized the program that had been developed by SSA career personnel. Initially, I slowed down the rate of cases called up for CDIs and I replaced the people who had been developing and running the program. I also exempted great numbers of cases from even having to go through the CDI process by classifying whole categories as permanently disabled. In addition, I required the examiners to use all medical evidence in making a determination of disability. For some reason, SSA had decided that only the most recent examination's findings would be used to determine continuing disability. So a beneficiary could have a file a foot thick with many pages of medical evidence and examinations saying he was mentally disabled and the last psychiatrist, in a fifteen minute interview, says he is OK and SSA kicks him off. I changed that. And finally, in late 1982, I required that all cases scheduled for a CDI had to have a face to face interview in the local District Office. I figured that if there was a face to face meeting, we would at least stop kicking quadriplegics and other people with obvious disabilities off the rolls.

I was completely frustrated by the constant stream of newspaper and television reports about mistakes. Common sense had gone out the window. It wasn't any one individual's fault. We were all to blame to a certain extent. The system was hidebound and mired in layer on top of layer of rules and procedures. I recall vividly a meeting in my office with the people who were running the program. We were discussing another sensational case. I finally said, "Damn it. If a guy is over fifty-five and he has had three heart attacks, he is disabled. Got it?" The response was "Yes sir." I think that that is still the rule.

One case that received quite a bit of national visibility was that of William "Bill" Schroeder. Schroeder filed an application for disability in March of 1984. His application was based on a heart condition. His application was still pending eight months later when Dr. William DeVries implanted the Jarvik-7 artificial heart in his chest and Bill became the first person to live with an artificial heart. Schroeder was well known at the local SSA district office and even while in the hospital getting the Jarvik, he called to inquire about the status of his application. He got no action.

But on December 12, 1984, just seventeen days after the surgery, Bill got a congratulatory phone call from President Reagan. During the call, Bill complained about getting the bureaucratic runaround from SSA and not getting any money. The Case-Worker-in-Chief told him that he would get right on it and find out what the problem was. He did.

When this occurred, I was the President's domestic policy advisor. I didn't get a whole lot of calls in my West Wing office from the President because most of our interaction was face to face. So when the red light on my phone lit up and the President was on the line, I was pretty surprised. I hadn't yet heard about the Schroeder call but he filled me in and asked me to check on it. I called out to Social Security and issued another edict "When a guy has a heart condition that is so bad that he needs an artificial heart, he is disabled!" "Yes Sir" was the response. The next day a representative from SSA visited Bill in his hospital room with a check for his DI benefits retroactive to his date of application.

In his diary, Ronald Reagan recalls it this way:

> "Yesterday I called Mr. Schroeder the man with the new artificial heart. He ended up telling me he had a problem with Soc. Security. I told him I'd look into it. Today he no longer has a problem."

I never did get the Disability Insurance Program fixed. Neither did any of my successors. Each one has tried but failed. JoAnne Barnhart (Commissioner from 2001 to 2007) made fixing the DI program her number one priority. Much progress has been made, but the administrative structure and process is essentially the same as it was when I was Commissioner. They don't shuffle the hard copy files around anymore, but today it can still take two years to get a final decision on disability. There are almost 1 million applications backed up in the state DDSs.

And the appeals caseload is still growing. A whole new industry has grown up for the lawyers. They advertise that only they can get your disability for you. SSA has made it easy for them because they pay the lawyers fee out of the retroactive disability benefit! It was a mess in the early '80s and it is still a mess ten years into the next century.

Chapter 12

Saving Social Security

The lines were drawn by our Social Security financing proposals of May 12 and it looked like it was going to be a long drawn out battle. The politicians saw the package as a way to get at Reagan and the interest groups saw it as a fundraiser. It was definitely controversial. As the *National Journal* reported:

"The bomb went off on impact. An outraged public and an election-wary Congress made their opposition abundantly clear. At the White House, officials set about trying to minimize the damage to the President.

Stories leaked to the press put as much distance as possible between Reagan and the reforms, leaving Schweiker and HHS holding the bag. It was HHS, the stories implied, that had put the proposals together and Schweiker who sold them to the President; top White House aides denied advance knowledge."

Nowhere was the rhetoric any louder and more vicious than on Capitol Hill. The Democrats, led by Tip O'Neil as Speaker of the House and Pat Moynihan on the Senate side fired away at will. Moynihan during a live appearance on ABC's Good Morning America characterized the package as "political terrorism." O'Neill called the plan a "rotten thing to do." He said that what the President was doing was "despicable."

Pickle and Archer were still intent on working out a bill in the Democrat controlled House, but real trouble was brewing in the Republican Senate. Just a week after our press conference announcing the package, Moynihan introduced a resolution in the Senate condemning our proposal and vowing that it would never pass. His resolution failed by one vote. Bob Dole, the Chairman of the Finance Committee then introduced a resolution which read in part "Congress shall not precipitously and unfairly penalize early retirees." It passed the Senate 96 to 0. Sounded so good that I would have voted for it! But Dole's resolution was played up in the press as a repudiation of the President's package for Social Security. An editorial in the *Baltimore Sun* summed it up:

> "That 96 to 0 Senate denunciation of President Reagan's proposed Social Security cuts presented the country with a nice piece of cynicism. Not that we hold any brief for the president's specifics, much less the way he rushed them forward to save his deficit-spawning tax cut plan. But the Senate vote, as unbinding as it was phony, was merely intended to take the legislators off the hook with elderly voters. It did not face up to the imperative for changes in the Social Security system, preferably this year, to prevent it from going broke or limping along through fiscal legerdemain."

While the reaction to our proposals was still unfolding, I went on the road doing interviews and giving speeches. I was trying to sell the administration's package by explaining the depth of the problem and debunking the myths that surrounded the program. Schweiker and I testified before Ways and Means on the House side and Finance in the Senate. I did the morning news shows and stayed up late to do Nightline. On Good Morning America in July I explained that we would not hurt current beneficiaries. I was followed by Pat Moynihan who repeated his comment that the administration's approach to social security was "political terrorism." He admitted that there was a financing problem but said that it could be solved through inter-fund borrowing and using some general fund money rather than relying on

Trust Fund money. Pat Moynihan was a brilliant man and a very effective orator. He was convincing.

We were getting hammered everywhere. On Nightline, Ted Koppel paired me up with Congressman Claude Pepper. Pepper then in his eighties was deaf as a post. He couldn't hear a thing and in order to do the show, the ABC technicians had to put a booster on his ear piece. In those days, Nightline had the two interviewees sit side by side with a camera on each person. Koppel did the interviewing from a remote location. Because there was a camera for each person, the television viewer didn't realize that the combatants were actually sitting side by side. On this evening, Pepper was at the top of his game. He railed against the President, shouting into the microphone. Koppel kept trying to break in but Pepper was having none of it. I was wondering what I was doing there. In the middle of the show I realized that I was holding the box that was Pepper's hearing booster in my lap. For a moment, I considered unplugging it but then I realized that if I did, neither Koppel nor I would ever get Pepper to stop talking!

Chairman Pickle called me in August. Jake was a pretty colorful fellow from Austin, Texas. On the phone he told me that he felt "like Richard Nixon during Watergate. I feel like I'm treed." He said that he was refusing to do any press interviews but that the House leadership had decided not to advance any legislation "at this time" and that O'Neill had decided to check the issue back to the Senate. "I'm not happy with that," Jake told me. He said that he needed the Administration to send up the legislative language for the President's proposals.* He was "confident that we will have meaningful legislation this year—we've got to!" A couple of days later he called to tell me that the "leadership met this morning and agreed not to do anything on Social Security. They're going to await action until the Senate or President acts. I could

---

* We never did send the package to the Hill. We drafted all of the language and put it in the format for transmission to the White House and then to the Congress. I took the entire package and locked it in my desk. It is still there.

tell you more but I better not. I am very sorry—it looks like this is going to be a more national political issue than before."

Boy was he ever right. Most of the Democrats in the House, under direction from Speaker O'Neill, demagogued their way through 1981 and 1982 right up to the November elections. When the elections were held Republicans lost twenty-seven seats in the House of Representatives. Exit polling showed that the Social Security issue played a role in twenty-four of those losses. Barber Conable, Republican from New York and ranking minority on the Ways and Means Committee at the time remarked to me that it was his toughest campaign. "All my opponent kept saying was, 'He wants to cut your Social Security' and all I could say back was, 'I do not.'" So O'Neill's strategy worked.

During the summer and fall of 1981 while the campaign against Republicans was being devised in the Speaker's office, the powers that be at the White House were doing all they could to distance themselves from "Schweiker and Svahn's" proposals.

Dick Schweiker was a good trooper. He supported the President's position, but he knew that our package was going nowhere. As a consequence, he pretty much let me do my own thing, running Social Security with little interference from the several thousand people in the "Office of the Secretary."

Occasionally, little dust ups would occur. It may seem hard to believe, but in 1981 facsimile machines were a hot new item. Since I had an office in Baltimore and Washington with a need to shuffle paperwork between the two, we bought and installed fax machines in both offices. Then an edict came from the Office of the Secretary, in this case from the Assistant Secretary for Management and Budget.

Fearing that there would be a proliferation of fax machines, the Assistant Secretary, Dale Sopper, directed that only his office would have a fax machine and that all faxes would go through his office. Other offices were not to have their own machines. Aside from the short-sightedness of his directive, it meant that all of our communications were going to be reviewed in the OS before I got a chance to look at them. That was unacceptable. So I told the staff in the Washington office to purchase two pigeons and put them in a cage outside my office in the hallway on the sixth floor and hang a sign on the cage that said: "Commissioner's Communication System." The word about the pigeons got around and we kept the fax machines.

I spent the four months between May 12 and September 12 educating members and the public alike about the realities of the program. We were still slipping into the financial abyss spending more money than we were taking in. During the summer, our projections showed that the fund would be unable to honor the checks that were delivered on November 3, 1982, the day after election day. But most members of Congress either ignored our warnings or didn't understand them. Our budget proposals unfortunately contributed to the confusion.

One area of controversy surrounded the elimination of the so-called minimum benefit. There were actually two minimum benefits: the regular minimum benefit and the special minimum benefit. The special minimum benefit had been enacted to provide a floor of benefits for people who worked at low paying jobs throughout their career. The regular minimum benefit had been originally established as an administrative simplification according to my deputy Bob Myers. SSA and Treasury didn't want to be cutting checks for small amounts so they set a minimum payment. Over the years, Congress had gradually increased the payment amount under the regular minimum benefit. The benefit had no relation to the beneficiary's earnings or work history. It was the regular minimum benefit that was terminated for current and future beneficiaries in the budget that had passed as the Omnibus Budget Reconciliation Act of 1981 (OBRA).

One day that summer I was briefing members of the House Republican Conference and one of the members questioned, "Hey Jack. What about the nuns?" I knew that what he was talking about was the furor surrounding the elimination of the $122 a month regular minimum benefit. And I explained what it was and who got it. Many of the people receiving it were retired government and non-profit employees. They worked outside the Social Security system for a career and received a pension from their non-covered employment. After retirement they took a job in the private sector and paid FICA taxes for a short time and then retired again thereby qualifying for the regular minimum benefit. It was a windfall for them and I said so.

I further explained that one sector of the non-profit world that found this windfall and took advantage of it was organized religion. Some denominations were not in Social Security but had discovered that as a member approached retirement age they could begin paying FICA taxes for that person for a short time and when the person retired they qualified for the regular minimum benefit. Apparently some orders of nuns were doing this. I explained that it was truly a windfall for them and that they were gaming the system. Satisfied with my explanation, I looked around the room for the next question and called on another member. He said, "What about the nuns?" It was a long hard summer.

The minimum benefit remained an issue for us throughout the debate. Even the President was hauled into the fracas. At an editorial board meeting at the now defunct Washington Star, he was asked if he was having second thoughts about eliminating the minimum benefit and whether or not he would go along with Congress to repeal it. The President readily replied with an answer that was as good as any one that I could have given. He then said it was not our intention to hurt anyone, just to remove the windfall. But in the end, he caved and said he would agree to Congressional action to reinstate the benefit.

Congress wanted to fix it and now the President wanted to fix it. It wasn't that easy; Congress had to pass legislation to undue it. The budget act required that SSA send a notice to all of the recipients who were being cut off informing them of the action. Those notices were supposed to go out in December and I was under pressure from the Hill to not send out notices "because we are going to take care of the problem." I got a call from John Salmon, Chief Counsel to the House Ways and Means Committee. The chairman of Ways and Means was Dan Rostenkowski from Illinois. I had a pretty good relationship with Danny and with John. Salmon told me that some of the minimum benefit was not going to happen. He told me that the Chairman didn't want to personally call me and tell me not to follow the law and delay sending out notices to minimum benefit recipients. But John said, "It would be too bad for you to lose your rapport with the Chairman over this little issue." They didn't want me to send out notices but they weren't going to act in time to stop them. Congress restored the regular minimum benefit in December 1981. We never sent the notices. The nuns were taken care of finally.

Meanwhile, with Tip O'Neill dumping daily barrages on Republicans, the Senate Committee on Finance started to take up Social Security. The Senate was controlled by Republicans. Howard Baker was majority leader and Bob Dole was Chairman of Finance. Bill Armstrong from Colorado chaired the Social Security Sub Committee. We began meeting with Finance looking at how we could salvage enough to keep the program solvent. Sometimes we met with members; sometimes with the staff. The Chief Counsel Robert Lighthizer and his Social Security staff person Carolyn Weaver were very intelligent, experienced staff people and had the confidence of Dole the Chairman.

On September 14 we met with Finance staff and Carolyn Weaver outlined a social security package that Dole believed would be acceptable to Democrats Long (LA), and Benson (TX), independent Byrd (VA), as well as to the six Republican senators who were up for reelection in November of 1982. Dole said that the package would have some of our original package but none of the "big ticket short term items." Read no reduction in early retirement benefits, not even on a phased in basis.

The other bombshell in the Dole proposal was that Finance was going to use the Intermediate set of economic assumptions. It made the financing gap appear much smaller than it really was. It looked like the Senate was going to go its own way.

On September 15, a chink appeared in our own armor. The President, in remarks at a White House reception on the South Lawn for business leaders said:

> "And let me silence those, those who would scare our older Americans. The budget will not be balanced at the expense of those dependent on social security. That system has serious problems; but we have sent our proposals to the Congress, and we have no plans to change them."

Right out of the blue. None of us who were working on the issue knew what caused the statement, nor did we know what it meant. The press picked up on it and speculated that it meant that there would be no cuts in Social Security.

I met with Schweiker the morning after the President spoke and we discussed the statement. Schweiker said that he had checked with the White House and that there was no change in our position regardless of the press speculation. We had the Administration's package and we were sticking to it. I heard him and went back into the fray but I could sense that something was brewing within the Administration. I got a call from Lighthizer at Finance later that day and he said that Dole was taking the package to the Republicans on the next day, September 17, and that they would go to markup on their bill the next week.

The next day I got a call from Jake Pickle. Jake wanted to know about the President's statement. He said he assumed it meant that Reagan was standing by his May proposals. I told him that yes that the President was sticking with his package. Pickle said that he was having a problem with Tip. Tip told him that he was too soft on us and

The 1982 Commissioner of Social Security's soccer team. I am standing in the center. The long haired gentleman on my left was the goalie for the professional soccer team in Baltimore. The Commissioner's team never lost.

The meeting in the West Wing's Roosevelt Room that started the big brouhaha about Social Security. From left, Jack Svahn; Undersecretary of Health and Human Services (HHS), David Swoap; Secretary of HHS, Dick Schweiker; the Vice President(partially obscured), Secretary of Education, Ted Bell; Assistant to the President for Policy Development, Martin Anderson; two unidentified persons; Murray Weidenbaum, Chairman of the Council of Economic Advisors; Bill Smith, Attorney General (partially obscured); the President; and Dave Stockman, the budget director.

177

Reagan could be very inquisitive when a subject tweaked his interest. We had just finished a discussion about the ins and outs of the Social Security system.

The President makes a visit to the 2nd floor of the West Wing. From my staff, on the far left, Jan Farrell, and behind the President and the author, Betty Ayers. Silver haired gentleman in the foreground is Lee Verstandig. Others are from Dr. Verstandig's staff.

The President plays a little joke on me aboard Air Force One. The plane was a modified Boeing 707 and now resides in a spectacular display at the Reagan Presidential Library.

Budget Reviews in the Cabinet Room after the 1984 election. From left, Jack Svahn, Assistant to the President for Policy Development; Edwin Meese III, Counselor to the President; The President; and James A. Baker III, Chief of Staff.

Three well known and one not so well known. From the left Jack Svahn, James A. Baker III, Chief of Staff, the Vice President and the President in an Oval Office discussion.

After a briefing in the residence, a return to the West Wing. From the left, Secret Service agent, Jack Svahn, the President, Secret Service, Edwin Meese III, and David Fischer, the President's personal aide who keep us all on time.

Sometimes briefings were done standing up. It made them shorter. Here, Lee Verstandig and I brief the President and Vice President prior to a meeting with the nation's Governors.

The Svahn family in the Oval Office prior to my departure party. From left, my father Albert R. Svahn, our daughter Kirsten, and son, John A. Svahn III, the President, Jill, myself, and my mother, Esther M. Svahn.

I frequently warmed up audiences before the President appeared. Here is one occasion in the beautiful Indian Treaty Room. The walk back to the West Wing almost became a disaster.

Debate preparations were not all work and no play. At Camp David, the author and Special Assistant to the President, Michael Baroody, do a mock debate with hand puppets of Reagan and his opponent, Walter Mondale. Reagan was much amused in his horse riding attire. I still have those paper bag puppets.

Richard G. (Dick) Darman makes a point during final debate preparations at Camp David. From left, Darman, the President, Nancy Reagan, James A. Baker III, and the author.

A bad day at Black Rock (actually it was in Louisville, KY). Watching the first debate with Walter Mondale. From left: Margaret Tutweiler, a Baker aide; Dick Darman; Ed Hickey, the head of the military office and someone who had been with us since 1968 in Sacramento; Jim Baker; Stu Spencer, long time Reagan political strategist; Paul Laxalt, Senator from Nevada and campaign chairman; Dan Rugge, the President's physician; myself; and Larry Speakes, the Press Secretary.

A meeting with the Vice President in his West Wing office. The author had some explaining to do.

Lunch at Table #2 in the State Dining Room.

The Shamrock Summit with Prime Minister Brian Mulrooney of Canada. The author is at the far end of the table between National Security Advisor, John Poindexter and Press Secretary Larry Speakes. The author had worked with former transportation secretary Drew Lewis to formulate a position on the issue of acid rain, the hot topic for this summit.

that he was "working with the enemy." Tip told him to hold a press conference and tell people that all we needed to solve the problem was inter-fund borrowing. Jake said that he wanted to be responsible and "I really think that the big problem is educating the people—including our members!"

On Monday, September 21, I met with Senate Finance members after a discussion with Lighthizer. Lighthizer told me that Armstrong and Dole were in disagreement and that "between us, he (Armstrong) is the problem. He is lobbying hard to get inter-fund borrowing and fold." At the 1:30 meeting Armstrong agreed that we needed to address the long term deficit but he felt that it was pointless to go forward with a reform bill unless it was bi-partisan. He felt that taking a partisan package to the floor was folly. He wanted reform but he wanted it all.

Lighthizer was still quite pessimistic about getting anything out. He didn't think that Armstrong had ever looked at some of the easy things in the President's package. I left the hill that day thinking that we were still alive. Then I got a call from Dave Swoap, the Under Secretary. Dave had previously been on the Senate Finance Committee staff and he worked for Armstrong. Dave told me that the Committee's Republicans had met on the eighteenth and concluded that "doing something is suicidal." They weren't going to do anything on Social Security. Dave said that Dole had notified Jim Baker, the White House Chief of Staff to that effect. I asked Dave what the hell was going on as I had just spent the day with Dole and his staff working on a bill. Swoap thought that the problem was a manifestation of a personal fight between Dole and Armstrong. On September 24, 1981, the White House threw in the towel.

Late on the twenty-third, I got a call from Bob Lighthizer asking about a draft of a speech that the President was going to give that asked only for inter-fund borrowing for Social Security. I told him that I knew of no such speech. I called Paul Simmons and told him something was up and we needed to find out what. Early on the twenty-fourth Simmons contacted Misty Church, one of the White House speechwriters and found out that indeed the President was going to give an economic speech that evening and that there was a section on Social Security in it! We got her to send us a copy and made some technical corrections to the section. But there was a real bombshell in the draft.

In the draft speech, at the end of his discussion of the economy, the President turned to the issue of Social Security. After having spent a few minutes explaining the proposals we released on May 12, and chastising those who had denigrated them and frightened seniors on Social Security, the President pointed out that "our feet were never imbedded in concrete on this proposal. We hoped it would be a starting point for a bipartisan solution to the problem." He said that had not been possible because House Democrats had "refused to join in any such cooperative effort."

He then asked for a restoration of the minimum benefit and interfund borrowing. In addition he asked O'Neill and Senate Majority Leader Baker to each appoint five members to a "task force" that would come up with a plan to assure the financial stability of Social Security. We were caving in.

I went to see Dick Schweiker with a copy of the draft speech. With the President giving in, we knew who the scapegoats were going to be. Schweiker said it had to be Baker and Darman who convinced the President to give in. We placed several calls to the White House trying to get someone's attention. Schweiker tried to reach Ed Meese. They couldn't be doing this to us! Yes they could. Craig Fuller, the Cabinet Secretary called us back and said that Ed had asked him to call. Ed couldn't return the call because he was in the Oval Office with the President going over the speech. The decision had been made. The President's diary for September 23 sums it up:

"I'm withdrawing Soc. Security from consideration & challenging Tip & the Dems. to join in a bipartisan effort to solve the fiscal dilemma of S.S.

without all the politics they've been playing. Since I'm inviting him on nat. TV, he might be persuaded to go on at 9 P.M. tomorrow night …"

The morning after the speech, Speaker O'Neill issued a statement congratulating the President on his "new flexibility" and on the fact that the President was now coming around to what the Democrats wanted all along. As for the "task force," O'Neill referred to it as a "new Commission." He said that, "This is a new idea, which the President has never discussed with me. The first notice I had of this was last night." So much for the new cooperation.

After nine months of working on the problem night and day, Social Security financing was on the back burner. The White House set about to put together its five nominees for the Commission and negotiations were begun with the House and Senate to put together the task force that was going to do what we had been unable to do, reach a bipartisan consensus.

There still remained the little matter of getting legislation to restore the minimum benefit for current beneficiaries and to permit inter-fund borrowing so that the November 3, 1982 checks wouldn't bounce. On Saturday, November 21, I got a call from Lighthizer inviting me to a meeting with Chairman Dole that afternoon to discuss the legislation to accomplish "what the President had asked for." The meeting with Dole didn't get anywhere. Dole suggested that Lighthizer call John Salmon, the Ways and Means Chief Counsel and see if we couldn't work this out. Lighthizer, Salmon and I met in H-208, one of the rooms on the House side. After an hour it became apparent that we were getting nowhere. Each side wanted the other to blink.

But it did appear that John Salmon was trying to get a solution. It almost appeared that he was under instructions to get it done. He had a summary of Unresolved Issues that the Conference Committee had. It all seemed so simple. They couldn't agree on how long inter-fund borrowing would be permitted and they couldn't agree on the date that prospective elimination of the windfall minimum benefit would become effective. They were sixty-one days apart.

But it was also clear that Salmon wasn't going to agree to any reduction in benefits. I chided him about the 1977 25 percent reduction in benefits that created the "notch." He laughed and said that he knew that they had reduced benefits then but that the good thing was that no one else did. We were getting nowhere and Lighthizer said that he saw no reason for getting the conferees together and the meeting broke up amicably.

The House was going to recess for the Thanksgiving holiday and wouldn't be back until December 9 so it was get it done today or wait until after the deadline for notifying recipients of the elimination of the minimum benefit. Bob and I went back to the Senate side and looked for Dole. We found him in the Senate dining room and briefed him on our meeting with Salmon. Dole said that he had called Rostenkowski and told him that we weren't going to meet that day. I was confident that when they returned we would get agreement and I decided on the spot that I wasn't going to send out the notices. Dole was pleased.

On December 14 the conferees reached agreement to authorize inter-fund borrowing through December 31, 1982, and to restore the regular minimum benefit to current beneficiaries. It was all over but the shouting. In a New Year interview by the *St. Louis Post-Dispatch* I summed up my feelings, "No one's going to write 'Profiles in Courage' on Capitol Hill this year."

Restoration of the minimum benefit was a simple task, because we had expended a lot of internal resources to plan and prepare to cut off benefits, but we had not done anything publicly to implement the provision so we just stopped planning.

Inter-fund borrowing on the other hand had never been done. Each of the programs, retirement and survivors, disability, and Medicare had a separate source of income and a separate trust fund. The new law gave us limited, specific authority to borrow between the funds.

In 1981, the vast majority of our payments to beneficiaries were done by paper check. Treasury cut all the checks. Everyone's check was delivered by U.S. Mail on the third of the month. Now of course most of the payments are made by direct deposit due to Treasury's campaign to get out of the check writing business and payments are spread out through the month. But in the early eighties, all checks were supposed to be delivered on the third and each month we braced for an on-slaught of calls and complaints due to lost and stolen checks. We are not talking onesy's and twosey's here. We are talking about hundreds of thousands of checks missing each month. On one occasion, an entire semi-trailer full of Social Security checks was missing on the third. Even today, on average, there are 70,000 missed payments each month, even when most people are on direct deposit.

On one occasion, I was asked by the White House to give my Social Security speech to a group of seniors in Santa Barbara. The President's ranch was outside Santa Barbara and he had been associated with the group in the past. I said sure and booked myself into Santa Barbara.

The group numbered about 250; most were affluent senior citizens. The format for the event was very interesting. The men ate together in one room and the women ate in a different room. The speaker, on this occasion me, was expected to give a speech to the men's luncheon first and right after that to go to a different ballroom and give the same speech to the ladies.

I went through my stock speech about the myths surrounding Social Security and the dire state of finances of the Trust Funds. When I concluded, the luncheon broke up and I headed for the ladies lun-cheon audience. But everyone was leaving at the same time and I was slowed by a couple of elderly guys heading for the door in front of me. Not knowing that I was behind them, the one man said to the other. "You know that young fellow was right. Social Security has become something that it was never intended to be." The second responded, "Yes it has. I don't need it and I get a little embarrassed going into the bank and cashing that check each month." The first guy replied, "I know just what you mean. I used to feel the same way, but they've got this new thing—direct deposit. You don't have to go to the bank. It goes right into your account!"

The process for sending out the monthly checks begins weeks in advance. When all the checks were delivered on the third day of the month, the Treasury Department knew exactly how much money it needed to transfer from the OASI trust fund in order to cover the checks. They also knew that everybody didn't immediately cash their check on the third so they would wait a couple of days before completing the transfer.

We didn't need inter-fund borrowing right away. The shortfall didn't come until the November 1982 checks went out. November 3, 1982, was a Wednesday. The day before, Tuesday the second, had been Election Day and the Republicans had lost twenty-six seats in the House. We knew and had been saying since May of 1981 that we were not going to be able to cover the checks in November of 1982. On November 5, we borrowed $581 million from the Disability Insurance Trust fund in order to have enough. Then on December 7 we borrowed $3.437 billion from the Health Insurance Trust Fund to cover the December checks.

The legislation that had been passed in December of 1981 that allowed inter-fund borrowing cut off our ability to borrow on December 31, 1982, but it allowed us to borrow up to six months of needed funds. Because we still didn't have a legislative fix and were continuing to lose money each month on December 31, 1982, because the authority to borrow was running out, the OASI Trust Fund borrowed $13.5 billion from the DI and HI Trust Funds to cover the payments through June 3, 1983. Before borrowing the money from the DI and HI trust funds, Treasury decided to first liquidate the remaining securities in the OASI fund. This early sale, where Treasury sold the securities to itself resulted in a loss of $329 million for the trust funds but saved the

Treasury an equal amount in future interest payments. It was as much as we could do. For years I joked about how I once borrowed $17.5 billion dollars on a signature note.

On the same day as the speech, the President formally wrote to O'Neill stating:

"Last spring, I proposed what I believe to be a fair, balanced and workable solution to the social security problem. However, it is now evident that there are so many proposal and so many different views of the problem that a comprehensive long-term solution is not possible in the immediate future."

He went on to call for

"the establishment of a bipartisan Blue Ribbon Task Force, to which you, the Majority Leader of the Senate and I would each name five outstanding Americans."

The White House immediately began to sort through a list of potential Presidential appointees to the Commission. The initial list included Schweiker, Myers, and me. They liked Jake Pickle and Dick Gephardt, the Congressman from Missouri although Jake's stance on using General Revenue to finance the system bothered a lot of people. Joe Waggner, a former Democrat member of Congress and Rita Ricardo Campbell, a senior fellow at the Hoover Institution and an expert in Social Security Policy, were also on the short list.

The White House staff decided that Schweiker and I, particularly me, were too damaged to be on the Commission and made a decision to have the President's appointees all come from outside government.

On December 16, 1981, the President signed Executive Order 12335 establishing the National Commission on Social Security Reform (NCSSR). That same day he announced the members of the Commission. The Chairman was Alan Greenspan. The other four Presidential appointees were Robert Beck, Chairman of Prudential Insurance, Alexander Trowbridge, President of the National Association of Manufactures, Mary Falvey Fuller, Vice President of the Shaklee

Corporation, and Joe Waggoner, the former Democrat Congressman from Louisiana. The Senate named Bob Dole, Bill Armstrong, chairman of the Finance subcommittee on social security, John Heinz, the Senator from Pennsylvania, Pat Moynihan and Lane Kirkland, the head of the AFL/CIO. The House nominees were Barber Conable, Congressman from New York and ranking minority on Ways and Means, Bill Archer, a member from Houston Texas and ranking minority member on the Ways and Means Subcommittee on Social Security. Both Conable and Archer were Republicans. The Speaker put Claude Pepper from Florida, Robert Ball, a former Commissioner of Social Security, and former Congresswoman Martha Keys to round out the fifteen members.

Two days before the President signed the Executive Order establishing the Commission, Bob Myers resigned. I tried to talk him out of it, but he, like me, thought that the Commission was a cop-out and that real reform of Social Security was not going to happen for some time to come. It turned out to be a fortuitous resignation. One of the first things that Alan Greenspan did as Chairman of the NCSSR was to find himself a knowledgeable Social Security expert to serve as Executive Director. He hired Bob Myers. And one of the first things that Bob Myers did as Executive Director was to ask me for staff and support. I told him that the whole agency was available to support the work of the Commission.

The first meeting of the National Commission on Social Security took place in February of 1982 at a Washington hotel. By law the Commission meetings were open to the public. I had been invited to attend the first meeting and to make some welcoming remarks. Unfortunately for me, an inexperienced reporter had misquoted me in the newspaper a few days before and both Moynihan and Kirkland had read the story. Kirkland said a few nasty words to me and then Pat, his cheeks turning red and foam on his lips shouted, "The best thing that could happen for Social Security would be for the Commissioner of Social Security to SHUT UP!" Then I got the floor and in very brief remarks thanked each of them for accepting and assured them that SSA was ready to assist the NCSSR in any way they liked. That was the only NCSSR meeting that I attended until the final one.

As it turned out, during 1982, Pat Moynihan was not the only one who wanted me to shut up. I made news whenever I gave my stock Social Security speech. Columnists wrote about it; editorial cartoonists did cartoons about it; and newspapers did stories and editorials about it. The one I delivered before the Town Hall of California in June of that year was published verbatim in Vital Speeches of the Day. During this time, Ted Turner's CNN was just up and running and they needed something to fill the air 24 hours a day. (Nothing has changed) Every time I would pass through Atlanta, we would schedule a trip over to CNN headquarters. Unlike the other networks CNN would let me talk forever.

By mid-summer, even the White House had begun to notice that I was making a lot of news with the speech and interviews. On August 9, Craig Fuller sent a note to Schweiker telling him that the senior White House staff (Jim Baker) wanted no talk about Social Security other than to say we are waiting for the NCSSR recommendations, and that those on Social Security must be protected. Attached to the note were clippings from the *Chicago Tribune* and *New York Times* about one of my speeches. It concluded, "Before releasing any statements, speeches, testimony or other material about the Social Security program, we should have an opportunity for review and comment." I had been muzzled.

Deciding to take this new development head on, we sent a copy of the stock speech, one that I was to deliver to the American Association of Retired Persons (AARP), to the White House for clearance. Fuller's office then circulated the speech to the Cabinet and White House staff for their comments. When we received the comments, they were mostly minor editorial changes which we incorporated. The only White

House staff to comment was Elizabeth Dole who said, "The speech is excellent. It is well-written, punchy and comprehensive. Suggest we take out the references to AARP so it can be distributed widely to other organizations for their use." I liked Elizabeth.

I don't know how many meetings that the NCSSR had during 1982, but there wasn't any action until after the '82 elections in November. The October meeting had been cancelled and the Commission was scheduled to have a three-day meeting beginning on November 11. We all believed that the NCSSR would adopt its recommendations at the November meeting.

The week before the election, a meeting was held in the White House to discuss what to do with Social Security and the Commission. In attendance were Ed Meese, Ed Harper, the domestic policy advisor, Jim Jenkins, Meese's Deputy, Craig Fuller, the cabinet secretary, Dick Schweiker, Dave Swoap and me. We discussed the likely outcome and Ed said that General Revenue was "absolutely out." But when it came to new taxes, he said we would generally oppose and would go along with them only as a "last resort." We decided that we would start working on a strategic and tactical package of actions on November 3, the day after the mid-term election. We would then get together with Greenspan before the NCSSR meeting.

The day after the election the issue was put back on the front burner. I had gotten a call from Pete Singleton, the Republican staff director for the Ways and Means Committee the day before the election. He told me that staff from Don Regan's office at the Treasury Department had come up to the hill with a bunch of proposals for fixing the financing problem. Pete said the he got the definite impression from the staff that Treasury Secretary Regan was behind the package and that he (Regan) liked it. Pete commented, "There's nothing in there that someone else hasn't thought of." Carolyn Weaver, who worked part-time for the NCSSR and who was on the Finance Committee staff also told me that Treasury staff had visited her with a package of reforms. A whole package. The staff told her that it "hadn't been cleared by Secretary Regan" but that they had a lot of copies and it was "clear that he is pedaling it." I got Carolyn to send me a copy of the Treasury package.

On November 3 I got a call from Bill Niekirk, a reporter for the *Chicago Tribune* asking about the Treasury proposals. Bill had been covering the issue and I had met with him on many occasions. Niekirk said that the Treasury staff told him that Regan had said that they would have to come up with their own plan because the Commission wasn't going to come up with one.

I was certainly surprised. Treasury was going on its own. And they were doing it before the election. The issue was the hottest one in Washington, the third rail, and Regan wasn't going to pay any attention to the President's policy; he was in charge and he knew better. Unfortunately, it was an omen of what was to come; I just didn't know it at the time.

Dick Schweiker called me at 3:00 PM to tell me that Treasury was going to do the inter-fund borrowing the next day. I filled him in on the Treasury package and Regan's rogue effort. Schweiker was surprised and indicated that he was on his way over to the White House and would fill them in on it. Things moved so fast for the next few days, that I never found out if the White House had come down on Treasury or not, but I didn't hear any more about the Treasury package.

On November 4, I got a call from Bob Lighthizer who floated a suggestion that the November meeting of the NCSSR should be postponed. He said that there weren't going to be any decisions and that there was no chance that a lame duck session of Congress was going to touch Social Security. He felt that Dole and the President had expended enough capital on the issue and that the Democrats would be holding the issue in abeyance to trot out before the 1984 elections. He said that Dole was putting out a statement that the NCSSR was not going to decide anything during its three day meeting. Later at lunch at the White House Alan Greenspan told Ed Meese that they had never contemplated that the November meeting would be a decision meeting.

All along, I had kept up with what the Commission and its staff were doing. Many of the staff was on loan from Social Security and almost all of the estimating and projecting was being done by us. Bob Myers and I would chat occasionally and he would bring me up to date. On November 9, Bob and I talked about the upcoming meeting. Bob told me that the liberals on the Commission, led by Bob Ball now had a package themselves. It added federal and non-profit employees to the system and raised taxes. The good news, Myers said, was that after a year of denying it, they now admitted that there was a problem and that in the short term it was almost $200 billion. Bob said that he was optimistic that "something is going to jell."

I was scheduled to go to an international Social Security meeting in Caracas, Venezuela and I called Dick Schweiker to see what he knew about what the White House was going to do if the Commission issued a report or adopted recommendations. I wondered if I should cancel the trip. Dick said there had been no action by the White House. He said that if there was "no change in the White House position, I might want to go (to Caracas) too."

The November meeting came and went with little fanfare. No packages were voted on and it resembled previous meetings with the members just discussing issues. Myers had told me that the plan had been to have short meetings in public and then have smaller secret meetings in other parts of the hotel to try to get something done. Apparently, that strategy did not work and the November meeting ended with an agreement to hold a meeting on December 10, hopefully the last meeting because the Commission expired on December 31.

The Wednesday before the scheduled December 10 meeting, Alan Greenspan attended a Legislative Strategy Group (LSG) meeting in Jim Baker's office. Stockman and Greenspan urged that it was time to get the President involved in the debate again. Baker and Darman were adamant that the President not get involved and that the Commission should fulfill its obligation. The Commission meeting took place on December 10 but nothing was decided. The liberals wanted to solve the problem by raising taxes and the conservatives wanted to solve it by reducing benefits. Greenspan recognized that he had to get the two factions together if there was to be bi-partisan support for their plan on the Hill. He postponed the meeting to some future date. He convinced Baker that there was still a chance for a package but that with the holidays approaching, they needed more time.

On December 20 Bob Myers called me and said that he was still confident that a report would be issued and that it would include elimination of the windfall that federal employees got under the current system, put federal employees into Social Security, remove Social Security from the unified budget, and require SSA to issue tamper-proof Social Security cards! Not the kind of report that I was looking for. On December 23 the President issued another Executive Order extending the life of the Commission to January 15, 1982.

Social Security lore has it that Moynihan and Dole got together and decided to give it one more try. They approached Greenspan and the White House and it was decided to put together a group of Commission members and White House staff to try to come up with a compromise. The group included Baker, Darman, and Stockman from the administration and Greenspan, Dole, Moynihan, Ball, and Conable from the Commission. Others got involved at times but the eight were the core of the negotiations. The meetings were held in the Blair House across the street from the White House.

I had wanted to participate, but my visibility and the fact that several of the Commissioners had visceral reactions when they saw me, meant that I had to remain in the background. Because they had to rely on me and the SSA staff for analysis and to keep Stockman honest, I spent much of the first two weeks of January 1983 in Jim Baker's office waiting for the team to come back from the negotiations. I was joined there at times by my deputy, Paul Simmons.

As the January 15 deadline approached, the secret meetings became more frequent and longer. January 15 was a Saturday, and the secret group was still meeting. I was over at the White House in Baker's office when he and Darman walked in and said they had a deal.

Greenspan had alerted the members of the Commission who were not in on the negotiations that something might happen on that Saturday as the deadline drew nearer and the call went out for them to return to the Commission offices early that evening. The meeting was scheduled for 6:00PM and I walked across the street to the Commission office on Lafayette Square to see what would happen. The street in front of the office was packed with TV trucks and reporters. The members filed in fairly quickly and when Alan Greenspan saw me in the crowd, he walked over and said, "Jack you were in this at the start and you might as well be in it at the end" and he invited me into the conference room with the Commission and staff. I was surprised that Kirkland or Ball didn't object.

Greenspan called the meeting to order and Myers went through the agreement point by point. They handed out a three page summary which listed eleven recommendations and showed the short term and long term fiscal effect of each.

At the conclusion of the Myers presentation, Claude Pepper, who probably couldn't hear any of it, shouted, "Is it OK? Is it OK?" Someone told him it was and Pepper was ready to take credit. A discussion began right away and I could tell that the conservative Republicans, Archer and Armstrong were not happy with the package. Archer, who had already taken a lot of heat about the "notch" Congress enacted in the 1977 amendments, argued strongly that the provision to tax Social Security benefits would create another unfair notch. If a person made $1 more than the limit, then 50 percent of their benefits would be taxed. He just didn't like the idea of taxing benefits. Armstrong quickly added up the numbers and said that the package was 63 to 75 percent new taxes and he objected to leaving one third of the long-range problem to future action.

Interestingly, Lane Kirkland objected to the package also. He was not in favor of adding government and non-profit employees to the program. Both Conable and Dole spoke in favor of the package saying that it was a good package to put into the legislative process. Dole stated that the package needed strong support from the President and Speaker O'Neill. He said it would take real effort by both of them "to pull this off."

After a year of deliberation, Alan Greenspan called for the first formal vote of the Commission. The vote was 12 to 3 with Armstrong, Archer, and Waggoner voting no. I looked at my watch and made a note. It was 9:06 PM.

The vote wasn't unanimous but it was bi-partisan and balanced: One Senate appointee voted no; one House appointee voted no; one Presidential appointee voted no. Two Republicans and one Democrat voted no. Bill Armstrong immediately put out a one page statement commending the process as getting closer to the goal of saving Social Security and at the same time outlining what he felt was wrong with the Commission package. Bill Archer put together a five page dissent to the majority package saying, "There is great danger that these proposals have made promises which the system will not be able to support." Several other members of the Commission issued statements opposing certain provisions of the compromise even though they had voted for it. Joe Waggoner went home.

The President issued a statement that evening after having reviewed the recommendations of the Commission.

"Each of us recognizes that this is a compromise solution. As such, it includes elements which each of us could not support if they were not part of a bipartisan compromise. However, in the interest of solving the social security problem promptly, equitably, and on a bipartisan basis, we have agreed to support and work for this bipartisan solution."

Speaker O'Neill and the rest of the leadership on Capitol Hill on both sides of the aisle put out similar statements of support and the deal was done. Now all we had to do was get legislation passed implementing it. No small order.

The Commission report was delivered to the President on January 20 and took on a life of its own. The Ways and Means Committee and the Senate Finance Committee held hearings and there was very little debate and few amendments offered to the Commission package. The big issue was how to fill the long term deficit that the Commission couldn't come to agreement on. The Commission left up to Congress to pick between two options: raise taxes or raise the retirement age. Bills passed both bodies and a Conference Committee was appointed to work out the differences between the House and Senate versions.

A Conference Committee is a necessary evil. Congress almost never passes identical bills on controversial subjects. The House and Senate versions always vary, sometimes on major sticking points. And the bills that passed HR 1900 in the House and SB 1 in the Senate had significant differences. In addition, the details of each bill contained nuances that cause the SSA bureaucracy heartburn. The Conference Committee is where the deals are cut—in real time.

The conferees were appointed by Speaker O'Neill and by Majority Leader Howard Baker. The Senate conferees were led by Chairman Dole and the House was led by Chairman Rostenkowski. It is fairly common to have a representative of the Administration in the room as a resource should the conferees ask for the Administration's position on any part of the bill. The key phrase in the previous sentence is "should the conferees ask"—the Administration spokesperson only speaks if spoken to. I was invited to be the sole Administration representative when the conferees met.

Conference Committee sessions are not a pretty sight. They are held in an office in the Capitol. The room is jammed full of people, the Conferees and every staff person who can get passed the security and squeeze into the room. This committee was no different. The House and Senate staff had met, agreed on the differences in the bills and had come up with recommendations. The staffs at SSA and OMB had analyzed the bill and I had a package outlining recommended positions on each item. I met with Stockman and we went over it.

The Conference Committee met on March 10. Once in the room, the process moves pretty fast. Each provision is brought up separately and either the House or Senate recedes to the other. I was asked about a couple of provisions and gave the Administration's position. There was a lot of discussion about raising the retirement age. Both bills contained provisions to raise the full retirement age from sixty-five to sixty-six but the methodologies were different. The Senate bill had a more gradual phase in and it also raised the age for eligibility for Medicare to sixty-six. We favored the Senate version. As it was, Pickle offered an amendment that gradually raised the age for full retirement to sixty-seven beginning in 2002. The final bill contained provisions to raise the retirement age beginning in 2002 for people born after 1938. My note from that evening summed it up:

> "At 2:00 AM on Friday, after 18 hours of intensive negotiations the Senate voted final passage of the Social Security reform bill. Only a few hours earlier I sat with Chairman Dole and Chairman Rostenkowski and worked out the final terms of this legislation."

The White House pulled out all the stops for the bill signing. On April 20, 1983, on the South Lawn of the White House, before a crowd of several hundred, the President signed The Social Security Amendments of 1983. I was up on the dais with him and the members of Congress who had been instrumental in passage of the bill.

Two interesting things happened in conjunction with the signing. The first was that this bill is signed "Ronald W. Reagan." The usual way he signed legislation was "Ronald Reagan." The 1983 Act may be the only piece of legislation that he signed using the W that stood for Wilson, his middle name. I asked him why he signed it with a W and he said he had forgotten that he was supposed to sign each letter with a different pen (so that they could be given away) and he didn't remember until he had written "Ro." He then compensated by adding the extra letter. Pretty quick thinking.

The other oddity was that Dick Schweiker wasn't on the podium. Schweiker had taken a lot of heat about the original proposals and had been the Secretary right up until the end, but he had resigned just as the bill passed and his successor, who had absolutely nothing to do with the legislation, replaced him on the dais.

I have a pen and a framed copy of the signed legislation on my office wall. The inscription on it reads:
"Jack – Much of this is thanks to you.
Best Regards,
Ronald Reagan"
I received a letter from Bob Dole in which he said, "I would like to express my gratitude to you and your staff for the expert assistance which was provided to the National Commission on Social Security Reform and to the Senate Finance Committee." And from the House I received a copy of the full house bill, H.R. 1900, inscribed "With our personal thanks and appreciation to our able SSA Administrator Jack Svahn" and signed Dan Rostenkowski, Barber Conable, and J.J. Pickle.

The fight to save Social Security was over. Our estimates were that the OASDI Trust Funds would be in balance until about 2040. The changes that we instituted were far out in the future and have not raised public opposition because people have had sufficient time to prepare for them. There is a lesson to be learned here. We can once again see the time in the future when Social Security will be facing bankruptcy. And most politicians are doing the same thing that they did almost thirty years ago—they are denying that we are headed for trouble. Policy makers in Washington should take action today so that people can plan for the future.

Chapter 13

Let's Put a Heckler in the Cabinet*

Things were going pretty well for us at SSA. We had cut a deal with Congress on the Social Security bailout and had made substantial changes in the program that would keep it solvent for the next fifty-five-plus years. It had sailed through the Congress without a hitch. No one wanted to touch that tar baby again. I was comfortable in my role as Commissioner and looking forward to being able to institute further administrative reforms and system changes that would make Social Security more responsive to the millions who relied on it and add a new perspective—make it more responsive and understandable to the millions more who paid into it each month.

Then, things took a downturn. Dave Swoap, the Under Secretary of Health and Human Services, announced in December that he was leaving Washington to join George Deukmejian, the new Governor in California, as Secretary of the California Health and Welfare Agency. Dave had been in California and took over the Department of Social Welfare after I left in 1973. He was still there when Brown came into office in 1975. After the November 1974 election I called Dave up and

---

* A little play on words. When Margaret O. Heckler ran for Congress, one of her first campaign slogans revolved around sending a Heckler to Congress.

asked him what his plans were. He told me he had known Jerry Brown for some time and that he thought that he might stay. I said, "Dave, you're Ronald Reagan's Welfare Director; you have to go." Dave stayed and on the morning of Brown's inaugural, the new Governor's Office put out a press release saying that Swoap had been fired. Dave seemed to have bad luck on the timing of his job moves, and so it was on this one.

In 1980, during the transition, I had been interested in the Under Secretary position. I had long admired working with Frank Carlucci in the '70s when he was Under Secretary to Cap Weinberger and thought that I could play the same role for Dick Schweiker. It was not to be, fellow Californian Dave beat me out.

When Dave announced he was going to California, I thought about taking another run at the position but decided not to for two reasons: First, I was pretty comfortable at SSA and had developed a good working relationship with most of the Administration and the Hill and second, Schweiker had a pretty close knit group around him and while he and I were quite friendly, I knew that I was not a favorite with his people. They had succeeded in all but cutting Swoap out of the running of the Department and I was not interested in becoming their next victim.

Then the whole landscape changed. On January 7, 1983, I got a call from Helene von Damme, the White House Personnel Director. I had known Helene from our days in California when she sat right outside the Governor's inner office as his personal assistant. Helene asked me to come over to the White House to discuss a matter of great importance. Now it was Friday evening, cold, rainy, and the end of a tough week and I really didn't want to drive back into Washington. I don't recall if I eventually did, but it doesn't change what happened. Helene told me "in utmost confidence" that Dick Schweiker had just notified the President that he was resigning. She further indicated that the President had decided to nominate Margaret Heckler, a fifty-one-year-old recently defeated House member from Massachusetts, as Dick's replacement. And she told me that I was to be nominated Under Secretary. Now she had my full attention.

I knew Peggy Heckler, both in person and by reputation and I wasn't thrilled. She was a liberal congresswoman from Massachusetts who had a long history of supporting liberal issues. She was an ardent supporter of the Equal Rights Amendment (ERA), and had a record of supporting increased social services and benefits to a plethora of publics—anyone who might vote for her.

She had been in congress for sixteen years and in November of 1982 she had been tossed out by her constituents in favor of Barney Frank, the openly gay liberal Massachusetts member of Congress who happened to be a Democrat. Her campaign slogan that fall had been something like, "I am not a Reagan clone." It didn't help her. She definitely was not a Reagan clone. She did support us on a couple of big votes early on in 1981, but before and after those votes, she constantly decried Reagan policies in committee and in private.

Heckler, known as Maggie or Peggy on the Hill, was always one of the last people to vote on an issue. She just couldn't make up her mind and always waited to see how others from Massachusetts and the leadership were voting. Trying to please her liberal colleagues, she even voted to override one of Reagan's vetoes in 1982. I really couldn't see how we were going to reward her with a Cabinet position.

She was also co-chair of the Congressional Women's Caucus and it was in that capacity that I first came into contact with her. One evening in November 1981, at her request, I went to Capitol Hill to meet with Peggy and her co-chair, the always "delightful" Patricia Schroeder of Colorado. Also at that meeting was Lindy Boggs, a pleasant and gracious lady from Louisiana who had taken over the seat of her late husband, Hale Boggs, after he was killed in a plane crash in Alaska.

I use the term meeting somewhat loosely. Basically it was a get together so that Peggy and Pat could beat up on me as the personification of everything that was evil toward women in the Social Security program (a creature of Congressional action) and in the Reagan Administration generally. Mostly they wanted me to understand that the Social Security program discriminated against women and they wanted me to do something about it. Without going into the details, the meeting resulted in Pat Schroeder putting out a press release headlined "Representative Schroeder Meets with 37 Year Old Social Security Svahngali." Needless to say, it was not complementary.[*]

So as Helene was telling me what a wonderful thing this was going to be, I was quite skeptical and wondered if she was talking about the same Heckler that I knew. Sensing that she might be losing this battle (probably due to my head shaking back and forth), Helene brought in my old friend Ed Meese to put a little pressure on me.

Basically, Ed said, the deal was all set. Heckler was to be Secretary and the "outside image" of the Department. It was felt by those in the West Wing that this was especially good as we were getting ready to go into reelection mode and the President had a perceived "gender gap" which Helene, if no one else, thought could be closed by putting women in highly visible positions in the Administration. She particularly wanted to put another woman in the Cabinet. Apparently Helene had convinced others of the efficacy of this strategy; hence they were going to offer Heckler the job.

---

[*] Sometime after that meeting, I was attending a Colorado reception hosted by Senator Bill Armstrong, the chair of the Social Security subcommittee of the Committee on Finance. There were a lot of folks in from Colorado and the room in the Capitol was quite crowded when who should make a grand entrance but Pat Schroeder. I don't know if Bill had invited her or she had just decided to crash the party. I maneuvered myself into position so that when she half turned, I was shaking her hand. Once in my grip, as the dawn of recognition swept across her face, I leaned in and whispered. "I am thirty-eight Pat, not thirty-seven." She laughed trying to politely pull away and said, "I'm forty." I laughed and said, "No kidding? You look a lot older." All this in front of a somewhat shocked constituent who said to me, "That's not a very nice thing to say to a lady." I replied, "She's not a very nice lady." With that, I let go of her hand and arm and Patsy Schroeder scooted to the other side of the room.

I, on the other hand, being known as a bureaucrat manager, was to be the chief operating officer of the department and handle all of the management duties. We were to collaborate on policy, but the unspoken underlying agreement was that I was to keep Heckler in line with Ronald Reagan's philosophy and policies. I was tempted and I think that they could recognize that, but I told Ed that I was not really interested. I couldn't see how anyone would honestly agree to be the figurehead just to get a job. I was wrong.

Ed said that I should meet with Heckler and talk it over. He said that he didn't want to impose this on me but that it would be helpful to him for me to agree. Helene told me that Heckler was going to be home over the weekend and that I should call her there and arrange to meet with her the first of the week when Heckler returned to Washington. Both of them cautioned me on the need for secrecy and indicated that they had told Heckler the same thing. This couldn't leak.

I went home and talked it over with my wife, Jill, and decided that I would call Heckler on Saturday morning. During our discussion over the phone, she couldn't have been a nicer. She had already told Presidential Personnel that she had never met me and on the phone that morning, she swore that we had never met. I reminded her of that very unpleasant evening with Patsy Schroeder and she told me it never happened!

I should have called the whole thing off right there. She either had a sieve for a memory or she was lying. I never figured out which was the right answer.[*] On the call I suggested that at the request of Ed and

---

[*] A Jack Anderson column in 1988 said that Heckler "is as adept at the amnesia defense as any top official in the Reagan Administration." He was referring to an incident where her last Chief of Staff in the Department was sent to federal prison on a conflict of interest charge. The COS claimed that he didn't have a conflict of interest and that Heckler had signed a waiver removing any conflict. According to Anderson, Heckler told the FBI she didn't sign any waiver. Later when the FBI read her a copy of the waiver, she said it was "as phony as a three dollar bill." Later when she was shown a signed copy of the waiver, she said that she hadn't read it before signing. Unfortunately, for the COS, it all came a little too late to keep him out of jail.

Helene that she and I get together when she got back to town. She agreed and looked forward to it. She asked where we should meet and I suggested the White House. She said that she couldn't do that "what if people saw me going in there, it might leak." I thought to myself, "A defeated congresswoman walking into the White House looking for a job was not going to make the network news." But she wanted somewhere "not in a government office." I suggested a hotel coffee shop or the like and we settled on the Mayflower hotel.

On January 11, 1983, I had the "secret" meeting with, as she now wanted to be called, Margaret Heckler. Only the meeting wasn't secret—she brought another guy with her. She led me into the closed lobby bar and for three hours we discussed the job of Secretary, her role in the Administration and my role in the Department. All this amid the smell of stale beer and cigarettes.

The White House plan was simple. There was a concern that we needed more women in high places in the Administration and that doing this would somehow narrow the so-called "gender gap" that had women supporting Ronald Reagan in less numbers than they should have. Heckler was to be the outside person and I was to be the inside person. She was the new face and I was to be the Chief Operating Officer of the Department. This strategy was designed to calm the nerves of those who were worried about Heckler's lack of management experience and her history of opposing the principles for which Reagan stood.

There was also a concern in the White House that under Dick Schweiker, the Under Secretary, Dave Swoap, had been cut out of the chain of command. It wasn't Dick who had done it; it was more a function of moving a legislative office into the Executive Branch and the creation of the position of Chief of Staff in the Department. Swoap was sidelined in a number of areas and was sometimes not included in the loop where his experience and knowledge would have been beneficial. Nevertheless, it had happened and the White House didn't want that to happen again. Thus there was the need for "an understanding" of our respective roles prior to the President making an announcement.

The guy she brought with her to our meeting at the Mayflower was George W. Siguler, also from Massachusetts. He seemed like a nice fellow, but the point was that he knew about Schweiker, Heckler, and me, and he wasn't even in the Administration! That was the least of my worries. Heckler told me that she had called several members on the Hill to feel them out about her taking the job. This after she had been explicitly told not to talk to anyone about it.

After the meeting I went back to the White House to report. Ed and Helene along with Jim Baker, the Chief of Staff, and Mike Deaver, Deputy Chief of Staff and I met in Ed's office. I told them that I had met with her for several hours and they asked me what I thought. I told them that "if you tell her that if she will take off all her clothes and run around Lafayette Park until you tell her to stop you will give her the HHS post, she will do it. But it will be the last thing that she does for you." Mike said, "Oh Shit!" We all talked it over for a while and then I left to go back to SSA. As far as I was concerned the deal was a non-starter.

Early the next morning, January 12, I got a call from Helene. "Jack, where are you?" she said in her distinctly Austrian accent. I told her I was in my Washington office. She said that I was supposed to be over at the White House so that the President could announce Dick's resignation and Heckler's and my nomination. This took me by surprise. I told her that I wanted no part of it, that I thought that I had made that clear the day before. I could tell by her voice that the anxiety level was rising. She insisted that I come over there right away. Again she enlisted Meese who got on the phone and suggested/asked/ordered me over to the White House.

When I got there, the President had just made the announcement of Schweiker and Heckler and I ran into all of them leaving the East Room. I congratulated Dick and Peggy. Prior to the announcement, there was some concern and confusion regarding the Under Secretary position due to my not being there. As a consequence, the announcement ceremony had been delayed for short time so that the President's statement could be changed. When he made the announcement about Heckler at 10:12 he said, "Later this morning I will announce my choice for the vacant position of Under Secretary of HHS …"

I had screwed up the President's announcement so I hustled over to report to Ed Meese's office. The cast of characters was the same as it had been in the earlier meeting, Meese, Baker, Deaver, and von Damme. And me. I felt like a rat. The only saving factor was that I hadn't really turned Reagan down. I had said my "no thanks" to Helene and Ed. Over the years, I had taken a lot of fire because I was a "Reaganite" and I felt bad that I was saying no to this new job. I was a loyal "Reaganite." Ed and Mike knew that and played on my sense of duty. I held out as long as I could. Then I made a big mistake.

I knew that I was weakening and I put up my last line of defense— Jill. I told them that I couldn't do it because I had promised Jill that I wouldn't take the job. Mike said, "Where's Jill?" I told him she was at home in Severna Park, Maryland. He said, "We'll get a car out there to pick her up" Mike knew that I might be able to say no to Ronald Reagan, but he had yet to meet the woman who could. I called Jill and told her that a car was coming to pick her up and bring her to the White House. She wanted to know why and I told her it would become apparent when she got there.

When Jill arrived a couple of hours later, no time was wasted. She came into Ed's office and we all got up and headed for the door. Jill said, "Where are we going?" I whispered to her, "I am not sure, but if we go into a room with no corners, greet the tall good looking fellow as 'Mr. President.'" We hurried down the hall and into the Oval Office. Thirty seconds later, I knew I was dead meat. As we entered, the President ducked the rest of us and grabbed onto Jill as only he could do. Big smile, a little aw-shucks and genuine warmth. He took her over by the fire and talked to her about how important this was, what a great guy I was and how much he wanted me to be the Under Secretary. I was a goner.

I had heard how women would swoon over him. And at the Inaugural Ball for Nixon's second inaugural, I was standing in front of the Reagan box with Ed Hickey, the head of the Governor's security, just before the Governor made his appearance. Hickey told me we had to watch out because when Reagan entered the box there would be a stampede of women heading for him. Darn if it didn't happen; just about knocked both Ed and me down. But I had never seen him—one on one—until that day. Jill didn't wash her hands for a week.

Then he talked to me. He told me that he had a great interest in this appointment. He knew that there were a lot of problems in the Department and for that reason he didn't want to go to an outside person for this critical role. He told me that I was to be his "personal emissary" and that it was the "highest priority." Today when I look at a photo taken of Ronald Reagan and me sitting in front of the fireplace in the Oval Office on that day, I do not look happy. I wasn't; my defense had failed. I had run out of excuses. I said yes.

That afternoon, January 12, 1983, the President announced his intention to nominate John A. Svahn of Maryland to be the Under Secretary of Health and Human Services.

Back at SSA, there was mostly shock. There had been too many short time Commissioners and Acting Commissioners in recent years and after having gone through the battle of financing and developing the Systems Modernization Plan, the Agency was looking forward to some continuity in management and I was disappointing them.

As we prepared for consecutive confirmation hearings before the Finance Committee, I continued to run Social Security. From the outset, things did not seem normal. Heckler did not talk to me much. She maintained her distance saying that she needed to learn the Department and its programs. That seemed quite reasonable. I offered to help but she seemed very distant and wanted to go through it herself.

During the period leading up to our confirmation hearings I began to hear from colleagues who were involved in briefing her about her abnormal work habits. Meetings scheduled in the evening, making Assistant Secretaries wait for hours for meetings, not showing up for meetings that she scheduled. I just chalked this talk up to early uneasiness with a new boss.

Since I was still the Commissioner of Social Security during this period, I was scheduled to testify before the full House Ways and Means Committee on an issue. When I arrived in the large hearing room, I was, as usual, early. I did this to get comfortable with the room and perhaps get a chance to chat with allies and opponents. The Chairman was Dan Rostenkowski, the Democrat from Chicago. I had developed a pretty good rapport with him and the other members of the Committee over the past two years. Danny motioned for me to come up to the dais to speak with him. He then called the ranking minority member of the Social Security subcommittee (and later an excellent Chairman of the full Ways and Means Committee) Bill Archer from Texas over also. We three put our heads together for the many cameras in the room and the shutters buzzed furiously. Important people conferring on important issues. Actually we weren't talking about anything. We were just a photo op.

Rosty then put up his hand signaling an end to the photo op and the photographers wisely backed off. Testing his mike to make sure it was turned off, he leaned over to me and said, "How in the fuck did you guys pick Maggie Heckler?" I was taken aback, Rosty was laughing and even Bill Archer was smiling. Danny quickly acknowledged that I needn't say anything and proceeded to tell some very funny stories about Heckler and her days on the floor of the House of Representatives. It seemed that her reputation was well known on the Hill.

But the public flap was just starting. Conservatives immediately reacted negatively to Heckler's nomination. The headline in *Human Events* (the weekly paper read religiously by Ronald Reagan) screamed: "Heckler Nomination Stuns Conservatives." Even in the White House, political director Ed Rollins challenged the decision asking how Heckler could possibly get political clearance for a Cabinet position when she had spent a career in Congress opposing everything Ronald Reagan wanted to do. Two years later, Lyn Nofziger, the President's long-time friend and political director for the first year in Washington, told me rather apologetically that he had in fact been the one that recommended Heckler to Helene. But as Lyn put it, "I never thought they would consider her for a Cabinet position. I just thought that we should find her a job somewhere."

To counteract the brewing storm among conservatives, the White House began putting out some of the details of our agreement. An unnamed person from the White House said that Heckler had promised to support all of the Administration's policies. And they put out the word that I was to be the one running the Department and that Heckler would do the outside work. None of this was done with any attribution, just White House official or senior administration official. And of course, none of this set well with Heckler and her staff. Before we were even confirmed, the *National Journal* did a story on the situation titled "Madame Figurehead?"

The Senate Finance Committee scheduled our confirmation hearings for the same day. Heckler went first and the hearing went pretty much according to plan. As a long-time member of the House, it was a foregone conclusion that she would be confirmed despite the negative press regarding her lack of managerial experience. Conservative opposition had diminished in light of the spin that the White House was putting on the tandem appointments.

My hearing on the other hand did not go nearly as well. I arrived early with my wife, Jill and our two children, Kirsten and John. I took the family up to the dais to introduce them to the Senators who were present. When talking to the Chairman, Bob Dole, we noticed Senator David Pryor enter from the back room. Dole called to him and asked him to come over and meet the family. Pryor declined and Dole asked him if he was going to go easy on me in front of my family. Pryor mumbled something and took his seat.

I had made the rounds of those Senators who wanted to see me as a courtesy call, but Senator Pryor did not indicate an interest in meeting with me. In fact, I don't believe that I had ever met him before the hearing and I certainly had not heard about any concerns that he had.

The hearing went pretty well at the start. I had a little dust up with Pat Moynihan which was not unusual. Moynihan and I had a relationship that went back to when he was in the Nixon White House as a domestic policy advisor advocating the Family Assistance Plan. Pat didn't hold it against me that we in the Reagan administration successfully worked to kill his baby. As a member of the National Commission on Social Security Reform, Pat had been highly critical of me for "needlessly scaring" the elderly. At the first meeting of the Commission, Pat had been quite vocal in his criticism. We frequently clashed but always in a gentlemanly manner and I viewed him as a friend.*

When Chairman Dole recognized Pryor the fur began to fly. Pryor went after me for everything that he felt had gone wrong at Social Security during my tenure as Commissioner. But his real gripe

---

* The last time that I saw Pat was in 2002 in a hotel bar in Los Angeles. I was with Phil Hawkes who had headed up the Refugee Program for me at HHS. We walked over and said hello to Pat and his wife and their two guests. Pat introduced me as "the greatest Commissioner of Social Security that we have ever had." We all had a good laugh, Phil paid our bill and we went to our respective rooms. The next morning, Phil told me that he was awakened by the telephone at about midnight by a crying waitress asking if he knew who the man we were talking to was. She was crying because he left without paying his bill and she was going to be charged for it. Phil told her he was Senator Moynihan from New York. About thirty minutes later he was again awakened, this time by the night manager, to confirm that it was in fact the Senator from New York. They were afraid to call his room without confirmation.

was that he thought that we were putting too much pressure on the Administrative Law Judges, particularly a couple of ALJs in Arkansas. (One of the administrative reforms that Lou Hays in the SSA Office of Hearings and Appeals had instituted was a little work measurement on the ALJs. They didn't like it.)

Of course Pryor couched his complaints in terms of human compassion (or rather my lack thereof) and the plight of the disability beneficiaries who were caught up in the congressionally mandated reviews. Most of the stuff he asked involved memos and actions taken in the bowels of the 83,000 person agency that I oversaw. Then he acted incredulous that I was not aware of them and accused me of being negligent. When the Committee vote was taken, he had convinced three other Senators to vote against me, Mitchell of Maine, Boren of Oklahoma, Baucus of Montana and himself, not enough to keep me from being sent to the full Senate with a favorable recommendation.

On March 8, 1983, the full Senate (after a floor speech against me by Pryor) confirmed me as the Under Secretary of HHS. The eleven votes against me read like a rogue's gallery of left wing liberals, including Pryor, Boren, and Mitchell. Senator Baucus remembered the name this time and voted for me.

All during the time that we were awaiting confirmation, Heckler had continued taking hits in the press for her lack of management experience and for her lack of knowledge of the nation's health programs. I didn't realize how much of an impact this was having on her and her staff, nor did I understand the undercutting of me that was going on by the outgoing personal staff of Schweiker.

I found out really fast. She and I met on March 8 at 11:30 in the morning. We had both been confirmed and were starting out our "team management" of the department. Or rather Margaret told me what she was going to do to run the department. She started by saying that she did not trust me. She said that she had been told that I had a "terrible" reputation and was known as a "games player." I would like to be able to say that I was surprised by her outburst, but I wasn't. But I resolved to try to make this political marriage work.

Our meeting went on until 2:00 PM. Other than our first meeting at the Mayflower, it was the longest meeting that I ever had with her. She said that she was going to run the Department and that she wanted the "power and the policy." I told her, "OK. You have it, what do you want to do with it?" She responded that she wanted to know all the issues before they came up. I tried to explain to her that it wasn't possible to be forewarned about everything but she wasn't listening.

She was paranoid about "end runs to the White House." She said that she had been told that Dave Swoap did that frequently and that she had been warned that I, being a Californian, would probably do the same. She told me she was not going to delegate any authority to me and that I would be "another staff person." She said that she wanted everything sent directly to her and nothing to come through me. She said she had been told by Schweiker's transition team that Swoap had sat on things and kept them from the Secretary. I knew that this wasn't true; that in fact that Swoap had been cut out of the action by Schweiker's staff, but given her natural paranoia; Heckler had bought it lock stock and barrel.

Nothing I said seemed to make a difference to her. We discussed our "arrangement" again. I told her that it took her three days to return my phone call and that I couldn't get a meeting scheduled on her calendar. In fact, I told her I wasn't even sure that she had a calendar. Her response was that she didn't like people to know where she was at any given time so her calendar was private.

Heckler had installed George Siguler as the Chief of Staff and we went over the role of the COS. I viewed the COS as her advisor and the head of her personal staff. The COS was not in the chain of command. But in fact, Heckler at that time viewed the COS position as the number two position in the department. She put out a position description for the COS which created a super staff position with department wide

218

portfolio. She didn't forget the agreement she made with me and with the White House; she just flat wasn't going to honor it. She told me, "The White House isn't going to run this Department. I'll show them who runs this Department." The problem was that Heckler didn't know the first thing about how to run anything, much less the largest civilian department in the United States government.

Margaret, as she was called from then on, surrounded herself with assistants, none of whom had been appointed by the President or confirmed by the Senate. Early on, she had thirteen of them all running around trying to figure out what needed to be done. She didn't pay attention to any of the other Presidential appointees in the Department. In fact, she reverted to a congressional office model because that was all she knew. She scheduled briefing sessions well into the night and often was late or a no-show. She had temper tantrums and routinely berated staff. Now this type of behavior is not unknown on Capitol Hill. Everyone who has ever worked there has a story about member temper tantrums. Unlike most, however Heckler didn't seem to care. She wanted everyone to report directly to her and she treated everyone as being of the same level. This despite the fact that many of the senior officials in the Department were distinguished nationally known professionals.

The first few weeks under the new Secretary were difficult to say the least. She and I continued to bang heads but it was strictly in-house as far as I was concerned. But for Heckler, there were problems, aside from me, that were more substantive. The Reagan Administration had been in place for over two years. Policies were being implemented, Ronald Reagan's policies. Many of those policies were ones that she had opposed as a member of Congress. And her prior opposition quickly came back to haunt her.

One of the first was the adoption of regulations to implement the "squeal rule." In short the "squeal rule" was a proposed regulation promulgated by Schweiker that required notification of a parent before a minor could be provided with prescriptive contraceptives. It was a regulation that Ronald Reagan strongly supported. Heckler had signed a letter in late 1982 urging the Department not to adopt the regulation. As soon as she became the Secretary, the dozens of members who had also signed that letter, led by liberal Henry Waxman, urged her to repeal the regulation. She was hung on her own petard.

The next was the issue of "Baby Doe" and on this one, she and I had our first knock down fight about her responsibilities and the function that needed to be served by the head of the Department. "Baby Doe" was the name given to a child born in Bloomington Indiana in April of 1982. The baby was born with Down's syndrome and the delivering obstetrician told the parents that the child would be severely retarded and recommended that treatment including food and water, be withheld. Conservatives and others who valued life fought the case in court, all the way to the U.S. Supreme Court, but before the Supreme Court could hear the case, Baby Doe died. The issue however did not. On March 17, 1983, only ten days after my confirmation, the issue blew up again and Heckler was nowhere to be found.

I got a call from my old California boss, Robert B. Carleson, now Special Assistant to the President and Executive Secretary to the Cabinet Council on Human Resources. Bob had tried to contact Secretary Heckler, but she was not available. Bob said we needed someone to be a spokesperson on Baby Doe that evening and he was suggesting the Surgeon General, C. Everett (Chick) Koop. Chick was a most distinguished pediatric surgeon and a worldwide authority on these types of cases and their treatment. I readily agreed with Bob and told him that I would clear it with Heckler. The problem was that I couldn't find her either. Finally, and within the timeframe, word came back from one of her staffers that she had cleared Chick to be the spokesperson that evening. But it wasn't over.

The next afternoon, I went in to see her about clearing a statement on the Baby Doe regulations and she blew up. She told me that she had misunderstood the request for Chick to make the press appearance and that I had tricked her into agreeing to it. She said she would have done it if her voice had been in better shape. Well, I don't know about the night before, but there was nothing wrong with her voice at 1:00 that afternoon. She told me that in the future the White House could contact her and no one else in the Department. She reiterated that she was in charge and that the "White House isn't going to run this department."

I told her that she couldn't be found when the issue had come up and that it wouldn't wait until she decided to surface. Further, I said it was inconceivable to me that she thought she could run the Department on a part-time basis, disappearing whenever she wanted to do so. She, in turn, implied that there was some sort of conspiracy between Bob Carleson and me to get her. She said that Carleson was trying to take over her Department and she wasn't going to let him. I told her nothing could be further from the truth. To which she responded, "Ahh, come On." This lady had a serious paranoia.

Things were not going well and apparently she realized that I was there and that she was going to have to let me do something. So, on March 21 she put me in charge of employee morale and the improvement of the operation of the outsourced employee cafeteria in the main HHS building, the Hubert H. Humphrey Building. Not the job that I signed up for and things didn't get any better. She never asked me for any advice on a matter and instead of being in the chain of command, she informed me that I would get copies of decision material and that I should feel free to comment on it.

To make sure that I had plenty to do, instead of working with the White House to get someone appointed to be Commissioner of Social Security, Heckler decided to have me remain in that position as well as the Under Secretary position. This caused quite a bit of angst among several people, me included. First of all, each of those jobs is more than full-time and it robs both agencies to have one person trying to do both. Second, it upset Paul Simmons, my long-time associate because he wanted to be named Acting Commissioner. But most importantly, it got Members of Congress riled up and they began an investigation as to the legality of it.

As the days grew into weeks, the situation did not improve and everyone in town seemed to want a piece of this action. Leaks ran rampant about our relationship. The stories did nothing to help. After the first three months, I was still trying to make it work, but Heckler was becoming more paranoid each day. She would schedule events and then cancel. When that is done to an outside group, you get egg on your face. When it is done to congressional committees, you get in hot water.

Her personality and quirks in management style started to be observed by others in the Department. The Agency heads and Assistant Secretaries who had been my peers in the Department looked to me for explanations and for answers. I didn't have any other than to say that she was a former member of Congress and they are generally not noted for their managerial skills. I decided to try to provide a little leadership to the Agency and began to schedule morning staff meetings with the Assistant Secretaries and the heads of agencies within the Department.

When I worked in the old HEW for Cap Weinberger, Cap would have a senior staff meeting every morning at 0830. When Cap was not there or otherwise engaged, Frank Carlucci, the Under Secretary would conduct the meeting. Very transparent and very worthwhile. The senior staff at HHS appreciated the meetings three times a week. But not Heckler and her staff. She complained to Helene Von Damme in the White House that I was trying to take over her position when in reality, I was just trying to do the job that the President asked me to do and do it while maintaining a working relationship with Heckler.

It was at one of these initial meetings that I asked the staff if they remembered the cry "Remember the Alamo" or "Remember Pearl Harbor." Of course the answer was yes. I said, "Henceforth in this

Department, we are going to remember MOMA." To quizzical looks I said, "That stands for Maine, Oklahoma, Montana, and Arkansas, the states with a Senator voting against me" in the Senate Finance Committee. I said that when someone from one of those states comes to you wanting something, you remember MOMA and send them to me. It was in jest of course, but on one occasion I was visited by Henry Bellmon, then Governor of Oklahoma and a former Senator from that State. He wanted some help with a health care issue in Oklahoma. I told him the "remember MOMA" story and we both had a good laugh. He said with a chuckle that he would pass it on to Senator Boren later that afternoon.

That spring, I got a call from the career international folks at the Department. Heckler was in Europe at the World Health Organization (WHO) annual meeting. She had apparently had a meeting with the Japanese Minister of Health, Yoshiro Hayashi and it had not gone well. The staff asked me that if the Japanese Minister came through Washington on his way home, would I meet with him and try to repair the damage that Heckler had done. I said, "Of course." One of the issues that the Administration was pushing with Japan was to have them allow the importation of more U.S. pharmaceuticals and I began to bone up on it in anticipation of the meeting.

Hayashi came to Washington and I hosted a nice reception for him and his party out on the National Institutes of Health campus in Rockville, Maryland. We hit it off pretty well and he invited me to a luncheon the next day at the Montpelier Room in Washington's Madison Hotel. At the time, the Montpelier Room was an excellent French restaurant. Our lunch was many courses, each paired with fine wine. During lunch, we discussed a number of issues including the issue of Japan's importation of our pharmaceuticals.

At the end of lunch, I thanked Yoshiro for the fine meal and his excellent selection of food and drink. Sensing that I was setting him up for another run at pharmaceuticals, he pushed back from the table and, through the interpreter, he said that if he were to eat like this all the time that he would die at a young age. He said that unlike us, Japanese have to watch what they eat because the Japanese body was different than the American body.

I sat my 6 foot 4 inch 225 pound body up straight in my chair and thought for an appropriate amount of time before coming up with a diplomatic observation. I told him that I agreed with him; I didn't fit in their automobiles. We both had a good laugh.

Meanwhile, the White House and others were watching the tense situation at the Department. Heckler was bucking the Presidential Personnel office—the same one that recruited her for the job—on every position open in the Department. And there were more positions opening almost daily. Dale Sopper, the Assistant Secretary for Management and Budget (ASMB) was one of the first to be ousted. His offense: When told that the velour seat covers in the Secretary's government car caught her skirt and twisted it, Sopper had the seats covered in clear vinyl. He didn't understand that the complaint was a request for a vehicle with leather seats. The next ASMB did.

Sopper was almost immediately followed by Pamela Bailey, the Assistant Secretary for Public Affairs who left to join the White House staff. And then there was a progression of high-level and mid-level career and political employees who started looking for positions elsewhere.

During one of our sessions, Heckler told me that she had been told that she could have her own people. It showed the naiveté with which she approached the position. Of course she could have her own people, but in any administration that I have been involved with, that means that you can recommend but you have to get White House sign off on any political appointments. And if the position was a Presidential Appointment, more than sign off was required. Most of the positions were appointed by the President and confirmed by the Senate and therefore involved substantial White House involvement culminating in a presentation of choices to the President himself. Heckler didn't seem to care. She told me that, "Helene is not going to tell me who I can have." I just shuddered as the woman seemed to be spinning out of control.

In May, I met with Craig Fuller, the Cabinet Secretary in the White House. He said that he had basically given up on trying to fix the issue and recommended that I meet with Ed Meese. Before I could do so, I got another call from Craig asking me to come to a meeting at the White House. When I got there, Heckler was also there. And we were meeting in Craig's office with Craig and John Herrington who had recently taken over Presidential Personnel from Helene von Damme. The meeting with Heckler and the White House took me totally by surprise. I didn't know what to expect.

Craig kicked off the meeting in his usual soft spoken diplomatic manner, explaining that we all needed to get along and work together. He tactfully tried to explain that the current situation was not working and it was causing problems for the President and the Administration. Heckler sat there stone-faced and not happy. You could see the determination building up in her face. Herrington could see it also. As a former Marine, John was much more direct in his discussion with her. He leaned over close to her ear, and in his best Drill Instructor bellow, he said, "You're supposed to be the fucking figurehead!" Heckler's head snapped so hard that the strawberry colored wig she wore most of the time tilted askew. And she must have been stunned because she did not re adjust it. For a minute or so, you could have heard the proverbial pin drop. I thought to myself, "Oh shit! If I think I've had problems up till now …"

The meeting broke up with Heckler agreeing to have her Chief of Staff and me work out a management plan for the department. Outside the West Wing, Heckler was madder than hell. I talked to her as we were leaving and explained that I had known nothing about the meeting beforehand and that I was as surprised as she was. It wasn't flying.

She told me not to work on any management plan and that the White House was not going to tell her how to run her department.

As the weeks went by, the drumbeat about our relationship continued. I never talked to a reporter, nor did I say anything to anyone other than those in my immediate office. I guess however, that long-time observers of the department could see that things weren't working. And the staff, both career and political, could see that decisions weren't getting made and morale was poor. Reports in the media were constant. The *National Journal* on May 28:

> "Tensions at the Top ... Relations are strained between the Secretary and under secretary of the Health and Human Services Department, sources close to HHS say. ..."

Evans and Novak on June 1, 1983, wrote:

> "White House insiders are betting that the newest member of the Cabinet – Margaret Heckler, secretary of health and human services (HHS) soon will hang a scalp on her belt by running her conservative deputy secretary, John Svahn, off her reservation."

The *Washington Post* on June 2:

> "FEUD AT THE TOP? ... Insiders say Secretary Margaret M. Heckler and (Under Secretary) Svahn have not developed the kind of 'close, warm working relationship' many had hoped they would in the three months since they took their current jobs."

McGraw Hill *Medicine and Health* on June 20:

> "SVAHN SAID TO BE DISCONTENT - Unable to exert any noteworthy influence on HHS Secretary Margaret Heckler and discouraged about his diminished role in the formation of HHS policy, Under Secretary Jack Svahn is reported by informed sources to be ready to hang it up and leave the Department. ... Inquiries are reportedly being made by the Secretary about a possible replacement for the number two slot."

It was true; I was discontent. But I figured that if that was the way the Administration wanted it, I'd have to make the best of it. Often, when I was at Social Security and feeling the pressure of work, I would blow off a little steam sailing on the Chesapeake. This time I was feeling a lot of pressure and so I went sailing—in Greece. Jill and I took a couple of weeks (unheard of for the Under Secretary) and went sailing. It gave me some time to think over the options and when I returned to the States, I wrote a letter to Ed Meese. In the letter, I reiterated the agreement that Heckler, Ed, Jim Baker, Mike Deaver, Helene von Damme and I had when this thing started. I outlined what had transpired in the interim, including the meeting with Fuller and Herrington. I told him that the situation, in my opinion was not salvageable. I said I had three options:

- Be the outside person—spend my time visiting facilities and kissing babies
- Move to a different position in the Administration
- Just leave

I ended the letter by saying, "I'm looking for some help. You can continue to count on my cooperation regardless of the outcome." And then I waited for a response. It was summertime in Washington, D.C., and things have a way of slowing down even more than normal. I didn't get an immediate response. Things didn't get better.

I went sailing again; this time on the Chesapeake Bay. About midway through the week, we were coming back from the northern Bay and anchored in a cove with a dozen other boats from the Sailing Club of the Chesapeake. I was immediately hailed by several boats and told that the United States Coast Guard had been calling my boat on the radio all day. Our radio was below on the sailboat and we did not monitor it during the day. I knew, however, that this was not a good thing. I went below and contacted the Coast Guard in Baltimore. After I identified myself to the duty officer, I could almost sense that he was coming to attention when transmitting. "Sir, this is United States Coast Guard, Baltimore Group, Sir." Yes. "Tantrum (the name of our boat) Sir, have you contacted the phone number 202-456-1414, today,

Sir?" I recognized the number as the administrative switchboard at the White House.

The White House telephone operators who man the "admin board" are a fantastic group of people who can find anyone anywhere at any time. They have the full resources of the federal government to help them do this. They had found me. I told the officer that I had not called them. He then switched me through several radio channels, I guess to try to lose anyone listening into the conversation, and patched me into the White House operator. The operator in turn put me through to James E. Jenkins, Deputy Counselor to the President and an old friend from California days.

Jim, being a retired Navy Captain, knew that because I was on a boat our conversation was probably being monitored by more than the Coast Guard so he was a little cryptic. He told me that some things were up and that Ed Meese had called him and asked him to contact me. He wanted me to get to a land line and call him back. He couldn't tell me much more but encouraged (read: ordered) me to weigh anchor and get to a phone.

When I called from a payphone in a marina, Jim told me that Ed Meese had talked to the President who was at his ranch in California and that the President had decided that he wanted me to move to the White House to replace Ed Harper as the Assistant to the President for Policy Development. Ed had been the Deputy Director of the Office of Management and Budget before he moved over to the West Wing to replace Martin Anderson. He had only been in his position for a year and had recently resigned. The Assistant to the President for Policy Development was the President's chief domestic and economic policy advisor. I almost fainted. My six months in hell was about to end.

Jim Jenkins asked when I would be back and I told him the end of that week. Jim said that I should plan to go to Santa Barbara to meet with Ed and the President. He said that Ed wanted me out there for the Labor Day weekend and that I would fly back after Labor Day on Air

Force One. I said great. I felt better than I had since the first of the year. I didn't care what the job was; I was getting out of HHS and away from Peggy Heckler. I had tried to make it work and now others at a higher pay grade than mine had concluded that it wasn't going to. I made reservations to visit Santa Barbara for the Labor Day weekend—1983.

Chapter 14

The White House

I was very excited about moving over to the White House, not just because I was getting out of a difficult situation at HHS, but also because of the portfolio that the Assistant to the President for Policy Development carried. In the Reagan Administration, the Assistant to the President for Policy Development had very broad responsibilities. As the President's chief economic and domestic policy advisor, the job handled all domestic activities, but wasn't, by original design, limited to only the domestic agenda. By including economic policy the portfolio broadened into the international arena, principally with regard to international trade, but it also included such diverse activity as our space program.

The position supervised the Office of Policy Development, the Office of Policy Evaluation, the Office of Policy Information and the Office of Drug Policy (the drug czar). It had the largest budget of the staff offices in the White House and probably had the largest full-time professional staff actually employed by the White House office. Although the National Security Advisor had more bodies on his staff, many of them were actually employed by other departments, most notably Defense, and "detailed" to the NSC staff.

The Assistant to the President for Policy Development was also a position holding the highest rank afforded White House Staff. In the White House pecking order, there were three levels of presidential commissioned appointments: Special Assistant to the President; Deputy Assistant to the President; and Assistant to the President. Each of those appointments was made with "commissions" from the President. And that made each one a commissioned officer. I was surprised one day when touring the U.S. Navy Academy in Annapolis Maryland. On the wall in John Paul Jones crypt beneath the floor of the Chapel was John Paul Jones' Presidential commission. It looked and read almost exactly like the four that I have in my office.

Each position can have something added such as "Assistant to the President for," but the commissioned ranks are limited to just those three levels. And the higher you go among the three, the fewer positions there are. All Assistants to the President were ES-2 appointments whereas Deputy Assistants and Special Assistants were ES-3 and ES-4 respectively. The Chief of Staff, the White House Counsel, the National Security Advisor, and the Press Secretary all usually hold the rank of Assistant to the President even though their working titles are different.

And nowhere does rank count more than in the White House. So being named Assistant to the President for Policy Development was a big deal. When you think of all of the people working in government at all levels in this country, the highest rank in the West Wing of the White House has to be close to the top of the heap.

When I moved over to the White House in September of 1983, the staff was headed up by the "Troika." I don't know who originally coined the term, but it pretty much summed up the operation. The Troika was made up of Edwin Meese III, James A. Baker III, and Michael K. Deaver. All of the functions and staff were divided up among these three.

Essentially, Mike was the keeper of the body; Ed was the repository of all Reagan policy and Jim's job was to make the train run on time. Ed was "Counselor to the President," Jim the "Chief of Staff" and Mike the "Deputy Chief of Staff. They were all Assistants to the President. And all three had offices on the main floor of the West Wing, the same floor that has the Oval Office on it. During the entire first term, one of the three would be with the President at every event and function he attended.

Baker was in the traditional Chief of Staff's office in the Southwest corner. Ed Meese had the office usually used by the National Security Advisor in the Northwest corner. Mike's office was much smaller but was located just outside the Oval Office. As they say in real estate—location, location, location.

Just to finish off the physical layout in late 1983, the Press Secretary, Larry Speakes, had an office on the first floor just up from the Briefing Room. The Press Secretary's office was strategically situated to allow him to repel attacks from the media who hung out in the Briefing Room. The National Security Advisor, Bill Clarke, had an office outside the Situation Room on the Ground Floor next to the West Executive Boulevard entrance. Dick Darman, Staff Secretary and Craig Fuller, the Cabinet Secretary were also on the Ground Floor.

My new office was the one designated for the Domestic Policy Advisor on the second floor of the West Wing. Also on the second floor were the offices of the Counsel, and the Assistants to the President for Intergovernmental Affairs, Legislative Affairs, Political Affairs, Personnel, and Public Liaison. If you are counting, that is only fourteen Assistants to the President and all were housed in the West Wing.[*]

---

[*] The Oval Office on the first floor of the West Wing is at the Southeast corner. My second floor office was directly over the President's study next to the Oval. Each Assistant to the President had a small staff of two or three that was also housed in the West Wing, but space was always at a premium. I once watched an episode of *The West Wing* series on television and had to laugh at the number of people and offices portrayed as being in the building. In reality, the West Wing is a very small group of offices and anyone walking at normal speed could get from any room in the West Wing to any other room in about ten seconds.

Even though the titles of the "Troika" implied some difference in position, they were in essence equals. And they worked pretty well together. Their staffs on the other hand were much more divided, and in some cases outright hostile to each other. Ed initially had all of the policy staff reporting through him, both domestic and national security. He also had the Cabinet Secretary reporting to him and therefore was the focal point for departmental policy input and direction. Jim had the mechanics of the White House reporting to him, including the staff secretary, the legislative shop, the intergovernmental relations staff, the administrative staff, the political shop, and the press shop. Mike had almost no staff reporting to him and he liked it that way.

As many have observed, Mike knew the President like no other person and because of this his position in the West Wing was secure. He didn't need to rely on titles or staff (not that the other two did). During the years between 1974 when Reagan left the Governor's office in California and 1981 when he was sworn in as President, Mike was a partner with Peter Hannaford in Deaver and Hannaford, the public relations firm that handled Reagan's weekly radio show and his travels. He had been involved with all the campaigns since 1968 and at one point he had unselfishly quit the 1980 campaign in order to reduce the early dysfunction. It didn't hurt that Mike was closest to Nancy Reagan either.

Ed Meese had staffed his organization with strong conservatives, many of them with ties to the California days. In addition to Jim Jenkins, he had Marty Anderson, Bob Carleson, Ed Gray, Ken Cribb, and Craig Fuller in key positions. Jim Baker's staff was made up of people he was comfortable with from many different backgrounds and political beliefs. His key lieutenants were Richard Darman, Jim Cicconi, and Margaret Tutweiler. Ed's staff referred to Baker's people as the "pragmatists" while Jim's staff viewed the Meese conservatives as not experienced in the ways of Washington and "hardliners" or "right wingers." There was a lot of anonymous sniping that went back and forth between the two camps in the early years. This was the situation that existed when I made my plane reservation to go to Santa Barbara to spend Labor Day Weekend with Ed Meese and the President at the Western White House.

Of course, the White House is wherever the President is, but in common parlance when the President is away on vacation, the area where he vacations is dubbed the "away White House." Nixon had San Clemente and Key Biscayne; Bush 41 had Kennebunkport and Bush 43 had the ranch in Crawford. The Western White House was a kind-of catch all phrase for Santa Barbara and environs during the Reagan Administration. The President and Mrs. Reagan stayed at Rancho del Cielo, the 600 plus acre ranch high up in the Santa Ynez mountains outside of Santa Barbara. The Ranch was a small house with a few outbuildings. It didn't have room for any staff other than those that took care of the President personally, and the Reagans liked it that way. Normally, the physician, the secret service, and the military aide with the "football" were the only staff that actually stayed on ranch property. In addition to the official team, there was the caretaker and Dennis LeBlanc, an aide to Reagan who stayed with him from his days as Governor and with whom Reagan did many "chores."

The senior staff stayed at the Biltmore Hotel* on the ocean in Santa Barbara as did a pool of senior media types. Junior staff and a lot of the press stayed at other hotels in town. I flew on a commercial flight and arrived in Santa Barbara late on the evening of August 31, 1983. I checked into the Biltmore and was given a large room in the duplexes that the Biltmore had throughout the property. The next morning, my first day as a White House staffer, got off to a quick start. After I got ready for work, I headed over to the staff office to meet with Ed. It

---

* The Biltmore has changed hands and names several times over the years. At this writing, it is the Four Seasons Resort. But it was plush duty for the staff that had to stand by while the President was staying at the ranch. Having just come off four years in Plains Georgia, the media liked Santa Barbara as well.

wasn't what I expected. Ed was there but he looked a little disheveled. I was happy and enthusiastic and he was harried and haggard. It looked like he had been up all night. And it turned out that he had been up for a lot of it.

He quickly told me that a report had come in that the Soviet Union had just shot down a Korean Air flight! There had been a large contingent of U.S. citizens including Congressman Larry MacDonald, a Democrat from Georgia, on the plane when it went down. Before I knew my way to the men's room, I was at the center of a major international crisis. As the day went by, the picture became clear: KAL 007 had been lost and it appeared that the Soviets had shot it down. As more evidence came into the office, including radio intercepts of the conversations between the Soviet pilots and their controllers, we were certain that the Soviets had destroyed KAL 007. And as far as the country was concerned, Ronald Reagan was on vacation.

Ed was very calm and deliberate as he assessed the situation. The President had been notified the night before that U.S. sources suspected that the Soviets had destroyed the aircraft. Ed had remained in contact with other senior staff throughout the night. As the day wore on, more of the senior staff arrived from various locations in Southern California. Mike Deaver from LA and Bill Clark from his nearby ranch. We talked about what kind of response we needed. It was generally felt that the President needed to change his plans and head back to Washington.

The President did not like the idea. He had planned on three more days at the ranch and he was not pleased about returning to the White House. In truth, the President could do anything from the ranch and could receive any information he needed while there; it was not really any less efficient than being at the White House. He often lamented that "in this job you don't take a vacation; you just change location."

But we all felt that his return to the White House would give a calming appearance to the nation and to the world. We packed up and headed back to Washington, D.C., on Air Force One on Friday the second. It was my first trip on the plane.

Flying on Air Force One is always a fun thing, but nothing replaces your first flight. Even today, every time I see that plane in the air, I recall Labor Day weekend in 1983. Air Force One is the designation given to any USAF aircraft that has the President aboard. During the time that I was in the White House, our primary Air Force One was a highly modified, extremely well maintained Boeing 707, or, in military parlance, C-135. Its tail number was 27000.

The plane was divided into seven compartments.* Looking aft from the forward door, the forward galley was on your left and the communications center was on your right. Two communications officers sat there to put through telephone calls and take messages. Each seat on the plane had access to a telephone. You have to remember that this was in the days before cellular technology. Being able to make a phone call from an airplane was cutting-edge technology. And every guest who flew on Air Force One would make a call to the ground somewhere to acclaim the technology and, oh by the way, the location of the caller. Made a lot of work for those guys up front.

Moving aft to your left was the President's cabin with Mrs. Reagan's just aft of it. There was a hallway that ran past these two cabins and the senior staff compartment down the left side of the fuselage into the general staff area. From the general staff area to the aft door, the plane had a center aisle. The general staff area could seat eight staff people at two tables and two administrative staff at two workstations. Behind this compartment was the guest seating for eight guests. Moving further aft, was seating for the secret service and in the back where it is easi-

---

* The aircraft most often used as Air Force One (Tail number 27000) by President Reagan is now on display at the Ronald Reagan Presidential Library in Simi Valley, California. The entire plane was brought to the Library and is housed indoors in a spectacular display due to the efforts of former colleagues Bob Tuttle and Fred Ryan. The plane has had some minor modification for display purposes, but looks very much like it did during Reagan's two terms.

est to get airsick, is seating for the media traveling with the President. People could feel free to move aft on the airplane from their assigned seat, but most needed permission to move forward. And I am sure there is a reason that twelve armed secret service agents separated the press from the rest of the airplane.

It is said in the White House that the staff can put the Seal of the President of the United States on anything. And that is true on Air Force One. Whether it is jackets, sweaters, notepads, jellybeans, matches, cigarettes (we're talking a long time ago), or playing cards, they all had the seal on them. And five minutes after the airplane is boarded you can't find any of it around. Guests, staff, and the media gobble that stuff up and stash it is their briefcases as soon as they sit down.

Unless you are the President of the United States, you fly as a guest on Air Force One. Even the Chief of Staff gets a certificate commemorating his first flight on Air Force One as "a guest" of the President of the United States. The same is true of the much rarer flight on Marine One.

In talking about taking the White House position, Jill and I had made the decision not to move into Washington, D.C. I was going to commute from Severna Park, MD, a distance of about thirty-five miles portal to portal. With two children, now twelve and nine, we felt that to uproot them from school and friends would be difficult.

Our home was in a delightful neighborhood right out of the 1950s where all the neighbors knew all the children and watched after them. It had a community pool and swim team and access to the Chesapeake Bay for the kids to fish, swim and boat. It was too neat a place to ask them to give it up for D.C.'s asphalt.

The Reagan administration, always looking to avoid bad publicity had severely limited "commuting" use of government automobiles and drivers. When I was at Social Security and HHS, my driver, Willie Falcon would often pick me up in the mornings or take me home in the evenings, either for security reasons or because I was not commuting but instead going to the airport or some other official function. He would do the same on days when time was split between Washington and Baltimore SSA headquarters. But if I were just going to D.C. or just to Baltimore, I drove myself or carpooled.

The same was true for the White House. Different administrations handle it differently but when I was there only a couple of people had portal to portal transportation. The rest of us had to get there and get home by ourselves. Once at the White House however, all your transportation needs were met, whether automobile or aircraft. You could get an airplane to London or a car and driver to drive you to New York and back, but he couldn't take you home.

One of the first signs that something was different about working at the White House was when the White House Communications Agency (WHCA) office called to arrange to install a couple of Signal telephones at the house. There were two telephone systems in the White House. The one that everyone hears about is the White House Administrative Switchboard or as we referred to it, the "admin board." This was staffed by an absolutely phenomenal group of operators who could get you anyone, anywhere, anytime.

The other system was the "White House Signal" who took care of telephones on trips, at Camp David, and at the Western White House. Signal had a separate switchboard that connected to the residences of all of the Assistants to the President. The Signal phones did not dial. You just picked up the receiver and the person at the other end said, "Yes Sir"; you told him who you wanted and they got the person on the line. There was, however, a pecking order. If I was calling one of the Troika, Signal would ring them first and tell them I was on the line and ask if they were available for me. If it was one of my staff people calling me, they would ask me the same question.

Perhaps one of my oddest experiences with WHCA Signal came one day while I was sitting in my office in the West Wing. The Admin

Board and Signal had separate sets of buttons on the telephone. The signal lines rang right into the office. On this particular afternoon, one of the lines rang and when I picked it up the operator said, "Mr. Svahn Sir, do you have a dog?" It took me a second and I asked him to repeat the question. He said, "Sir, do you have a dog at your residence." I said yes (we had an Irish setter named Maude). The Signal operator said, "Well Sir, the dog is on the line." Maude was at home by herself and had apparently knocked the receiver off the hook of the phone in the family room. When the Signal operator on the other end had said, "Yes Sir, Mr. Svahn," Maude heard it and started barking at the receiver. And she was still barking. Signal couldn't cut the connection. I laughed pretty hard and the Signal operator was laughing but he asked if there was some way to get the phone placed back on the cradle so that they didn't have to listen to the dog all afternoon. I called a neighbor and she let herself in and fixed the phone. After that, every once in awhile, a Signal operator would ask me, "How's your dog, Sir?"

I learned during my tenure in the White House that when those Signal lines lit up, it usually meant that there was a problem. I was sitting in my office one Friday afternoon when one of the red buttons on the signal line started ringing. My nicely paneled office on the second floor of the West Wing had a closet in the back of it. The closet was built into the room. Why it was there, I never figured out but one of my predecessors, Melvin Laird had found a use for it. Laird, who was Secretary of Defense before he moved to the White House as President Nixon's domestic policy advisor, had requested the Department of Defense to build and install a two-step heavy-duty set of metal stairs in the closet. They raised you up to a double set of opening windows. You could step up the stairs, open the windows and step outside onto a three foot wide balcony. The windows faced south and west but you could continue around the corner to overlook the roof of the Oval Office, the South Portico, and part of the South Lawn—the part where Marine One landed and took off when the President was aboard.

On this particular Friday afternoon, I had been visited by my wife and a couple of friends of ours. Sitting in the office they heard Marine One come in to pick up the President and Mrs. Reagan to take them to Camp David. I was involved in something and didn't have time to escort the three of them through the West Wing and out on the lawn to see the President off. Jill asked if it would be all right if they went out on the balcony to see the departure and I said, "Sure." They went into the closet and out onto the balcony overlooking the South Lawn. Jill had done it several times before without any problem. Two minutes later, one of the Signal lines lit up. I answered it and the person on the other end said, "Mr. Svahn, there is someone on your balcony." I said, "Yes, it is my wife and two of my guests." He replied, "Sir, could you go out on the balcony so that we can identify you?" Then I understood what was going on.

There were secret service agents on the roof of the residence at all times. They didn't wear dress uniforms or plain clothes like the agents in the West Wing. They were outfitted with camouflage uniforms and rifles with scopes. When the President is scheduled to leave via the Diplomatic Entrance onto the South Lawn, they are on high alert. On this day they spotted three unknown people, albeit two women and a man, where they shouldn't be. I guess they wanted to make sure that the three weren't some kind of threat to the President. I went out on the balcony and told my wife and guests to please wave at the man on the other roof, the one with the rifle pointing at them. The agents recognized me and returned to scanning the area. I stayed out on the balcony until the President had left.

There are no easy answers for the issues that come to the White House. If there were, some Cabinet member or Assistant Secretary would have solved them. My first month or so was an eye-opener. Right on the heels of the KAL 007 shoot-down, we had problems with the situation in Lebanon and our Marines presence there. They were constantly being shelled by the militants and their position at the airport was vulnerable. And Congress had tied the administrations hands in terms of eliminating the threat. There was a lot of dissension within the White House and between State and DOD about the Marines presence in Beirut. Interestingly, Cap Weinberger, Secretary of Defense was the one opposed to having the Marines located at the airport there. At the same time, Bill Clark had announced that he was leaving the post of National Security Advisor and a scramble began among several West Wing staff to replace him.

Tragedy struck the third week in October when a suicide truck driver drove a truck full of explosives into the Marine barracks headquarters in Beirut. Cap had been right. Over 240 U.S. service personnel, most of them Marines died as a result of the bombing. Forty-eight hours after the bombing, we had a military action at the request of the Eastern Caribbean States to clean out some of Castro's troops and to rescue a group of stranded U.S. citizens who were medical students at the St. Georges University Medical School in Grenada.

That action was carried out in secret with no leaks and it was successful. It caught most of official Washington, and for that matter the rest of the country, completely by surprise. It was over before the usual opposition had a chance to scream. When the first of the rescued medical students got off the airplane on U.S. soil and kneeled down to kiss the tarmac, we knew we had a winner. The successful action in Grenada complicated the task of the critics who were gearing up their opposition intending to use the bombing in Lebanon as ammunition.

But the incident in my first few weeks that had the most impact on me personally, and that shaped my resolve and actions for the next three years occurred on October 19, 1983. It involved a press conference.

Ronald Reagan was often criticized by the media for not having regular press conferences while he was President. When he was Governor, he had press conferences frequently. But they were different than the ones in the White House. It seemed to me that the Sacramento media used press conferences to gather information. The White House press corps used press conferences to play "gotcha" and to get face time on the networks. They were more an exercise in who can get to ask a question and who can look good to the world than they were an opportunity to gather information.

To prepare Reagan for a press conference, the Press Secretary would set up a series of briefings, usually in the Family Theatre in the East Wing. These took the form of a "practice" press conference with the President standing at a podium in the front of the theatre and several press office staff sitting at a table asking questions. The President always tried to lighten up these practice sessions with a little standup comedy. When asked:

"Mr. President, in light of recent senior staff changes, do you see a different role for the Vice President in the second term?"

The President: "Well, not if I stay healthy."

Or:

"Mr. President. Are you disappointed by Panamas' refusal to take (Philippine President) Marcos?

The President: "If the SOB living here before me hadn't given the Canal away he'd be living in Panama now!"

I always thought that Larry Speakes, the de facto press secretary, canvassed the White House press corps as a press conference drew near to get an idea of what questions they were going to have for the President. It could be, of course, that the press office staff was clairvoyant, but it was amazing how they could come up with some of the most off the wall questions during the rehearsal, and then some correspondent from the White House Press Corps would ask the identical question when called on by the President.

Sitting in the front row of theatre seats would be a dozen or so of us, mostly Assistants to the President, who would listen to the President's answer to a question and then critique it. On October 19, a press conference was scheduled for 8:00 PM in the East Room of the

242

White House. It was the first one that the President had had since June and it was the first one that I was to attend.

We held a practice session that afternoon in the Family Theatre and the President seemed at ease and very facile with his answers. Just as we were breaking up, Larry Speakes spoke up and reminded the President that a bill was pushing through Congress to make Martin Luther King's birthday a national holiday. Then he asked the President if he agreed with Senator Jesse Helms' assertions that Martin Luther King had communist associations. The President answered, "We are just going to have to wait thirty-five years to find out, aren't we." I was stunned. He was of course referring to the fact that an agreement had been reached between Dr. King's family and the government to seal the FBI files on Dr. King and not release them to the public until 2027. But he couldn't say that!

We had had several discussions about the bill moving through Congress. The President didn't want to sign a bill making Martin Luther King's birthday a national holiday. It wasn't because he didn't like King, but instead like so many things that he thought through for himself, he had concluded that it might be popular, but it wasn't good public policy.

Aside from the hundreds of millions of dollars that each federal holiday costs, he felt that it was wrong to name a federal holiday after an individual; it raises the question of where do you stop. What about John F. Kennedy or Franklin Roosevelt? But the politicos on the staff were arguing that the bill was on a freight train, that it would be unpopular to oppose it, even arguing that a veto might be overridden in light of the upcoming election year. They had pretty well convinced Reagan that he would have to sign the bill. But some of us weren't convinced that it was over; the bill hadn't passed yet and there was still time to let the President return to his preferred conclusion.

I looked to my left and everybody was laughing. It was a joke. Meese, Baker, Deaver, and the communications guru Dave Gergen;

everyone was enjoying the joke. I thought to myself, who am I to pipe up and say something. I'm the new guy on the block and they have been through this for two and a half years. So I remained silent and I didn't say anything about his quip.

The fourth question asked of the President at the press conference:

"Mr. President. Senator Helms has been saying on the Senate floor that Martin Luther King, Jr. had Communist associations, was a Communist sympathizer. Do you agree?"

The President. "We'll know in about thirty-five years, won't we?"

This time, there wasn't any laughter—anywhere. It was a disaster. He went on to explain why he didn't think that it should be a national holiday and how he would like to see King recognized, but the damage was done. The bill would be signed. The President called King's widow and apologized. Instead of a quiet signature on Friday afternoon, we scheduled a big signing ceremony with King's family in attendance. We got in front of the crowd and led the parade.

And I decided that night that I would never let something like that go by again without giving him my best unvarnished advice. And I kept that promise to myself. Reagan recognized it, because for the next three years, just before offering a quip he would sometimes look at me and say, "Now I'm not going to say this Jack."

Sometimes I had to suck it up to keep that promise. During the second term, after the President's colon cancer surgery, we were preparing for a press conference in the Family Theatre. It was to be the first one since the surgery. Don Regan had replaced Jim Baker as Chief of Staff and the atmosphere in the West Wing had definitely changed. It was again right at the end of the rehearsal when Larry asked another of his "possible" questions. It was innocuous. "Mr. President. How do you feel?" The President answered that he felt fine. And then he expanded on it: He said that he would like to thank all of the people who had written and sent cards, but he "didn't suffer from cancer." He didn't have cancer, he just had an operation and now he was fine.

Don Regan jumped up, moving for an end to the preparation and said, "That's a great answer Mr. President." I looked at Don and said, "Mr. President, it is not a great answer. You shouldn't use it. I know what you mean that you didn't 'suffer' like so many do when they have cancer. But if you say you didn't have cancer that way, the press will go out and get some doctor who will say that you have the typical denial syndrome that many cancer patients have." The President looked at me rather quizzically, not sure about it, but he agreed not to use that answer. Don Regan was just staring daggers. He didn't like to be contradicted, particularly in front of others. Later, before he went to pick the President up in the residence, I reminded Don to remind the President not to use the "I didn't suffer from cancer" answer.

One thing about Ronald Reagan, once he had analyzed something and come to his own conclusion (which he did frequently on a wide range of subjects), he would store the conclusion away and be ready to use it at a moment's notice. Some of these he stored on little cards that he kept in his desk, but for a lot of them, he just kept them in his head. He kept his answer to the "how do you feel question" in his head. Several weeks later he was being interviewed by a print reporter and was asked the question. His answer was the same one that he gave in the press conference preparation. And the story that came out of it was all about the typical response of patients to deny that they have cancer.

The average workday in the West Wing was full of meetings. There were certain scheduled events that occurred every day and others that occurred every week. Many of them involved the President, but many were meetings that involved other policy makers and Cabinet members.

On a typical morning, I would arrive at the White House before 0700 and review what had transpired the night before and read the news summaries. Then I usually started off with breakfast at 0730 in the senior staff White House Mess with Craig Fuller, the Cabinet Secretary, and Dick Darman, the Staff Secretary. Occasionally, we were joined by David Stockman, the Director of the Office of Management and Budget. We would discuss the issues of the day and other weighty subjects.

The White House Mess is operated by the U.S. Navy. The manager was a Chief Warrant Officer and all of the stewards there were high-level enlisted personnel, most of them at the E-9 level. The Mess had two dining rooms and a takeout window. Seating was by rank. The President (although I never saw him eat there), the Vice President, the Assistants to the President and the Director of OMB all had privileges in the Senior Mess, a small wood paneled room with about eight tables. Deputy Assistants and Special Assistants and the Associate Directors of OMB could eat in the larger staff Mess. Those who were not commissioned but still had the coveted green White House pass used the takeout window.

Politics even plays a role in the White House Mess operation. During the Carter Administration, Coca Cola products were served in the West Wing. Coca Cola, with its headquarters in Atlanta, was a favorite of the people from Georgia. When Reagan became President, Coke was out and Pepsi was in. Pepsi and its management were big supporters of Republicans and Ronald Reagan in particular. Thursdays were Mexican day in the Mess in honor of all the Californians in the Reagan Administration. And to keep the tobacco states happy, much to the chagrin of the Surgeon General, you could get a pack of cigarettes from the mess (with the Seal of the President of the United States on them, of course).

The Mess was not free. Every month you got a bill for meals and service that you had from the Mess. My father, who was director of safety for Pacific Southwest Airlines, came to Washington fairly often for meetings of the Air Transport Association. When he came to town, he liked to come over to the White House for lunch and bring along a few friends. I think he thought it was free. It wasn't. You paid for everything that you or your guests ordered. The same applies to the President in the residence. He has to pay for all his personal food.

After we finished up breakfast in the Mess, we had the 0800 senior staff meeting in the Roosevelt Room. The Roosevelt Room is one of two meeting rooms in the West Wing, the other being the Cabinet Room. It is conveniently named Roosevelt as there were two who were Presidents, Franklin D. and Theodore X. Franklin was a Democrat and Teddy a Republican. That meant that the party of the current President could emphasize *their* Roosevelt in furnishing the room.

The senior staff meeting was chaired by Chief of Staff Jim Baker, and attended by all of the Assistants to the President and on an as needed basis, other staff personnel. The main purpose of the 0800 staff meeting was to go over the President's schedule for the day, discuss any other issues that might come up and just generally make sure that everyone was on the same page. There was a lot of serious stuff discussed at this meeting but it could also be an opportunity for a little fun.

At one point during the first four years, it was pretty widely known that Jim Baker was tiring of the COS job. In fact, when Bill Clark left, Baker had wanted to take Bill's place as the National Security Advisor. Later on, it was rumored that he was going to become the new Commissioner of Baseball, leaving government altogether. The rumor had hit the papers, but no one in the West Wing was talking about it. One morning, Jim came into the 0800 staff meeting and sat down. Immediately, Dick Darman said, "Hey Jim" and tossed him a baseball. We all roared—and that was the last anyone heard about him going to the major leagues.

Baker had a pretty good sense of humor. On another occasion, he walked into the meeting with a big glass fishbowl and set it down in front of me. Sitting on a rock at the bottom of the bowl was a frog. Baker announced that the frog belonged to his daughter, Mary Bonner and that we were going to have a "Friday Frog Feeding." He then slid a baggie with a few crickets in it over to me. "Jackie, when I give the signal, you're going to drop the cricket into the bowl, and we are going to bet on how long it takes for the frog to eat it."

Each guy around the table put a predicted time on a piece of paper and Darman ran across the hall to the Oval Office to get the stopwatch that the President kept in his desk drawer. When all was ready, I held a cricket in my hand over the bowl and Baker said, "Drop!" I opened my hand palm down and nothing happened; the cricket was firmly attached to my palm, upside down. I couldn't shake it off. When I finally got it dropped into the bowl, it was gone in a nanosecond. But everybody's time was off because of my delay. Baker said I wouldn't ever be allowed to do it again and took the bowl and frog back to his office.

Later, either that day or the next, I had a guest joining me for lunch. I went to the small reception area where Dottie Dillenger greeted all guests to the West Wing to get my guest and take him to the Mess. As we went through the hall door, Jim Baker was standing outside the Vice President's West Wing Office with Vice President Bush. Baker looked down the hall and said, "There he is Mr. Vice

President. Jack stole the frog!" My guest was truly bewildered. I didn't know it, but apparently the frog was missing and Baker was blaming me. A search was conducted of the entire floor looking for the damned frog. Several days later, the frog was found behind an air conditioning unit—very dead. I had nothing to do with it. [*]

After the morning staff meeting, I, along with Joe Wright, the Deputy at OMB, and Craig Fuller would join Ed Meese and his lieutenant T. Kenneth Cribb in Ed's office to follow up and to discuss Cabinet activities. Then I would meet with my staff and finally at about 0930 roll into the regular day. On Tuesdays, instead of going to the senior staff meeting, I would walk through the East Wing and across the street to have breakfast with Don Regan, the Secretary of the Treasury, Dave Stockman, the Director of OMB and Martin Feldstein, the Chairman of the Council of Economic Advisors. Sometimes, by invitation, Paul Volker, the chairman of the Federal Reserve Board would join us at these Tuesday breakfasts. The focus of these meetings was on the economy and it was as a result of spending so much time with him, that I came to respect Don's knowledge and predictions about the economy. He did know Wall Street.

There also were regularly scheduled meetings with members of the Congressional leadership, sometimes bi-partisan and sometimes just the Republican leadership and meetings of the Cabinet and Cabinet Councils several times a week.

The Cabinet Councils were instituted right at the start of the Administration. In California, Governor Reagan used his cabinet extensively. Meetings were held frequently and Cabinet Secretaries advised the Governor on most issues. In California however, the

---

[*] Christopher Buckley in his very funny novel, *The White House Mess*, has an episode where the fictional President Tucker's kid loses a pet hamster in the White House and a full search is conducted until they find it. It was as dead as the frog. I have often wondered if Chris, who was a speechwriter in the Vice President's Office during this period, had heard about the Friday Frog Feeding Fiasco.

Cabinet Secretary had several departments under him but he did not have responsibility for everyday management. That was left to the Department Directors. And the Secretaries themselves were in the position because of Ronald Reagan, not because of a party organization or geographic balance or anyone of the other reasons Cabinet members in the federal government are selected.

In Washington, there were many more Cabinet members than there were in California and a goodly number of them were in positions because of the politics of the appointment, not because they knew Ronald Reagan nor had any loyalty to him or his policies. Margaret Heckler was not the only member of the Reagan Cabinet over the eight years to fall into that category. Every high-level appointee had come from somewhere and owed someone. Only those who came from California or had been deeply involved in the 1976 and 1980 campaign really felt that they owed Ronald Reagan. *

As a result, during Reagan's first term, using Ed Meese and Marty Anderson's design, the President established the Cabinet Council system. The purpose of the Cabinet Council was to provide smaller groups of somewhat like-minded Cabinet Secretaries to meet on issues and to make recommendations to the President. Initially, there were five Cabinet Councils: Human Resources, Natural Resources and Environment, Commerce and Trade, and Economic Policy. The fifth Cabinet Council was the National Security Council. It was

---

* In 1981, the President recognized this and made the decision to try to staff each of the Departments with a high-level Californian who had been in the administration in Sacramento. It worked in some places, like Defense and it had an intended impact as with Bill Clarke as Deputy Secretary at State under Al Haig, but in other departments it didn't turn out so well. Swoap and I as Undersecretaries in HHS are a good example of the latter category. And besides, there just weren't enough of us to go around. Plus, the White House wanted to avoid the perception that too many Californians were being appointed by the President. Hence, the four commissions hanging on my wall in the office all read: "… hereby appoint John A. Svahn of Maryland."

a little different than the others in that it had been established by Statute after World War II. Three more Cabinet Councils had been established by the time I moved over to the White House. They were the Cabinet Councils on Food and Agriculture, Management and Administration, and Legal Policy.

The President was the chairman of all the Cabinet Councils although he appointed a Chairman pro tem from the Cabinet to head each one of them up in his absence. The Vice President, the Chief of Staff, the Counselor to the President, and the Assistant to the President for Policy Development were ex-officio members of each Cabinet Council. Each Cabinet Council was staffed by an Executive Secretary from the Office of Policy Development (OPD). Some Cabinet Councils met frequently while others rarely met.

These meetings gave Cabinet members the opportunity to engage their peers in discussions and were frequently preceded by one-on-one discussions. Since all meetings were held in the White House, usually in the Roosevelt Room, it gave Cabinet members an opportunity to be in the building on a regular basis and made them feel an integral part of the administration. A side benefit of the Cabinet member trip to the White House is that it would boost his or her stature with the department's bureaucracy. Departmental staff is always concerned with their status and it helps to think that the boss is being seen and heard by the President. Most importantly, the meetings gave the President what he wanted and needed—input from the people that he had appointed to run the government.

There were several other groups that met periodically outside of the Cabinet/Cabinet Council structure. The first was the Legislative Strategy Group (LSG), an ad hoc group that was chaired by Jim Baker and which met periodically to strategize the tactics used to implement the President's policy. While its name implies that the LSG only dealt with matters before the Congress, in reality, any problem or issue that was hot would be addressed by the LSG. The LSG meetings would be held in Baker's office and included relevant Cabinet members, and involved White House Staff, usually the legislative liaison, staff secretary, cabinet secretary, and myself.

Another group that I served on was the President's Economic Policy Advisory Board, or PEPAB as it was known. This was a group established by Executive Order by Reagan in March of 1981. It was modeled after the President's Foreign Intelligence Advisory Board (PFIAB) established by President Eisenhower. PEPAB was chaired by Walter Wriston, Chairman of Citibank at the time. It included noted economists Milton Freidman, Arthur Laffer, Alan Greenspan, Herb Stein, Arthur Burns, George Shultz and my predecessor Marty Anderson among others. I served as the Secretary to the Board.

PEPAB was designed to give the President unvarnished advice on the economy from people who were outside the Administration. Some people within the Administration who were involved in economic policy resented this outside group with direct access to the President. The staff at OMB and CEA was among this group, but Treasury and most notably Secretary of the Treasury, Don Regan was the most vocal in their opposition. Reagan on the other hand enjoyed the repartee involved with his periodic meetings with this group. No decisions were made at these meetings, but it gave Reagan an opportunity to bounce ideas off of his "fellow economists."

Another reason for formulating the Board was somewhat defensive. Having all the noted Republican economists have periodic meetings with the President might temper their public remarks about economic policy. After all, they had all had a chance to tell the President what they thought in person.

PEPAB almost came to an untimely end in 1985. By October of that year, Don Regan had been Chief of Staff in the White House for a little over nine months. Regan still harbored a dislike for PEPAB.

He felt that it was a waste of the President's time to have them meet in the White House to discuss the economy. One morning I got a telephone call from one of my predecessors, Martin Anderson. Marty had left after a year in the White House and had returned to the Hoover Institution at Stanford. He had retained his membership on PEPAB and had been appointed to PFIAB upon leaving the White House. Marty asked me about a meeting with the President by a group of outside economists. I told him that I had not heard of one and that it wasn't on the President's long-range planning schedule. Marty said that Milton Friedman had been invited but that he didn't think it was a PEPAB meeting. I thought that it was odd and I told him so. I promised to check it out and get back to him.

I called Beryl Sprinkle, Chairman of the Council of Economic Advisors (CEA) thinking that the CEA might be having some sort of session. Sprinkle said he didn't know of any meeting. I then went to see Regan to ask him but he was not in the office. One of his assistants told me that in fact, Regan had scheduled a bi-partisan group of economists to attend a meeting with the President. When I asked him how that fit in with PEPAB, he told me that Executive Order 12296 that established the PEPAB had expired a few days before and that **Regan**, not Reagan, had decided not to renew it. I was dumbfounded. Don Regan was making a big mistake and I told his assistant that he was. The President enjoyed meeting with PEPAB and I felt that he needed to know that a decision had been made on his behalf to abolish it. Never mind that no one had been told of the decision. I told the assistant that Regan needed to call me to discuss it.

When trouble was brewing in the White House and Regan's fingerprints were on it, he had a way of disappearing until the flap blew over. He didn't call for a couple of days. When he and I finally discussed PEPAB, he told me that it had been a "mistake" to allow it to expire and that the President would be reissuing the Executive Order. And the meeting with the outside economists had been cancelled. He never said that he was the one who made the mistake, but we both knew that he had gotten caught with his hand in the cookie jar.

One of the most perplexing issues during both terms was the issue of "leaking to the media." Ronald Reagan spent eight years complaining about leaks and trying to figure out how to stop them. Unfortunately, most of the time, the people he was complaining to and the people he charged with stopping leaks were in fact the leakers themselves.

A lot was made of the President's propensity not to make decisions in a meeting of the Cabinet or in the Roosevelt Room. Critics cite this as proof that he couldn't or didn't make decisions and that when decisions came out at a later time, they weren't his. They said that he left the room and let staff make the decisions. They were wrong. The reason that he didn't like to make decisions in those venues is because they LEAKED. Reagan knew this as he watched time and time again where what was said in the West Wing was repeated almost immediately in the media.

Sometimes things were leaked on purpose with the President's full knowledge. These weren't really unauthorized "leaks" because the people doing the talking on "background" or "not for attribution" were in fact authorized to do so. The annual briefings for the State of the Union Speech (SOTUS) fell into this category.

In the evening, just before the speech, the National Security Advisor, the Chief of Staff and I would appear in the White House Briefing room to go over the speech with the White House press corps. We were on the record, but not for attribution by name. Any quotes had to be from "a White House official" or perhaps "a senior administration official" in order not to upstage the President. We would outline the speech and answer questions. I'd take the domestic

254

and economic sections and the National Security Advisor, either Bud McFarlane or John Poindexter during my years, would take defense and foreign policy.

Each year on the day of the speech we would have a lunch in the Roosevelt Room for the television networks. Invited would be the network anchors and their White House correspondents. In those days, networks meant ABC, CBS, CNN, and NBC. Those in attendance from the Administration would always include the Press Secretary, the National Security Advisor and me. Sometimes the Chief of Staff would participate.

During the lunch, we would go over the speech with the networks and outline the themes and try to spin the speech in the way that we intended it to be covered. The briefing was more thematic than the later briefing. It was always a fairly congenial session and the President would always drop into the room for a little informal chat. But the sessions were never without surprises and in some cases a little controversy.

The SOTUS lunch in 1985 happened to occur on February 6, the President's seventy-fourth birthday. As we had done for the 1984 speech, we gathered in the Roosevelt Room with the anchors and chatted through lunch about the speech. It was the first SOTUS after his landslide victory in November and we, on the Administration side, were feeling pretty good. As we were finishing up lunch and getting into more substantive discussion, a staff member from the press office announced that the President would be joining the group shortly and commented that it was his birthday. She suggested that we might want to sing Happy Birthday to him.

This seemed like a good idea to everyone until Daniel Schoor, the controversial correspondent from CNN, spoke up. Schoor in a fit of pique said, "I am not going to sing Happy Birthday to that man." It was apparent from his words and demeanor that he did not like Reagan and his outburst immediately put a dampener on the meeting. No one said a word. The silence was uncomfortable. Before anyone could recover from his comment, the President walked in and greeted the group. As soon as Reagan had said welcome, CBS's Dan Rather (of all people) said, "Mr. President, I understand today is your birthday?" The President smiled and said it was whereupon Rather started to sing "Happy Birthday." The rest of us joined in; even Schoor mumbled something. I guess the peer pressure was too great for him.

The State of the Union Speech is delivered in the House of Representatives Chamber to a joint session of Congress and it usually starts at 9:00 PM so that more people across the country are able to watch it after work. The senior staff all rode up to the Hill in the President's motorcade. It is kind of eerie riding through Washington, D.C., at night at 50 MPH. Riding in the motorcade is an experience in itself. You have to be in the car when the President hops in the limo or you are left behind. When the radio crackles "We have Crown departure," the line starts moving. On one occasion I can recall Bud McFarlane, the National Security Advisor, hopping on one foot trying to get in the car as it pulled out from the South Lawn.

Once we got to the Capitol, we, the staff, would file into our assigned seats in the gallery. I use the term seats loosely. Because we were the last to enter and the first to leave, we actually sat on the concrete steps in the gallery in the area where the First Lady and honored guests sit. SOTUS's are very regimented. Rarely does the entire audience engage in applause. If you watch closely, the party of the incumbent President does the applauding and in our case, because Republicans were in the minority they had fewer people to applaud. But they made up for it with raucous noise.

At the end of the speech we would jump up and run through the Capitol to get to the motorcade before it took off for the White House. I can vividly remember one evening when Dick Darman and I literally ran through an eerily deserted Capitol building startling a number of Capitol Police and just made the motorcade back. I always wondered why we were never stopped.

The 1986 SOTUS network anchors luncheon is one that I will never forget. The lunch was scheduled for noon on January 28. Before the President dropped in, a watch officer from the Situation Room came into the Roosevelt Room and told us that the space shuttle Challenger had exploded right after liftoff. We immediately had a television brought into the room and collectively watched again and again as mission control ordered the vehicle to "Go with throttle up" and seconds later traveling at Mach 1.92 at 46,000 feet, Challenger disintegrated in a huge fireball and the pieces began a slow descent into the Atlantic Ocean. The harsh reality was that among the crew of seven on mission STS- 51-L was Christa McAuliffe, a bright young woman with two children. She was the first participant in NASA's Teacher in Space Program.

It seemed like an eternity, but it was really only a few minutes before we decided to break up the luncheon so that the anchors and reporters could get in contact with their networks. We offered phones and told them that we would get back to them as soon as the President decided what he wanted to do about the speech. As everyone headed for the doors, Sam Donaldson, ABC's White House correspondent turned to me and said, "I want my name taken off the list to be the first 'Journalist in Space.'" I was dumbfounded. He wasn't laughing but I couldn't tell whether he was making a joke out of the tragedy or whether he was so scared by it that he wanted to make sure he wasn't number one on the list.

The President was very upset about Challenger. He was personally committed to what the teacher was trying to do and like on so many other occasions, he felt that he was somehow responsible for the loss of life. Whether it was Christa McAuliffe, marines in Lebanon, victims of highjackers, or Americans kidnapped by terrorists, Reagan took each and every one of them personally.

I cautioned that we shouldn't overreact; that the military lost people in accidents every day. I suggested that the President issue a somber, serious statement and that we move forward with the State of the Union Speech. The President decided to postpone the SOTUS and instead went on national television that evening to address the nation regarding the tragedy. Sometimes I get it wrong.

The speech that the President gave that evening was memorable. It was drafted by Peggy Noonan and is, along with the speech he gave in Normandy on the fortieth anniversary of the D-Day invasion, arguably the most well known of the speeches that she drafted for Reagan. My only contribution to the speech was to change one phrase, and Peggy fought me on that. She wanted to refer to the seven astronauts as "the magnificent seven" and I thought that inappropriate. In a discussion I flat told her that the "magnificent seven" were a bunch of drunken gangsters in a movie and that we weren't going to have anyone compare the Challenger astronauts to some Western movie characters. She didn't like it, but realized that the speech wasn't going to the President with that phrase in it, so she took it out.

She didn't forgive my interference however. A few days later, I got a note from her with a clip from the *New York Daily News* with a screaming banner line "Magnificent Seven had lived for their big dream." The note suggested that maybe I better give the *Daily News* a heads up on the flak they might be receiving for their choice of words.*

Leaks to the media, as opposed to authorized "backgrounders," were perplexing and greatly bothered Reagan. You can read in his dia-

---

* The Challenger speech was one of Ms. Noonan's best works for Reagan. Another of Ms. Noonan's famous speechwriting efforts was written for Vice President George H.W. Bush. It was the acceptance speech Vice President Bush gave at the 1988 Republican National Convention in New Orleans. Its most notable line was "Read my lips; no new taxes." I almost fell out of my seat when I heard it; I knew he would later regret the statement.

ries how consumed he was about leaks. He believed that if you signed on for a tour of duty, you were committed to the Administration. He didn't understand how "our" people could be doing it. But he constantly saw internal discussions laid out the next day in the newspaper. And you can also read how happy he was when he had made a decision and it hadn't leaked. In his diary, he almost sounds like a little kid getting away with something when something doesn't leak. He really relished being able to have a secret kept until it was time for an announcement.

After one egregious leak of what went on at a National Security meeting in the Situation Room, he was urged by Ed Meese and Bill Clark to order an FBI investigation into the leak. During the investigation, the FBI wanted to do polygraph tests on a number of administration officials. Reagan almost ordered the lie detector tests for the participants. George Shultz, then Secretary of State, said that he would take the test. But he would only take one and then resign. In the end, Reagan decided not to order anyone to take a lie detector test. As a result, like most leaks, he never found out who the perpetrator was. In his diary, he said that he had decided not to order staff to take lie detector tests because if he had ordered it, *that* would leak and cause a bigger flap!

Leaking was done for a variety of reasons. In the first term, the staffs of Baker and Meese would leak little tidbits about each other's mistakes to try to diminish the role each had in the Administration. A lot of the leaks during the first couple of years of the administration were personal attacks on Ed Meese and his staff most likely done by Stockman and by my good friend Dick Darman, Baker's chief lieutenant and the Staff Secretary. Craig Fuller, the Cabinet Secretary and I once told Darman that we were going to put a red light over his office door that flashed "Do Not Disturb—Leak in Progress" when he was hosting a reporter.

On occasion, as I found out, leaks are expected. During one August I was out in Santa Barbara as the senior staff person on duty while the

President was up at his ranch in the Santa Ynez mountains. I accepted a lunch invitation from Eleanor Clift and Thomas DeFrank. At the time, both of them were with *Newsweek* magazine. *Newsweek* had a little section at the front of the magazine called "Periscope" that used to publish some real "inside" leaks each week. When the magazine came out Sunday night, White House staff couldn't wait to get their hands on it to see the latest items in Periscope.

Things tended to slow down somewhat during those August visits to the ranch and both the White House staff at the Biltmore and the White House press corps have time to relax, so I didn't think much about two of them asking me to join them for lunch. As we sat in the sunshine on the patio of the little restaurant after lunch, Eleanor asked me to give them something. I wasn't sure of the drift in her request but I said I'd be glad to answer any of their questions, figuring that we were going on the record. She responded that no, she wanted something "juicy" and implied that the whole purpose of inviting me to lunch was for me to honor tradition and leak something to them. I told her that I was on the record and glad to answer any question. DeFrank * didn't say anything, but Eleanor got snippy about it as if it was a quid pro quo and that I was expected to leak something. I didn't and was not asked to lunch again!

Sometimes leaks are just a rookie's mistake. I was responsible for one leak in my three years in the West Wing. I didn't know that I was leaking at the time but I should have been more careful. It had to do with a portion of the President's 1984 State of the Union speech. It all started in November of 1983 when I read a clip from the news-paper that Senator Charles McC. (Mac) Mathias, a Republican from Maryland had met with Dave Stockman "of the White House" and had been disappointed in Stockman's response to his entreaties about

---

* I don't think that it was just coincidence that Tom DeFrank wound up co-author-ing the memoirs of two of the most notorious White House leakers, Jim Baker's *The Politics of Diplomacy* and Ed Rollins' *Bare Knuckles and Back Rooms*.

the dire condition of the Chesapeake Bay. When I was younger, I was a pretty active environmentalist and I was still kind of a closet environmentalist. I lived in Severna Park, Maryland, in close proximity to the Bay and was active in several boating organizations so I called Mathias to see what he was talking about. Mac said that he had met with Stockman because the EPA had testified against the part of reauthorization of the Clean Water Act that would have earmarked money to clean up the Bay. He was convinced that EPA Administrator Bill Ruckelshaus didn't oppose the project but that Stockman did. I told him that the President had not made up his mind on the subject and invited him and a delegation from states that bordered the Bay to come meet with me in the White House.

Mathias agreed and got my own Congresswoman, Marjorie Holt, along with Virginia Senator John Warner to come to my office in early December to discuss the case for cleanup. I didn't make any commitment at that meeting other than to assure them that the President hadn't been presented with the issue and that he hadn't made any decision on it. Apparently that was enough because the local papers quoted all three of them saying the President hadn't made a decision. Mathias went further in an interview with the *Baltimore Evening Sun* after the meeting saying, "It's clear from our conversation here today that the Chesapeake Bay has a friend in the White House."

Stockman was not pleased with my interference in what he considered was his prerogative, but I knew that the environment was going to be an issue in 1984 and that Reagan had unjustly been given a bad rap on the environment during his two terms as Governor and that reputation had accompanied him to the Presidency. Other than the appointment of Bill Ruckelshaus to fill the job at EPA when Ann Gorsuch was driven out of town, nothing had been done in the first three years to change that reputation.

So as we got back to working on the SOTUS after the first of the year, I raised the issue in terms of the President's undeserved reputation on the environment and we inserted a line in the SOTUS recognizing the importance of the Bay and pledging to clean it up. It read:

> "Though this is a time of budget constraints, I have requested for EPA one of the largest percentage budget increases of any agency. We will begin the long, necessary effort to clean up a productive recreational area and a special national resource - the Chesapeake Bay."

Even though the President had made the decision to fund the cleanup, I was still surprised that the original language made it through all of the edits and the night before the speech was to be delivered, the Bay cleanup language was finalized. That evening, I was attending a black tie event and ran into Senator John Warner. He asked me how we were doing on our little project and after I swore him to secrecy, I told him that the President had decided in favor of the Bay cleanup and that he would announce it in the SOTUS the next night.

The next morning, the *Washington Post* carried a story quoting my good "friend" John Warner as saying that the President was supporting the Bay cleanup and would announce it in the SOTUS. When I walked into the senior staff meeting at eight o'clock that morning, everyone seemed to know that it was my leak. But it was my only one, and that may explain why later in my tenure at the White House, I myself, became the subject of a lot of leaks.

One leak that still makes me laugh occurred after a rather heated meeting of the Cabinet Council on Trade and Commerce meeting on textile trade policy. The issue came about because of an industry filed unfair trade practices case against China. After some negotiation with industry representatives, we got them to agree to suspend their case until the administration could work out a compromise. The deadline for our compromise was the close of business (COB) on December 16, 1983.

A lot of negotiation went on between the departments involved and the White House staff. Essentially, Malcom (Mac) Baldridge, the Secretary of Commerce, favored helping the industry, while Bill

Brock, the U.S. Trade Representative, and the National Security apparatus favored a more market oriented approach given the promises that the President had made at the Economic Summit to resist artificial trade barriers. Others, like the Chairman of the Council of Economic Advisors, Martin Feldstein, and Don Regan, the Secretary of the Treasury, were involved as well.

Senators Strom Thurmond and Jesse Helms, both of them from textile producing states, had made entreaties to the President to protect domestic textile companies. Thurmond in particular was very adamant about it. Strom Thurmond could turn anything into a discussion about protecting the domestic textile industry. Defense budget, a favorite of Reagan's—"Where are you going to get the uniforms, Mr. President?" Motion picture industry—"You need costumes, Mr. President." Welfare to Work Programs—"People need clothes to go to interviews." Sometimes it was hard to keep a straight face when he started up.

The meeting took place over a two-day period in December of 1983. After a particularly argumentative session late on December 15, the Baldridge plan was defeated and a compromise agreement was reached by the members of the Cabinet Council on a plan. The agreed upon plan was not going to make anybody happy as it called for more study. A lunch meeting of the Cabinet Council with the President was scheduled for the next day in the Cabinet Room. At the meeting, Baldridge reneged on his agreement to go with the plan agreed to the night before and proceeded to pitch protectionism to the President. All hell broke loose. The arguments continued and when the meeting time was up, Jim Baker suggested that all of the combatants retire to my office and work it out before the five o'clock deadline.

Dick Darman and I had passed notes back and forth during the fracas making projections on how long it would take for the story to leak and in what media it would first appear. Also how long it would take before we got the first call from Strom Thurmond. Our consensus was that it would hit the *Wall Street Journal* on the following Monday and that Thurmond would call within five minutes of the decision being made. We were right about the *Wall Street Journal.*

On January 6, 1984, under a "Behind the Scenes" heading with "Bickering in the West Wing" sub-heading, *Wall Street Journal* reporter Art Pine wrote a front page story over forty column inches long about the issue. He included in his article a blow by blow description of both Cabinet Council meetings and of what transpired in my office. It was very apparent that whoever had leaked the story to him had been in all three sessions. But his leaker wasn't in the *last* meeting. Here is the way Mr. Pine described it:

> "No one is sure precisely when it happened, but somewhere between 3:00 PM and 4:00 PM the drafters diluted the Baldrige plan by adding two critical ingredients: First, they exempted smaller low-wage countries, concentrating the import-tightening on larger textile-producer such as China, Hong Kong, South Korea, and Taiwan. Then they inserted a crucial 'and' …
>
> The revised version was carried by hand to presidential aides Edwin Meese and James Baker, who approved it without comment. The time: minutes before the industry-agreed deadline, late Friday afternoon, Dec. 16."

It didn't happen that way. Whoever leaked the story to Pine only told him one true fact about how the decision was made, the part about "no one is sure." What actually happened was that as the bickering between Cabinet members and their representatives continued, Dick Darman came to my office a little before four and asked how it was going. I told him that the group was never going to agree on language. Darman said we had to get it done before 5:00 PM. He asked me where the decision paper that had been developed for the President was. I was holding it in my hand and Darman said, "Let's go."

We left the rest of them still arguing in my office and headed downstairs to find the President. We asked a secret service agent on the way for the President's location and he told us that he was at a dentist appointment and pointed in the direction of the residence.

I am not sure that I could find the room again. We followed the trail of secret service agents, passed the bowling alley, and walked down a very narrow flight of stairs. About half way down an agent was posted at a door that opened right into the stairway. The agent said the President was inside and Darman knocked on the door. The dentist (I think he was Navy) opened the door and there sat the President, with his mouth open, half reclining in the single dentist's chair. The room was so small that Darman and I couldn't get in it to talk to him so we stood in the hall and explained the situation and the time deadline once again. He asked me a few questions about the options and what had transpired in my office. I told him that the principals were still up there arguing. He then took the decision memo, ticked off his decisions, signed it, and handed it back to me. I thanked him and apologized again to the very pissed off dentist.

Dick and I took off at a fast gallop back to the West Wing. We grabbed Larry Speakes, the Press Secretary, and told him what the President's decision was and Larry put it out about five minutes before the deadline. Darman was right about the *Wall Street Journal*, but by that time it wasn't important to try to find out who the leaker was. It wasn't Dick, because he wasn't in my office. And since the President and I knew how the decision was really made, neither of us would have made up the Meese-Baker fib.

Even in the event that we found out who the leaker was, there was never any disciplinary action taken. The most prominent and egregious example of that was David Stockman's leaks over a period of time to William Greider. Stockman, while acting as the administration's point man on the economic plan in 1981, engaged in a series of meetings with Greider. Greider then wrote an article for *Atlantic Monthly* in which he recounted the meetings with Stockman. The article proved that Stockman didn't believe in the Reagan Economic Program.

Some of us already knew that Stockman was disloyal. Most of the people that I knew in the Administration thought that he ought to have been fired. Apparently, many of the powers in the West Wing thought that he should have been fired also. But Jim Baker prevailed on the President's good nature and Reagan did not fire Stockman. It might have been an even more successful Presidency had Reagan let him go.

Chapter 15

Life in the White House

Alot has been written about Ronald Reagan's work habits. He was routinely criticized for having a short work day, for coming into the office late, for spending too much time at Camp David, for napping in the afternoon and for delegating too much authority to staff. Most of it is wrong.

In fact, Ronald Reagan arrived at the Oval Office between 8:50 AM and 9:00 AM every day he was in town. You could almost set your watch by it. He didn't nap and he was a voracious reader. Whether he was in the Oval or in the residence, he was always working. It is true that he didn't like to sit in meetings for long periods of time while people around the table talked to hear themselves talk. He liked to get crisp thoughtful briefings and if there was a difference of opinion on a particular subject, he wanted to hear all sides.

If an issue was one that he had thought about and analyzed, he could carry on the discussion and be quite forceful about it. On the other hand, if it wasn't something that he was familiar with, he would just listen. Most of the time, when an issue was up for decision, he would listen to the discussion and would not make a decision at the table. He would think on it a little and decide later. A lot of the time he would double check things to make sure he fully understood. People mistook this delay as a sign that he wasn't actually making the decision. Not true.

If it was an issue that he had already come to a conclusion on, he rarely reversed his opinion. He was comfortable with his own decision-making capability. You never knew when an issue would really spark his interest. He rarely let politics play any role in making decisions. Frequently when the discussion would drift in that direction, he would remind those in the discussion that "we didn't come here to make political decisions; we need to make the best decision for the country."

Some of his set opinions were based on personal experience. Everyone knows that Reagan did not like high taxes. He was successful in lowering tax rates to the lowest level that they had been in decades. He believed that low tax rates encouraged economic activity and growth. His belief was based on his own experience making movies. Whenever the discussion would turn to raising taxes he would tell the story about his movie days when the top marginal tax rate was 90 percent. He would make just one or maybe two movies in a year and then wouldn't work anymore. His comment: "I wasn't going to work for ten cents on the dollar!"

He would also point out that because he didn't make any more films in a year, that meant that all of the other people associated with making his films, the camera men, the makeup artists, and all of the rest from director to clerk, didn't work anymore that year also. And they weren't in the 90 percent bracket. When people would continue to argue, usually Democrats in Congressional leadership meetings, Reagan would smile and remind them that he was one of the few, if not the only one in the room, who had a degree in economics.

The issue of abortion is one of the most perplexing in our society. No other issue has had such a lasting impact on the modern American political scene. Ronald Reagan's position on abortion was well known and he had come to it, not for political reasons but through logical examination. Throughout America, he was either loved by the pro-life people or hated by the pro-choice segment of our society. But I would not classify Ronald Reagan as a radical pro-lifer. He knew it was a divisive issue that spawned very irrational behavior in some people. He despised the violence and radical forms of protest that characterized both sides. It was something that he had given a lot of thought to and his position made perfect sense. Ronald Reagan, for a variety of reasons, had concluded that life begins at conception. His thought was that if life had begun, the only legal reason for one person taking another person's life was self defense. Therefore, if the mother's life was in danger, the pregnancy could be terminated in self defense. If it wasn't self defense, it shouldn't be allowed. Pretty simple.

On a trip to New York City with the President, I was warming up a crowd of female magazine editors and publishers. I frequently got the assignment of talking to a group while they waited for the President to make an appearance. The President was there to make a lunch speech at a women's business group and he was going to drop in on the magazine folks for a little discussion before the big luncheon. On this occasion, I made a few remarks and then opened it up for questions. One of the first came from a woman who wanted to know about Reagan's position on abortion. The question was not asked in a friendly manner.

In all the years that I worked for Ronald Reagan, in all the different positions I had, no one ever asked me what my position on abortion was. And it is probably rightly so, because my position on the issue wasn't relevant. Ronald Reagan was the President and over the years, I had become very comfortable in explaining his position and his rationale for it. That is exactly what I did to this group. I explained his position and his rationale for it. Then I added that almost anywhere you traveled in this country, you would find people on both sides of the issue. Now, I had seen a list of who was attending this briefing session and I gambled that like America, there were probably people in the room on both sides of the issue, so I said so. Sure enough, the women started to argue amongst themselves. After a few minutes of them arguing back and forth, I interrupted the clamor. I said:

> "Ladies, if I might have your attention. I notice that the guys with the guns
> (the secret service) have entered the room and that means that the President
> is not far behind. When he gets here, if you want, you can raise this issue
> with him. I have told you his position and you have seen what the discus
> sion can lead to, even in this room. But it is your choice."

The President arrived, said a few words, and they loved him. The whole crowd. And not one of them asked about abortion.

Another area that Ronald Reagan had thought through thoroughly was that of nuclear weapons and nuclear war. He often expressed his thoughts and commented on man's latent propensity to engage in self-destruction. When it came to the possibility of nuclear war and the use of nuclear weapons, his conclusions sometimes confounded his closest advisors and caused him to be held up to ridicule by those who were confused with the conventional wisdom. The latter group included the powers that be in the Soviet Union.

Reagan had concluded in his own mind that all nuclear weapons should be banned. His rationale for it was that man had always been able to build a defense for each new weapon that came along, starting with the cave man's clubs and shields. The problem as he explained it time and time again was that there was no defense against a nuclear weapon and therefore, like the poison gas used in World War I, the nuclear weapon should be banned.

Along those same lines, Reagan's support of the Strategic Defense Initiative, derisively dubbed "Star Wars" by his opponents and the mainstream media (that may be redundant), was geared toward averting a major threat, that of the intercontinental ballistic missile. And when Reagan would indicate that if we were successful in developing such a technology, that the U.S. would make it available to all countries for their protection, people just couldn't believe him. SDI was a real sticking point in his negotiations with Gorbachev. When the

President returned from Geneva and his first summit with Gorbachev, he commented on how surprised he was at how strong Gorbachev's opposition was to SDI. In his return briefing for the Cabinet and staff, Reagan said that Gorbachev "believes that the danger of SDI is that the research will accidentally discover an offensive weapon for space."

Reagan had vision, more than any other politician I've ever met. Perhaps it was the times that he had lived through or perhaps it was just that he was a dreamer. Whatever it was, he rarely backed away from an idea that he believed possible, even when others ridiculed him. Who would have thought when he decried, "Mr. Gorbachev, tear down this wall" in front of the Berlin Wall, the symbol of Soviet determination and the cold war, that it really would have happened? I never talked to him about the Wall after it came down, but I am sure that if I had, he would have talked about how he knew that would be the result at some point in time. In his mind, it was inevitable.

He liked to tell a story from his early days as Governor in California. There was a lot of unrest about the Vietnam War and nowhere was that more pronounced than on the campuses of the University of California system. We had had riots and student uprisings particularly at the Berkeley campus to such an extent that Governor Reagan had called out the National Guard to restore order. As the unrest grew, he agreed to meet with a group of students in his offices in Sacramento. To hear Reagan tell the story, the students showed up unwashed and clothed in typical hippy attire of the day. Their spokesman went into a diatribe about how Reagan couldn't understand their generation; how they were different having grown up in an age of television, space travel, and jet planes. Reagan without blinking an eye agreed with them. He said, "You're right, I didn't grow up with those things; my generation invented them."

There is an interesting side note that came out of Reagan's first meeting with Gorbachev in Geneva, Switzerland and I think that it shows a lot about Reagan's self confidence. Leading up to the day there was a lot of media hype about the first meeting between the two. The Soviets had their number one American watcher, Georgi Arbatov, later the head of the Moscow-based Institute for the Study of the U.S.A. and Canada, out in full force. Arbatov had a reputation within Washington circles as the long-time Soviet player whose job it was to watch the U.S. society and economy and translate it for the Soviet mind. He was so good, so facile on American television, it was hard to tell that he was a Russian. In preparation for the summit, he was spending a lot of time commenting on the Soviet view and what they expected out of the meeting. The U.S. media loved it. During one pre-summit session, a reporter asked Arbatov about Gorbachev's preparations for the meeting. The reporter said that he understood that President Reagan was watching films of Gorbachev as part of his preparation and he wondered if Gorbachev was watching films of Reagan. Arbatov replied, "General Secretary Gorbachev has no need to watch Grade B movies." The statement created quite a stir in parts of the White House.

The meeting in Geneva took place the third week of November 1985. When Reagan returned to the White House, he was in a really good mood. His only regret about the meeting was that one of the goldfish that were left to his care by the little girl who lived in the villa that was borrowed for his stay in Geneva had died. Other than that, the meeting was a success. The next morning he was scheduled to brief the Cabinet on his trip. The meeting was set up with only one agenda item, the Summit.

As he entered the Cabinet Room for the Cabinet meeting everyone congratulated him. His first report was not that Gorbachev was polite or that Gorbachev made reference to God and quoted scripture on two occasions, or that Gorbachev had said that his wife, Raisa, was an atheist. He told us all of that later. Instead, he opened the meeting by telling us about the newly famous walk down to the pool house where they were to sit by the fire and talk one on one. He said that they stopped half way down and had a few words. We all knew that had happened, but we also knew that it wasn't in the minutely choreographed schedule. Reagan said that he stopped Gorbachev and told him to "tell that Arbatov that I made some pretty good movies. They weren't all grade B!" The President said that Gorbachev laughed and replied that he knew; he had seen one—"the one where you got your legs cut off," meaning Reagan's best film, *Kings Row*. The room erupted in laughter. And that is how he began his briefing of the Cabinet.

I always told new staff people in the White House that you had to be careful with what you gave the President. It had to be correct because he read everything AND he remembered it. Some of them took my advice and some didn't. I figured that it must have been a trait he picked up in the movies or in television, reading scripts and memorizing parts, because he truly did have a photographic memory.

During the early to mid 1980s, the situation with American farming had reached a critical period. There was a drought in West Texas and cattle were dying; drought in the Midwest; farmers being foreclosed on, you name it and it was a problem in the agricultural section of our economy. During this period I spent a lot of time with farm state Governors, farm groups, and agri-business interests trying to work out a solution. Of course, when you say farmer, it immediately conjures up a Norman Rockwell image of a family tilling the soil. Well that was not what farming was in the United States during this period. Farming was big business. But even the big businesses wanted the politicians and policy makers to continue to think about the family farmer when making farm policy.

In fact, some family farmers were in trouble, but the number, when you considered agriculture as a whole was pretty small. A lot of the little guys during this period got into financial trouble by carrying too much debt. The debt in a lot of cases was generated by buying the farm from retiring parents at a high price with the assumption that the value could only go higher. Some bought fancy expensive farm equipment like tractors with air conditioning and high end stereo in their cabs on credit. After all, we had seen double digit inflation for the past several years and no one thought that anything would get cheaper in the future.

On one occasion, Jack Block, our Secretary of Agriculture, requested a meeting with the President to discuss the issue. Jack was a great guy and a good Secretary of Agriculture. I figured that he was going to come in and try to convince the President to do something more for the family farmer. He had been a farmer in Illinois and I knew that his arguments for the federal government doing something (something means put more money into it) for the farmers were based on the Rockwellian model.

Before the meeting took place, I asked the OPD staff to put together a succinct briefing paper, one page that outlined the true picture of the family farmer in modern day agriculture. The document was a full page long with statistics on the number of family farms in the U.S., what they produced, how many were in financial trouble, and how most of them got there. I sent the paper to the President and suggested that he might want to take a look at it before the meeting with Jack. I didn't think any more of it and the President and I didn't discuss it before the meeting.

When Jack came in, we sat down in the Oval Office and he began his pitch. Reagan, sitting as usual in his straight back chair listened attentively. Block, sitting in an identical chair, the one to the President's left that was usually reserved for the guest, took the approach that I had assumed he would take. When he had finished, or at least stopped for a breath, the President said, "Well Jack, as I understand it ..." and he went right down the briefing paper, point by point, from memory. That pretty well wrapped up the discussion. As Jack and I were leaving the Oval Office, he very quietly said to me, "Boy, you sure have him briefed on Agriculture!" I just smiled. Ronald Reagan was a quick study.

One way that I found to raise issues with Ronald Reagan directly usually occurred on Monday. When I moved into the West Wing, I was advised by my assistant, Betty Ayers, that just about every week on Monday or sometimes Tuesday I would attend an "Issues Lunch" with the President.

The lunch was an informal gathering in the Cabinet Room with the menu predetermined by the White House Mess. In addition to the President, it was attended by most of the Assistants to the President and by the Vice President. So you had about a dozen people sitting around the table for a luncheon discussion of issues, which any one of us could raise. I viewed the issues lunches as an opportunity to raise policy issues that were just on the horizon, not those being debated in the Cabinet Councils or those that were ripe for decision. Each week, I would prepare notes on two or three issues and would use the notes to start a discussion. Sometimes the discussions would be pretty animated and sometimes the President and the others would just let me talk, probably hoping that I would be brief. Sometimes my issues would be preempted by the priorities of the day, but I could usually find time to get what I thought was most important onto the table.

In late 1984, I raised an issue with him during an issues lunch that had far reaching implications and eventually caused quite a debate within the Administration and among the White House Staff. I raised the issue of the internment of Japanese Americans during World War II. In law school,* I read the Korematsu decision handed down by the United States Supreme Court in 1944. Korematsu was a Japanese

---

* My Constitutional law professor was Anthony Kennedy, now a Justice on the U.S. Supreme Court. I take a little credit for his appointment to the Court. In late 1972 Chuck Hobbs, who had been with us in Social Welfare, was working on California Proposition One, the original California Tax Limitation Initiative. One evening Chuck told me that he was looking for a conservative, strict constructionist, Constitutional lawyer. I told him about Kennedy who was practicing law and teaching at night. Chuck contracted with Kennedy to assist on the project. The project failed at the polls, but Tony Kennedy became known to the Reagan Administration and was eventually appointed to the U.S. Supreme Court by President Reagan.

American who was convicted of defying the curfew excluding Japanese Americans from certain military areas, in this case, the West Coast of the United States. The Supreme Court upheld his conviction and thus started a discussion that lasted another forty-plus years. Arguments raged back and forth for years.

I had been raised on the West Coast; I've lived in Washington State, California, and Hawaii. I had known and worked with a lot of Japanese Americans, many of whom had been uprooted from their homes and interned in the camps during World War II. A couple of friends had even been born in the camps. Many were bitter about the experience and felt that a real injustice had been done to them solely on the basis of their race. During the war, no comparable action was taken against German Americans and Italian Americans. Only Japanese Americans were singled out and only those who resided on the West Coast. Supporters of the decision argued that only Japan had pulled a sneak attack and that at the time, it was felt that they might attack the West coast with assistance of Japanese American residents. I personally felt that it was pure racial discrimination.

I had been visited in the office by Frank Sato, the Inspector General at the Veterans Administration and the then President of the Japanese American Citizens League (JACL) on several occasions. President Carter had appointed the Commission on Wartime Relocation and Internment of Civilians (CWRIC) and directed the Commission to study the issue. The Commission recommended an apology on behalf of the nation and payment of a nominal sum to the survivors. Frank and other representatives of the JACL were making the rounds trying to drum up support for redress legislation and for an apology from the federal government. Louis B. Hays, my assistant, was interested in the issue and was the main point of contact for the JACL.

Lou Hays and I had a long history. He had been an attorney with the Los Angeles County Counsel's Office during the welfare reform battle in California. He served on a task force that Carleson and I set

up and when we went to HEW, Lou was one of the few that we recruited to accompany us. When Child Support law passed in 1975, he
became a key person on the implementation team. He was the first official Deputy Director (the person who ran it day to day) of the Office
of Child Support Enforcement. Lou then became the head of hearings
and appeals for Social Security when I was Commissioner and he came
over to the White House to be my Special Assistant in 1984.

I did a little research and at a Monday Issues Lunch, I brought the
subject up to President Reagan. I filled him in on the background and
the fact that the issue was well known on the West Coast with its large
population of Japanese Americans, but that it had received little attention elsewhere in the country, especially in Washington, D.C.

I reminded him of a day in 1945 when he appeared in the Hollywood
Bowl at a function honoring a fallen Japanese American member of the
U.S. Army's 442nd Regimental Combat Team. His remarks had become
part of the Ronald Reagan lore in the Japanese American community.
On that day, U.S. Army Captain Ronald Reagan was quoted as saying:

> "Blood that has soaked into the sand of a beach is all one color. America
> stands unique in the world, the only country not founded on race, but on
> a way, an ideal."

The President vaguely recalled the appearance but didn't really comment too much on the subject. I felt that at least we had raised the
issue and I was certain that the JACL would continue to push their
cause. What I didn't realize was that there was a competing interest in
the issue that had not raised its head at lunch, but which would pressure Reagan to oppose the redress issue and legislation for the next four
years. I didn't know it but they pressured Reagan by making the issue
one of international relations with Japan.

I raised the issue with him for the final time at an Issues Lunch
in 1985. I reminded him of the 110 thousand Japanese Americans
who had been deprived of liberty and property during the War. I also

reminded him of the 18,000 or so Japanese Americans who served in the 442nd during the war and that the 442nd was the most decorated combat unit in American history. And I told him that he had become memorialized in the writings of the Japanese American community for what he had said at the Hollywood Bowl in 1945. I completed my pitch by saying:

> "Mr. President. There is little doubt today that the actions taken over forty years ago were unnecessary and unjust. Some of us think that it's time to put forty years of resentment and frustration to rest in the Japanese American community. Perhaps (next) Veterans Day President Reagan could say again what Captain Reagan said so long ago."

Again, he seemed to be very interested but also noncommittal. No one at the table raised an objection or made any comment. Even those who were opposing the redress issue who were sitting around the table kept quiet. I think they did this because they knew that if Reagan got into the issue, his natural inclination would be to right the wrong. This would have been strengthened by the fact that he had already come down on the issue once—in 1945. But his comment in his diary about the meeting was, "Our issues briefing lunch was more or less routine."

After I left the White House, the legislation, HR 442, was introduced and started moving. I went to Capitol Hill and visited with Robert Matsui, the Congressman from Sacramento. I first met Bob when he was on the Sacramento City Council and renewed our friendship when he served on the House Ways and Means Committee during my Social Security days. We discussed the redress legislation and I gave him my assessment of the President and that in my opinion, in the end the President would sign HR 442. In a later note, Bob told me how much he appreciated the inside assessment of the President's feelings on the issue.

There was a lot of pressure on the President from the Japanese American community to sign the bill. The efforts within the Administration to get him to veto HR 442 were from various sources. OMB opposed it on fiscal grounds and the national security and foreign policy people opposed it feeling that it would impact current relations with Japan for some odd reason.

I always thought that the precedent issue probably transcended all others even though it was never specifically brought up in my presence. The underlying, unspoken concern was that if you did this for this group that was discriminated against on the basis of race, would you be setting a precedent for African Americans to receive an apology and payment for past discrimination based on the history of slavery? I could certainly separate the two in my mind, one being a formal action of the federal government and the other having existed before the country was even founded, but I suspect those in the Administration who opposed the redress legislation could not.

Reagan changed the mind of his administration about vetoing HR 442. He signed the bill into law with a signing ceremony on August 10, 1988. At that ceremony, he finished by using the same words that Captain Ronald Reagan had used at the Hollywood Bowl in 1945.

Sometimes the Issues Lunches resulted in unintended consequences. At one lunch, in the middle of February 1984, we had just finished eating and were still talking. The food at these lunches was always filling. Usually, there was a salad and then an entrée, perhaps a broiled half chicken, and then it was followed up by some fabulous dessert. By the time you finished dessert, you knew that you had eaten. The President, on the other hand, almost always had a bowl of soup and a few jelly beans for dessert. On this particular day, he watched us finish up the dessert (he loved desserts) and he commented, "You know fellas, if I ate lunch like that every day, I'd be fat!" He didn't mean anything by it, but as you looked around the table, the President, Vice President Bush and Jim Baker were the only guys at the table who didn't have a bulging waist and double chins. Some of us were working on triples.

It didn't take long for Dick Darman, the Staff Secretary, to come up with a Darmanesque solution to the problem. He convinced his

West Wing basement cohort Craig Fuller to join him and they announced the **Pre/Post Convention Olympiad.** The rules were pretty simple. Participants had to sign up and have their starting weight taken and witnessed by a permanent employee of the White House either in the gym or in the medical office. At that time the individual had to declare a target weight. There was to be a Bronze Medal awarded to the individual who lost the most pounds in the first fourteen days of competition; a Silver Medal to be awarded to the competitor who reached his/her pre-selected target weight in sixty days and a Gold Medal awarded to the competitor who maintained his target weight and won a three mile foot race to be held in Dallas the day before the Republican Convention started in August.

The Olympiad was open to all White House staff and to members of the press corps. Fifty-three participants signed up including such notables as Bill Plante from CBS (target -12 lbs.), Elisabeth Blumiller of the *New York Times* (target -2lbs.), and Bob Woodward of *Washington Post* fame (target -16 lbs). Betty Ayers, my assistant, was the only participant that wanted to gain weight to reach her target (+8lbs). These were all pikers compared to those of us sitting around the Cabinet Room at lunch that day. Our targets were:

> Dick Darman - 40 lbs
> Jack Svahn - 32 lbs
> Ken Duberstein -20 lbs
> Ed Rollins -28 lbs
> Larry Speakes -16.5 lbs
> Fred Fielding -10 lbs
> Craig Fuller -25 lbs
> Bud McFarlane -9 lbs
> B. Oglesby -20 lbs

The competition was fast and furious but at the end of the first two weeks, the "Rules Committee" put out a statement that I had won the "race for the bronze" with a weight loss of 17 pounds for the period.

I issued a statement myself. "The Second Floor West Wing is back ---- Standing Tall --- and Thin!" The Silver Medal was a little more difficult. On May 26, under the heading, "Trimming the Real Fat," the *New York Times* reported: "An anonymous White House source reports that Richard G. Darman, an Assistant to the President … is a poor loser who has refused to announce the winner of the latest contest. … At the risk of touching off a round of polygraph tests in the White House, the winner, it can be reported, is Jack Svahn … he has shed 35 pounds."

Darman didn't release the results until August 10 when he declared a postponement of the Race for the Gold (George H. W. Bush and I were the only ones who met the criteria to compete). In commenting on my win of the Silver Medal at that time, Dick wrote, "NOTE: New York Times reporting on this event was somewhat misleading." Whatever the results of the competition, there was a lot of weight lost that summer in the White House and it wasn't over worry about the upcoming election.

Working in the White House had some definite fringe benefits. A lot of people just want to come there and see it. President Reagan was a popular President and people wanted to meet him. He, in turn, enjoyed meeting people. He liked for them to visit "the people's house" as he called it. Consequently, we had a constant flow of people from all walks of life coming through the White House. It was interesting to be able to meet a lot of people who, even though they didn't know you, you knew who they were. From sports stars to Hollywood celebrities to Afghan freedom fighters they all wanted to come through the White House.

Carlton Turner, a Deputy Assistant to the President, who worked for me heading up our Office of Drug Policy, had arranged to have Michael Jackson be present at one of Mrs. Reagan's anti drug campaign events on the South Lawn. This was when Jackson was at the top of his career and very popular; he had not become too much of a kook yet. It was a big event and afterwards, Jackson was in the Roosevelt Room greeting staff and families. Betty Ayers and Janice Farrell in my office asked me if I was going to go there and get my picture taken with Michael Jackson. I told them, "Of course not." They badgered me into going down to the Roosevelt Room and grabbing the hand of the gloved one and having our picture taken.

A few weeks later, I was at an event and talking to Ursula Meese, Ed's wife. She said that their daughter Dana had been in that day, had her picture taken and sent it to Jackson. Jackson had autographed it and sent it back. Ursula asked me if I had gotten a photograph with Michael Jackson. I said, "You mean the guy with the one white glove?" She said yes and suggested that I should send it to him to autograph. I told her, "The picture was in my in box. I asked Betty who it was and she told me. I wrote on it 'To Michael – With Best Wishes,' signed it and sent it to him." Ursula looked at me like I was nuts. Maybe she had it right.

Or one evening at a state dinner for the Nation's Governors we made a midnight run at the Oval Office. After the dinner in the State Dining Room, everyone adjourned to the East Room for the entertainment. On this evening it was going to be Lee Greenwood and his band. Greenwood was a favorite of Reagan's and he didn't let the President down that evening. The finale was his hit single, "God Bless the USA" and it had the house cheering. After the show was over, Jill and I were standing with Lee Verstandig, the Assistant to the President for Intergovernmental Affairs, and his wife, Toni commenting on the performance. Greenwood was standing there with his wife and we walked over to complement him.

He was very appreciative and very much in awe of the White House. He commented that he never thought that he would be in the place and he asked where the Oval Office was. We told him that it wasn't in the Residence, but that it was in the West Wing. He and his wife were disappointed that they would not see it. To which I replied,

"Would you like to see it?" He said, "Yes!" Now this was late in the evening and we had consumed a few glasses of wine, but the six of us traipsed through the Residence, up the Colonnade and into the West Wing. Once we got there, we were hassled a little bit by the Uniformed Secret Service agent who stands guard at the Oval Office twenty-four hours a day but we eventually got Mr. and Mrs. Greenwood the tour of the West Wing.

That wasn't the only time that I found myself in an awkward position at a State Dinner. One evening after the dinner was over, Jill and I were in the East Room for the entertainment. I don't recall who or what the entertainment was that evening but I do recall that we were seated in the second row right behind the President, Mrs. Reagan, The Vice President and Mrs. Bush. When the entertainment was over, the President and Vice President got up and led the crowd out into The Cross Hall, the hall between the State Dining Room and the East Room. Leaving the East Room works kind of like a wedding with each succeeding row following in step.

We were right behind the Reagans and Bushes when we got out to the Cross Hall where they served after dinner drinks and cigars (yes cigars), when the U.S. Marine Band, "The President's Own," started to play dance music. President and Mrs. Reagan walked into the Entrance Hall at the North Entrance and started to dance. Jill and I were standing there watching the graceful couple twirl around the floor as the rest of the guests filed out of the East Room. Suddenly, someone grabbed me by the arm from behind and said, "Come on, Jack. Let's get out there on the dance floor." It was the Vice President and he was moving out to the floor with Barbara. I asked Jill if she would like to dance and we followed.

Then I looked around. There were only three couples on the floor. The entire group of guests, roughly a hundred people, were standing in the Cross Hall and watching the three couples dance. I tried to scrunch down and become unnoticeable and I whispered into Jill's ear that I might be unemployed the next morning. Fortunately, no one important took notice and eventually several others ventured out onto the floor. I felt like I had dodged a bullet. I didn't even have a cigar that evening.

Sometimes access can result in some interesting happenings. While I was at the White House, I had two White House Fellows in my care. I had just picked the first one when I was at HHS. He was U.S. Coast Guard Lt. Cdr. Craig Coy. I don't think he was too happy to being fended off to the Under Secretary of Health and Human Services rather than something more in line with a Search and Rescue pilot's career path, but he was taking it in stride. Right after the selection process, we both took a week off. When he returned I was no longer at HHS and he was a White House fellow in the White House. His spirits improved. When we had originally discussed his tenure as a White House Fellow, I had told Cdr. Coy that he was free to come and go with me and that he was there for a learning experience so he should make the most of it. He took me at my word.

Shortly thereafter, I was attending a pre-press conference session with the President and the other senior staff in the small theatre in the Eisenhower Office Building otherwise known as OEOB 450. During the session, the President answered several questions regarding foreign policy that needed a little touching up. It just wasn't his day and Bud McFarlane had gone through some fairly extensive debriefing.

A couple of days after the session, Fred Fielding, the White House Counsel, came into my office and showed me a photograph of Cdr. Coy, asking, "Do you know who this is?" I said of course I know him. Fielding said that he was in the briefing with the President. I was pretty surprised and said that he couldn't have been. The security is pretty tight around the President and clearly he wasn't authorized access. I called Craig and asked him about it. He said he was there. He said that he had come over to my office and asked Betty where I was. She told him and he decided to follow. When challenged by the Secret Service at the door, he showed them his White House pass and said he was with me. They let him in.

I then swore him to secrecy and told him that if he ever told anyone what went on in the room (not that there was anything bad, maybe just a little embarrassing) that he would spend the rest of his life in a helicopter. Being a very smart and ambitious young man, Craig promptly forgot the whole incident.

My other White House fellow was not selected by me but was the choice of my predecessor. Her name was Elaine Chao and she was a banker from Citibank in New York. When I came on board, she was just arriving also. Elaine was an extremely bright young woman with an interest in all things governmental. She was a naturalized American citizen, having come to the United States from Taiwan with her parents when she was a young child. I knew that Elaine was headed for a great career in whatever field she chose, but my assessment was brought home to me shortly after we started working together.

Jill and I were attending a session of The Business Council at the Homestead, a plush resort in the Virginia mountains. The Business Council is an association of Chief Executive Officers of the world's largest corporations. It was formed during the Great Depression for government officials to be able to interface with business leaders. We were talking to Walter Wriston and his wife at an evening function when I mentioned to Walter that I had just hired one of his analysts. He asked who it was and I told him it was Elaine Chao. Without batting an eye he exclaimed, "She's wonderful." I had to chuckle to myself, I figured that if the Chairman of Citicorp knew the then thirty-year-old analyst she must indeed have a great future.*

---

* Elaine Chao has succeeded in everything she has attempted. Since she worked for me, she has served as the Chairman of the Federal Maritime Commission, the Deputy Secretary of Transportation, the Director of the Peace Corps, the CEO of United Way of America and as the nation's twenty-fourth Secretary of Labor. She is married to Senator Mitch McConnell of Kentucky.

The social life for a high-level Presidential appointee is almost non-stop. As an Assistant to the President, you are automatically on the "A-List" for invitations to social functions. You are listed in the Social List of Washington D.C., the so-called "Green Book." You attend a lot of functions in the White House and are invited to most black tie events held during the fall and spring social seasons in the city.

People think that it must be a glamorous life. And for a while it is. But after awhile it gets to be somewhat tedious. I wouldn't trade the privilege for anything, but like business travel, it gets to where it wears on you. I used to go to receptions and dinners several nights a week. I attended many functions by myself as we had two young children at home. As the kids got a little older, or if it was a really big deal, Jill would drive into the office and we would leave from there. If it was a formal affair, I would just change clothes in the office.

We really enjoyed functions in the White House Residence. Since our time together at home was limited due to my schedule, we took full advantage of an evening in the White House. Instead of rubbing elbows all evening with the guests, after the perfunctory social rituals were observed, Jill and I would take a glass of wine and sit before the fire in the Red Room. We would discuss family matters, bills, the kid's school and other things that people leading normal lives might discuss in the evening. All this while the guests wandered in and out.

If it was a function outside the White House, we were always the guest of someone or some organization so it was not nearly as convenient to talk to each other. In fact at those kinds of events, it was usually impossible to talk to each other because you were always seated apart and many times not even at the same table. We always joked about having dinner with two thousand of our closest friends, but it was amazing at how closed a society Washington is. You actually did run into a lot of friends at these events. Of course at other times, you run into new people; and that can be either good or bad.

I recall one dinner at the Washington Hilton with more than two thousand friends there. Jill and I were just sitting down when Jill saw Justice Sandra Day O'Conner at the table next to us. O'Conner had only recently been appointed to the court and was probably as recognizable as any woman in Washington at the time. Certainly she was in that ballroom and because of her celebrity status; she was seated with another popular Washington celebrity John Riggins, the star running back for the pro football Redskins. Jill walked over to O'Connor's table to introduce herself and to congratulate her on her confirmation. When she returned to our table I asked her if she had said Hi to Riggo. Jill, not being a fan, had no idea who he was. Later in the dinner, when I turned around in my chair I found the star running back for the Washington Redskins taking a "nap." I didn't find out until the next morning when the *Washington Post* reported that prior to napping, Riggins had in conversation with Justice O'Conner, uttered his most famous statement: "Lighten up, Sandy baby!"

It wasn't the only time that I learned of an incident after it took place, even when I was at the event. One evening we were attending a state dinner during a visit by Canada's Prime Minister, Brian Mulroney. The guest of honor was Vice President Bush and the dinner was being held at the Canadian Ambassador's residence. The Ambassador, Allan Gotlieb, and I knew each other pretty well having worked together on the issue of acid rain. Acid rain was another of those subjects that crossed both domestic and foreign portfolios and it had big economic and political ramifications for both Mulroney's administration and our own. Within the Reagan White House, I had the lead on acid rain, and had worked with Allan in trying to resolve the issue to both principals satisfaction. The dinner followed meetings on the subject between the President and the Prime Minister.

Gotlieb and his wife, Sondra, were well known as a power couple in the federal city. Sondra periodically wrote a somewhat tongue-in-cheek column on her impressions of life in Washington for the *Washington Post*, and she was known as a preeminent hostess on the social circuit.

The event began with a rather lengthy cocktail party and then Jill and I went to our respective tables on opposite sides of the room. Before taking my seat I, as usual for these types of events, went around the table and introduced myself to the guests whom I did not know and greeted those who I did. As the dinner started, I noticed that the lady sitting to my left, a Washington socialite and friend of the Ambassador's wife, was a little tipsy. She inquired as to what I did in order to be invited to this dinner. I engaged her in a little chit-chat and told her what my job was. Her voice then got a little sharper and demanded to know why we, the Reagan Administration, were "supporting the Contadoras." I told her that the Administration did not support the Contadoras.* She said, "Yes you do!" in a fairly loud voice. I then realized that she might be more than tipsy. I replied, as politely as possible, that she was mistaken and that we did not support the Contadoras. She insisted that we did. I told her that she probably was referring to our support for the Contras, a totally different group engaged in fighting the Sandinistas in Nicaragua. She just glared at me and said, "I am going to slap you!"

Now, I wasn't sure that in her condition, she could aim well enough to actually hit me, but when she said it a second time, I quietly suggested that slapping me would not be a good thing to do. I told her that I would probably slap her back. She just looked at me with a wobbly stare and then got up from her seat and walked to the other side of the table to complain about me to some guy from Hollywood. Lynne Cheney, the Chairman of the National Endowment for the Arts at the time, was sitting next to Mr. Hollywood and suggested that she trade

---

* The Contadora Group was made up of representatives from Columbia, Panama, Mexico, and Venezuela. It started at the suggestion of Swedish Prime Minister Olaf Palme and was trying to establish a peace in Central America. The U.S. did not support the group or its objective because it would have prohibited U.S. unilateral involvement in the region. President Reagan called the Contadora Group's plan for Central America "fatally flawed."

seats with the woman. Lynne came over and after I explained what had happened, we enjoyed dinner together.

After dinner, I met up with Jill and on the way out the door, I commented to the Ambassador, "Allan, I am a little perplexed about the guests you invite to these things; the woman sitting next to me wanted to slap me in the face." Gotlieb just gurgled a little bit and tried to smile. He didn't really have a response and I thought it odd because we had always been able to joke a little together. I found out what Allan's problem was the next morning in the *Washington Post*.

It appeared that a really coveted guest at A-List Washington parties, Mr. Richard G. Darman, then Deputy Secretary of the Treasury, had cancelled his attendance at the last minute. When the Social Secretary at the Embassy had approached Mrs. Gotlieb with the news, Sondra was so upset that she slapped the Social Secretary hard across the face. The event was witnessed by a reporter and it was the talk of the town the next morning. So then I knew why Allan had almost fainted when I told him about my close call. Two slappings at one function just won't do in Canadian diplomatic circles.

Dick Darman and I had a pretty friendly relationship. I rather missed him when he went to Treasury with Jim Baker. When Darman showed up at a White House meeting a day or two after the incident, I passed him a note: "Dick – Thank you so kindly for attending today." He sent one back: "I came for humanitarian reasons. No telling who'd get hurt if I didn't show."

Chapter 16

1984

It was time to test the public's faith in the Reagan presidency. Are you better off now than you were four years ago? That was the battle cry that candidate Reagan had used in 1980 against President Jimmy Carter. Now we were going into an election year and were concerned that the same question was going to be used against us. But as luck would have it, Ronald Reagan's luck that is, 1984 became "Morning in America," a bright new day. But that didn't stop us from worrying.

The preparation for the 1984 campaign initially got underway almost as soon as I arrived at the White House. In early October 1983, Ed Meese called together the policy side of the White House to talk about planning for the Platform Committee and to set up a process of issue identification and resolution going into the 1984 campaign. We talked about who we should get to begin drafting for the Platform and how we should organize the committee structure and hearings. Ed recognized that we weren't going to write the draft; that was the responsibility and the proper role for the Committee itself. But we wanted to have materials put together for the Committees deliberation when the time came.

In discussing what we should do in the lead up to the Convention, we were looking at it from the standpoint of the Administration rather than from the party's perspective. There wasn't much question as to who the Republican Party would nominate at the convention in Dallas in August, so we felt pretty secure in planning at least the policy aspect. On the other hand in late 1983, the President was keeping pretty much to himself as to what his plans were. We knew that Nancy might not be favoring a second term, but we thought that Reagan felt that he could continue to make a contribution and therefore would run. I think that the reason he held off telling the rest of us about his decision was that he wanted time to make Nancy comfortable with it.

I had responsibility for putting together papers on the issues that might arise at the Platform and recording the President's positions on them. In addition, as we proceeded through the spring, I was to work with the Cabinet Secretaries to develop positive testimony for them before the committee hearings.

I set up a small group in the White House that met on "The Future of the Republic." We identified many issues that needed to be addressed from a policy standpoint. I had the staff thoroughly comb the records of the 1980 campaign and tally every promise Ronald Reagan had ever made. And we did our best to catalogue what he had done on each and every one of them. Joe Wright, the Deputy Director of OMB had a long list of issues both legislative and regulatory that were probably going to pop up during 1984. Each was categorized as Priority 1, 2, or 3 and analyzed for probability of becoming an election issue.

Just about the time that we were getting things off the ground, in January of 1984 William French Smith announced that he was leaving the administration and the President announced his intention to nominate Ed Meese as Bill's replacement at the Justice Department. I was happy for Ed because I knew that Justice, and law enforcement in general, was his life's work and I knew how much he wanted to do it. But again, just as in the Heckler move, I thought to myself, "How come when things seem to be smoothing out, someone has to go and upset the applecart." That probably isn't exactly what I thought, but it will do to show my frustration. I figured that with Ed leaving, he would take Jim Jenkins and Ken Cribb among others, and leave me to deal with the pragmatists on my own.

As it was, Ed wasn't sworn in as the seventy-sixth Attorney General of the United States until a year later. His confirmation was delayed by members of Congress and the media as they mounted personal attacks against him. Ed fought them with his usual resolve, and in the end, after exhaustive investigations by a Special Counsel appointed by the Justice Department, Ed was cleared of all the accusations made against him. But just the accusations themselves and the necessity of taking time to defend himself cut down the time that Ed had to engage in White House business during that year. I think that if he hadn't been nominated to be Attorney General, his detractors would not have gained traction and none of it would have come up. That probably would have been better for the President. On the other hand, if Ed hadn't been so engaged in his defense, I probably wouldn't have been given the latitude and breath of responsibility that I ended up with that year.

The campaign staff had been established and had opened a campaign headquarters in October, even before the President had made or at least announced his decision to run for re-election. He had however, signed the papers authorizing the establishment of a re-election committee and to allow it to spend money. The campaign chairman was to be Paul Laxalt, the Senator and long-time friend of the President. Ed Rollins would be the campaign director and actually run it. Ed had taken over the political shop in the White House as Assistant to the President for Political Affairs when Lyn Nofziger left in 1982. Ed was from California and had come to the White House as a protégé of Lyn's.

Within the West Wing, it became apparent that Jim Baker was taking over responsibility for coordinating the White House and the campaign. Baker and the President specifically told us that we were two distinct entities, the White House and the campaign. We, on the staff, were to continue to perform our jobs and conduct the people's business while the campaign would perform all functions political. When Rollins moved out at the end of 1983, he took the political shop with him. We did not have a political office in the White House again until early in 1985. But that did not stop us from discussing it and from making sure that events that we could control would put the President in the best light. Nineteen eighty-four was full of them and Mike Deaver made sure that they reflected well on the President.

The year started out with a trip to the President's birthplace in Dixon, Illinois. He was met there by his brother "Moon" and they did a nostalgic trip down memory lane. The next big trip was to China in late April with all the great footage of Reagan at the Great Wall and viewing the newly discovered terra cotta soldiers at Xian. On the way back from China, there was a quick meeting with Pope John Paul in Anchorage, Alaska. The Pope was on his way to South Korea.

Then in June, he was off to the Economic Summit in Europe but managed first to stop off in Ireland. He went to Ballyporeen, the little town where his great grandfather had lived when he left Ireland to immigrate to the United States. While there, he stopped at the Ronald Reagan Pub to have a pint with the locals. Lots of camera shots there too. Then it was dinner with the Queen in Buckingham Palace and on to a joint commemoration of the fortieth anniversary of D-Day in France. The pictures of Reagan standing atop the cliff at Point du Hoc were almost as moving as the tale he told of the Rangers who stormed that cliff on June 6, 1944. In 1984, there were over fifty of them who were right there beside him.

In July, Reagan opened the Summer Olympics in Los Angeles with an extravaganza that could only happen in California. And even Jimmy

Carter helped out with that one. Carter had decided that the U.S. would boycott the 1980 Olympics in Moscow in protest of the Soviet invasion of Afghanistan. The Soviets decided in the spring of 1984 that they would boycott the Summer Games in Los Angeles in retaliation. Fifteen other countries, mostly Soviet bloc countries, joined them in the boycott. That was fine with us. It almost guaranteed that U.S. athletes would come away with the bulk of medals from Los Angeles. That is what happened. The United States won 83 gold medals and a total of 174 medals in the XXIII Olympiad. West Germany was second with 59 total medals. When the games ended with Lionel Ritchie singing "All Night Long" all night long, there was the definite feeling around the country that America was back.

Right after I arrived at the White House, Dick Wirthlin, Reagan's pollster, had pointed out an issue that caused some consternation—the so-called gender gap. In every poll, Ronald Reagan did much better with men than he did with women. Reagan was viewed as a "man's man" by the public.

This apparently was causing some concern in the residence because I got a call from Mike Deaver. Mike didn't usually get involved in policy matters, but on this occasion he asked for a meeting. We met in his office, the little one right off the Oval Office. Mike had also asked Nancy Risque to attend. Nancy was the Deputy Assistant to the President for Legislative Affairs but had interests that far exceeded her duties as a legislative liaison. Nancy and I were friends and worked pretty well together. Neither one of us took ourselves too seriously.

Mike wanted us to take charge of the "women's issue." He said that the President's daughter, Maureen was going to working it from the Republican National Committee side and he wanted Nancy and me to coordinate the White House effort to close the "gender gap." That started an almost year long series of events that focused on women and were geared to boost the President's image among women. I had the staff put together a list of gender-based initiatives that the

President had supported or accomplished that benefited women both directly and indirectly. We cited reduction in the "marriage tax penalty," establishment of spousal IRAs, the President's appointment of the Task Force on Legal Equity for Women, many child support provisions that had been enacted, the establishment of a White House Coordinating Council on Women, a Cabinet Council Working Group on Pornography, and a Federal Task Force on Domestic Violence. Plus he had appointed three women to the Cabinet and the first ever female Supreme Court Justice.

Early on, Nancy set up a meeting in my office to which she invited a number of Congresswomen, all of them Republicans. The purpose of the meeting was to address "economic equity issues." The group included Bobbi Fiedler from California, Olympia Snowe from Maine, Lynn Martin from Illinois, and Nancy Johnson from Connecticut. I was a little apprehensive about meeting with them because of the relationship that I had had with several of them while I was at Social Security but Nancy assured me that they would not bite.

We met on several occasions and looked for common ground on what the President could support in the way of legislation. We were finally able to come to some agreement late one Friday in October 1983. We immediately scheduled a meeting for Monday with the President to get his signoff. Barber Conable from New York was the ranking Republican on the House Ways and Means Committee and he had sponsored a bill, the Women's Economic Equity Act, which incorporated many of the things that we had agreed that the President would support. The Treasury Department was scheduled to testify on the bill on Tuesday and we wanted to get the President's decisions before that testimony.

Unfortunately, that was the weekend that a suicide bomber drove an explosive laden truck into the Marine barracks in Beirut, Lebanon. It was not a good time to be meeting with the President. Nevertheless, the meeting took place at 5:00 PM that Monday. Reagan was in a somber mood but he focused on what the group was presenting and agreed to support those provisions of the bill.

The members were happy that he had endorsed the provisions because there was some speculation that he was opposing them. That was not the case, but as so often happened during those years, it was OMB and Dave Stockman who were opposing the bill but Reagan got the blame.

After the meeting, we, the members of Congress, Nancy and I, went into the briefing room to brief the White House press corps on the President's decisions. All of the members were very positive about the meeting with the President and with his decisions on the legislation. Each member made a positive statement with Lynn Martin summing it up by saying, "As a member of the Budget Committee and as a woman, working with the White House has been an experience because they were intense about doing something …" I figured that she must have been talking about Nancy Risque.

The press on the other hand was mostly focusing on the fact that the meeting with members of Congress wasn't included on the President's daily schedule. They saw something sinister in that. I tried to explain that we had only reached an agreement on Friday and had immediately scheduled the meeting. Marlin Fitzwater, the deputy press secretary, said it was just an oversight given the events in Lebanon. They weren't buying it. We didn't get an inch of ink out of the meeting or the effort to change the perception of a gender gap.

We scheduled a lot of events with women that year. We did a Women's Business Conference, a women's basketball team, and the first female graduate of the United States Naval Academy to name a few, just to show the "diversity."

Meanwhile, Maureen was traveling around the country drumming up support. She was like a small tornado. Maureen thought that not enough attention was being paid to elected women officials around the country, particularly Republican elected women. So she set up a series of briefings and lunches for these women during the first part of 1984. Maureen and I got along pretty well, but she was really good friends with Nancy Risque. For whatever reason, whether it was Maureen or Nancy, I was always asked to these lunches as the host of one of the tables. I enjoyed these events because it gave me some perspective that was not tainted by a lifetime in Washington, D.C.

I should mention here, that dining in the State Dining Room is quite an affair whether it is a state dinner or luncheon. The only noticeable difference is the china and the fact that the latter is conducted in daylight. There were usually eleven tables in the State Dining Room. Each table sat ten people close together. Very close together. Sitting at one of those tables gave true meaning to the phrase "rubbing shoulders with." Since I was always the senior person at a table, and usually the only one from the White House, I was the host of the table. At Maureen's lunches I was also the only male at the table.

Meals in the State Dining Room are pretty fancy. The host is always served first. That means that the waiter brings the dish to you and holds it between your head and that of the person sitting on your left, just barely missing your ear lobes. You then retrieve the serving implements from the tray and take a portion of the dish and put it on your plate. Figuring out how to cut/spoon/slice or otherwise dig into the dish usually was fairly easy with the entrees, but some of the dessert concoctions were pretty flamboyant and required a moment's study. Then with either course, extreme caution was needed to move the portion from the plate in your left ear to your plate on the table without dumping some of it in your lap, or worse yet, in your neighbor's lap.

You also had to know which eating implement to use with each course because most people at the table were watching you so they would know what to do. No one wants to make a mistake and look like an everyday American. The most important thing that the host has to do during the meal is to make sure that as soon as the wait staff puts the finger bowl down, you put your hands in it. It doesn't make any difference if you are in the middle of a sentence; get your fingers in that bowl. If you don't, it is a mathematical certainty that one of the nine people at your table is going to think it is soup and put a spoon in it.

One of the luncheons is still quite vivid in my mind. It was one of Maureen's lunches for elected Republican women. I was working in my office when my assistant, Betty Ayers, said that I needed to get over to the residence or I would be late. When I got up to the second or main floor of the residence, I stopped as usual at the white-gloved usher's desk to pick up the little white envelope with my name on it in calligraphy. In the envelope was a little white card with my table assignment for the event. The card just had a number on it designating the table. (I said these were formal events.) The usher recognized me and handed me the envelope. When I opened it and looked at the card, it said "2." I looked at the usher and said, "Two, where's two?" He replied, "Just inside the door Mr. Svahn."

In the State Dining Room, the President sits against the west wall facing east, right in front of the fireplace. He is in the middle of the room with tables to his left and right. There is a table directly in front of his and then a table behind that one against the east wall of the room. That is table 2. It is Mrs. Reagan's table. As I walked into the room I realized this and thought to myself, "Uh Oh." I wondered to whom I would owe thanks for this honor and whether or not I would make it through the lunch. Mrs. R had a pretty tough reputation with the West Wing staff and I was never anxious to test it.

I walked over to the table and proceeded to go around and introduce myself to each of the women sitting there. I apologized for being tardy but no one seemed to care; they were all waiting for the President and Nancy to arrive. We did a little chit-chat and when Mrs. Reagan came in, I got up and went to the opposite side of the table and held her seat for her. We exchanged pleasantries and I went back to my seat. One thing that I forgot to mention about tables in the dining room is that they each have a very large, very beautiful floral arrangement in the center. Table 2 had just such an arrangement so I couldn't see Mrs. Reagan well and vice versa. The President arrived and the meal service began. I spent most of the time talking to the ladies on my left and right with a couple of others occasionally joining in the conversation. Since all of these lunches were for elected women and since the White House represents the highest elective office in the land, the conversations always centered on what it is like to work in the White House. This day was no different. Somewhere between the entree and dessert, one of the women asked me how much time I had for family while working there. I replied that I tried to keep a balance and in fact that very evening I was going home to cook a Chinese dinner for the family. Two or three of them thought that was marvelous and just then, this head leaned out around the floral display and Mrs. Reagan said, "I didn't know that you cooked, Jack." Uh Oh. I was on the radarscope. But the lunch went fine; I survived and went on to eat many meals in the State Dining Room although I never again sat at table 2.

Meanwhile back on the campaign, after Mondale, the Democrats nominee, picked the liberal New York Congresswoman, Geraldine Ferraro, to be his Vice Presidential running mate, we got even more concerned. The polls were not changing; we still had a gender gap. All of the events, policies, and appointments geared toward the gap didn't seem to make a difference. Later in the year, many women's groups endorsed Mondale. Reagan just couldn't understand it. He felt right up until the election that there had to be some mistake; that there was no reason for women not to be favoring him. In the end it didn't make any difference. When people went to the poll that counts, he won forty-nine states.

Another assignment that year involved the so-called Mexico City policy. It is funny when you look at today's news and see an issue that you were involved in twenty-seven years ago and it is still news. In 1984, I got a call from Jim Baker. He wanted me to take over the policy position drafting for a delegation to the International Conference on

Population being held in Mexico City. The President wanted the delegation to be headed by James L. Buckley, the former Senator from New York and the brother of noted conservative and Reagan friend, William F. Buckley, Jr.

Jim Buckley would only lead the delegation if the statement he was to make met his requirements with regard to family planning. The feeling was that by providing federal funds to domestic operations of various family planning organizations, we were freeing up their other monies to be used to provide and promote abortions overseas, particularly Third World countries.

Carl Anderson, on my staff at HHS and in the White House, was thoroughly familiar with the issue and worked well with Buckley's former staffer, Bill Gribben. We added Baker's chief policy guy, Jim Cicconi to the team and after much back and forth and editing drafted a statement that both Buckley and the President could endorse.

When we had a draft of the document, we circulated it to the White House staff for comment. The NSC sent the draft over to the State Department for their comments. I got an immediate call from Ken Dam, the Deputy Secretary of State. He was concerned that the statement was a change in U.S. policy. I told him that the draft was a change and that after receiving comments that we would circulate a final before sending it to the President for decision. State, not liking the draft, leaked it to the media and tried to blame me for doing an "end run" on U.S. foreign policy.

In the end, the statement that the President approved was a strong one. It prohibited federal funding to public and private organizations that promoted or funded abortion in foreign countries. Buckley had been a proponent of just such a statement when he was at the State Department, but had been unable to get it implemented because of intra-departmental in-fighting with the Agency for International Development (USAID).

Buckley delivered the statement in Mexico City that summer. As a result of the policy, many non-governmental organizations lost a good percentage of their funding. Most notable of them was Planned Parenthood, which estimated the decrease in funding at about 20 percent. The statement was immediately dubbed "The Mexico City Policy" by the press and the "Gag Rule" by the pro-choice sector. It was a short intense period of deliberation, but the policy was drafted, Baker accepted it; Buckley was happy and it was in line with the President's position on the issue. I didn't think anything more about it.

Then in January 1993, on the anniversary of Roe versus Wade, the United States Supreme Court decision that legalized abortion in this country, President Clinton rescinded the Mexico City Policy. It had stood for ten years. But the fight wasn't over. On January 22, 2001, President George W. Bush issued an Executive Order *reinstituting* the Mexico City Policy. So for the next eight years Reagan's policy was in effect until President Obama, as one of the first tasks he undertook after his inauguration, issued a new Executive Order rescinding the Bush Executive Order. ABC News captured the current U.S. policy:
"Obama Overturns 'Mexico City Policy' Implemented by Reagan. U.S. Can Now Give Federal Funding to International Family Planning Groups That Provide Abortion Services." Based on its history over the past twenty-five years, it is likely that we have not seen the last of this issue.

We spent 1984 working with many issues to try to shore up the President's standing with the voters while still maintaining a separation between the normal White House operations and the campaign. We had regularly scheduled meetings with Rollins and his deputy Lee Atwater but they basically ran all things political.

We continued to work on the President's environmental image. It was an image that had hounded him since his days in California. Reagan liked to toss off one-liners like his famous quote, "I've signed legislation which outlaws Russia forever. The bombing begins in five minutes." It was delivered for a microphone check during the campaign in 1984. The problem was, the microphone was live. He made the same kinds of remarks about environmental issues. Saying, "A tree's a tree. How many more do you need to look at?" is not a way to endear yourself to most folks. We could kiss off the left wing enviro nuts, but we still wanted to let the rest of America know that Ronald Reagan was an outdoorsman. He respected and enjoyed the outdoors just like most Americans did.

We did several environmental trips that summer including a trip to the Blackwater National Refuge on Maryland's Eastern Shore. The trip followed his call in the State of the Union Speech to clean up the Chesapeake Bay. During the trip, the President met with naturalists and visited the fleet of Skipjacks, the only working sail fleet in America, on Tilghman Island.

While he was there, Lee Verstandig, Assistant to the President for Inter-governmental Affairs, and I met with the three Governors bordering the Bay, Richard Thornburg from Pennsylvania, Chuck Robb from Virginia and Harry Hughes from Maryland to discuss the Bay cleanup. Hughes and Robb were most interested in the issue as it was popular at home. I think that Dick Thornburg was there to protect Pennsylvania. Pennsylvania doesn't actually border the Bay, but the Susquehanna River is the largest tributary to the Bay, carrying pollutants from all of Eastern Pennsylvania's farmland into the Bay. The five of us met in the garage at the Volunteer Firehouse on Tilghman Island. It was kind of humorous. The truck was not there because that was where the limo would bring the President when he finished his tour.

Here were five guys in suits sitting on folding chairs in a circle deciding how to spend the $50 million that the President had committed to start the task. Chuck Robb wanted to know if the President was serious about the cleanup. I told him that the EPA was opening an office in Annapolis, MD; that we were committing $50 million and that Reagan was here on the Bay to show commitment. It seemed to impress all three of them. We had to jump up as the door opened for the Presidential limousine and then we all went into the firehouse to have an Eastern shore lunch done by the Ladies Auxiliary. The traveling press corps thought it was all pretty hokey, but there hasn't been an event that big, before or since, on Tilghman Island.

We tried not to miss a constituency that year. Some of them were tough, the Japanese and the UAW in particular. We instituted the Voluntary Restraint Agreements (VRA) in lieu of quotas against Japanese automobile manufacturers. Even those didn't satisfy the UAW or the Big Three CEOs. Roger Smith of General Motors and I were not friends and Lee Iacocca sat in my West Wing office one evening with uber-lobbyist Bill Timmons and told me that if "you don't do something about the Japs, I am taking my company offshore! Chrysler will not go under." He did. They didn't. Yet. The plight of the farmers, the steel industry, small business, and the elderly—all took up time and effort during the year. We didn't forget anyone or anything.

As August approached, the President, along with the Troika, decided that I should go to Dallas to represent the President at the hearings and deliberations of the Platform Committee. Initially there were to be a number of us including my predecessors, Marty Anderson and Ed Harper. I had never worked the Platform Committee before and I called Marty to see what he was going to do. He told me, "Platforms are for young people." I wasn't sure what he meant.

The Platform Committee meets the week before the convention to hammer out the planks upon which the Party's candidate will run. Depending upon the situation within the party, it can be rather dull and boring or it can be quite feisty. It used to be all closed door with only the party regulars aware of what was going on. With the advent of CNN and particularly C-SPAN, platform deliberations became televised and that required one face for the nation and another for the party. The '84 Platform in Dallas was going to be one of the first to be televised gavel to gavel on C-SPAN. We knew that meant that the deliberations of the committee had to be orderly and deliberate.

Trent Lott, then a congressman from Mississippi, was to be the Platform Committee Chairman. Senator Paula Hawkins of Florida and Governor Kay Orr of Nebraska were Co-Chairs. The Committee Chair rotates between a Member of the House, a Senator, and a Governor. It was the House's turn in 1984 and Trent was running the show. I was really looking forward to going to Dallas because it meant that we were getting closer to the election and hopefully a resumption of the Reagan Revolution. I didn't think that there was going to be much of a fight as Ronald Reagan had run on the Republican Platform in 1980 and there was no reason to think that 1984 should be any different.

The Platform Committee, actually the correct name is the Committee on Resolutions to the Republican National Convention, is a party organization. Frank Farenkopf, then the Chairman of the Republican National Committee asked Drew Lewis, the former Secretary of Transportation, to represent the RNC and the Reagan/Bush campaign at the meeting. Drew had recruited a cadre of political operatives to monitor and work the members as the week was to wear on.

Because the deliberations of the whole committee were to be televised, we decided with Trent that it wouldn't look good to have the White House being the focal point on positions. It couldn't look like we were unduly influencing the Committee. Consequently, Drew and I took up station at a table off to the side of the risers upon which the Committee was perched. There was a stage curtain that separated us from the members of the committee and from the cameras. But we needed a way to be able to communicate with members as to what the Administration's position was on each issue as it came up so we picked one member to be the "signal." He was Stanton Anderson, a long-time Republican lawyer from Washington, D.C. Drew had set up a whip structure with Charlie Black, Kenny Kling and other political operatives to notify members that Stan was our man. When in doubt about how to vote on an amendment, look to Stan who was seated just outside our curtain in the upper-left quadrant and see how he was voting. Vote the same.

Each state plus the District of Columbia, the Virgin Islands, Guam, and Puerto Rico has two delegates on the platform committee so we are talking about a lot of people and a lot of opinions. There are members of Congress, Senators, Governors, state party workers, and other activists. There are no shrinking violets. I naively thought that since we had a very popular sitting President that the deliberations would be pretty tame. I was wrong.

The week started off with hearings and testimony before the seven subcommittees. Ken Cribb from Ed Meese's staff and Paul Simmons from my staff, along with Mike Baroody from the White House communications staff, had come down to help me keep track of things. They and others attended the subcommittee meetings to see what issues were coming up and to alert Drew and me so that we could be ready when a particular issue came to the floor.

The actual draft of a platform had been circulating at the White House since it was put together in early June. By the time we got to Dallas we had seen and commented on two drafts. They had been tightly held and had not been seen by the participants in the hearings and by most of the Committee members. A notable exception was Lowell Weicker, Jr., at the time a Senator from Connecticut. Weicker had been given a draft of the language by Drew for some reason and he announced that he had some twenty amendments that he wanted to introduce at appropriate times. His amendments dealt with abortion and the Equal Rights Amendment among other subjects and Weicker knew that they would be controversial.

Bill Gribben, the editor of the document, was quietly working on the draft skeleton of the platform so that final production would not be held up. If you think about it, a couple of hundred people, some with partying on their minds, coming to town to debate, agree and draw up a document in less than seven days is an awesome task.

The first few days were pretty hectic. Drew was trying to keep things in line, but the Committee members and the hundred or more "kibitzers" had minds of their own. Things started to get out of hand and we didn't want to be too heavy handed. He and I were there to do damage control, to keep things from getting way out of hand. The platform is the Party's document; it is not the President's document. Some conservative pundits heaped abuse on us for not "controlling" the Platform. Right from the start, Trent gave us the "you didn't hire me, you can't fire me, and you don't sign my paycheck" speech and made it clear that he would work with me and with Drew where he could but that some things that we didn't like were going into the document no matter what we said. He couldn't have been clearer about it.

When the Committee met in plenary session, the amendments started to fly. I don't mean literally, but sitting side by side at the table behind the curtain, Drew and I were besieged with people and paper all seeking either the campaigns or White House approval for their introduction. Some of the amendments had already been rejected at the subcommittee level and the proponents knew they didn't have a chance with the full committee, but they were going to try anyway.

The issues were all over the map. I never realized that there were three factions all claiming title to the Republican Party in Puerto Rico—those in favor of statehood, those for independence, and those for the status quo! Maureen Reagan sent me a message; she wanted language put in supporting the ERA and the concept of "comparable worth," a controversial step up from "equal pay for equal work."

Cabinet members were faxing in suggestions and pushing us to get them included in the platform. The scene behind the curtain was pure bedlam. People were handing in handwritten amendments, typed amendments, amendments on napkins, almost any vehicle. Voices were raised and there seemed to be as many people behind the curtain as there were out front. To Drew's credit, he referred all questions and requests for positions of the Administration to me. He spent most of his time trying to make sure that the members knew how we wanted them to vote.

Somewhere in deliberations, Lowell Weicker had gotten Trent Lott to agree that he could bring up the planks that he wanted the Committee to consider. Weicker was joined in proposing a number of amendments by five other Senators so he had some backing from the liberal wing of the party. The Platform Committee, on the other hand, was heavily weighted with conservative party activists and Drew and I knew that Lowell's amendments on abortion and the ERA were going nowhere. Normally, on most floor amendments, we would signal a position that we wanted our people to vote for but when it became apparent that Weicker was going to get some time to introduce his issues, Drew turned to me and said, " I think this would be a good time for you and me to go get a cup of coffee." And that is what we did. Weicker went down in flames. When he put forward his abortion language, Holly Coors from Colorado immediately made a motion to table Weicker's amendment and the voice vote for tabling was strong.

After the commotion had died down, Drew and I were back at the table when the curtain flew open and a really mad Senator from Connecticut came thundering at us. Weicker is a big guy and I thought he was going to come across the table and engage in some physical violence. He was wild, accusing us of having set him up. I was having a tough time keeping a straight face while at the same time telling him that Drew and I were on a coffee break when he was defeated. We didn't have a thing to do with it.[*]

Before the platform deliberations began, a lot of talk was going around the hall about a secret plan that we had to raise taxes in 1985. Nothing could have been further from the truth but even some of our Republican friends were talking about it and it got picked up by the media. Once that happened, it wouldn't go away. Wirthlin was beginning to see where the "secret plan" was gaining traction and we made a decision to knock it down hard and get it behind us.

The President was at the ranch and Jim Baker was with him. Darman was in the White House and I was in Dallas. Darman had the staff put together a draft statement for the President and we jointly edited it by telephone. The President signed off on it and it was released to the press in Santa Barbara and to the Platform Committee on August 12, the day that the committee first met. It didn't leave any room for doubt. He said:

> "I have reduced the tax burden on the American people and I want to reduce it even further. I have no plan to raise taxes nor will I allow any plan for a tax increase. My opponent has spent his political life supporting more taxes and more spending. For him, raising taxes is a *first* resort. For me, it is a *last resort*."

The statement took the wind out of the media's sails. It eliminated the topic in Dallas and the story, per Wirthlin's prediction, went away. It wasn't the unequivocal statement that George H. W. Bush made in 1988—"Read my lips. No new taxes."—but the meaning was the same. President Bush had his statement thrown back in his face when he decided that he had to raise taxes. But when Reagan did likewise in his

---

[*] I agree with Ronald Reagan's assessment of Lowell Weicker: "He's a pompous, no good, fathead."

second term, he was not constantly reminded of his August 12, 1984, statement. It had some "wiggle room" that President Bush's didn't.

In 1988 I did the platform committee at the request of Frank Farenkopf, the head of the Republican National Committee. Frank asked Mike Baroody and me to attend as "senior advisors," or as Judy Van Rest, the Executive Director of the platform committee said, "to provide the gray eminence." It was a lot easier being the gray eminence than it was four years earlier. But it was not without its problems and difficult moments. Several of our nemeses from the '84 platform exercise were there and it is sometimes tough to get otherwise reasonable people to behave reasonably. A case in point.

In 1988, it was a Governor's turn to chair the Committee on Resolutions and that task went to Kay Orr, then Governor of Nebraska. I had met Kay four years before and I had heard good things about her. The co-chair from the Senate was Bob Kasten from Wisconsin and the House co-chair was Jerry Lewis from California. Judy Van Rest, as the Executive Director had the task of keeping all three of them happy while putting together the document. Right from the start, there appeared to be problems, not so much with the process, Bill Gribben was Editor in Chief and Judy had it set up pretty well, but from the standpoint of leadership. The three principals seemed to have separate agendas and Governor Orr didn't seem to know how to mesh them.

It came to a head as the draft was being put together. The Bush campaign was arriving in New Orleans in the evening and John Sununu, Bush's liaison with the Platform Committee and later his Chief of Staff, requested that a copy of the platform draft be made available as soon as he arrived. We were in a meeting and Kay said, "No, he can't have it." She went on to say that they, the campaign, weren't going to tell the Party what went in the document and that no one from the campaign could see it until it was presented to the Party for adoption. Wow!

After the meeting was over, I took Kay aside and explained that there was no uncertainty as to who the candidate was going to be and that it was not unreasonable for the candidate's representatives to look at a draft. I told her that if there was something in there that Bush couldn't live with, it was better to try to fix it now rather than have him repudiate it later—better for the Party, better for the candidate, and better for Governor Kay Orr.

She came around and decided that I and only I could have a copy to share, one on one with Sununu, and that I had to retain possession of the document. I figured that was better than nothing and I told John that I would meet him when he got in that evening in one of the trailers that was used as an office off the convention floor. And that I would have a copy with me. Being a sitting Governor, John knew Kay and was not overly surprised by this development. When he showed up he had a couple of campaign people with him, one of them being Charlie Black. Just after Sununu arrived, Kay came in. I figured she must have been waiting to see how many people came with John. She and Sununu had a discussion about protocol and procedures and Charlie Black suggested that since they knew me and had worked with me, I would make a fine liaison to the campaign and Kay agreed. Blowup averted.

As history shows, the document was adopted and no one was the worse for wear. Judy Van Rest and her deputy, Barb Sido did a great job holding all the disparate pieces together. Late on the last night, the night before the actual convention began, Mike Baroody and I were having a drink at the Hilton and he asked me what I was doing for the convention. I said, "Nothing. I am going home tomorrow." He was surprised but I told him that I had had my convention in 1984; it could only go downhill from there.

The Republican National Convention in 1984 in Dallas was a terrific experience. There was no drama involved; no suspense; just a lot of like-minded (well mostly) people in town to have a good time and send Ronald Reagan on to a second term.

When Jill joined me for the convention, I had already been in Dallas for over a week developing the platform. I was assigned a room on the twenty-fifth floor of the Anatole Hotel upon arrival and didn't think much about the fact that there weren't many others on that floor.

The day after Jill arrived, the Vice President, George H. W. Bush, was scheduled to arrive and there was a large rally planned for him in the hotel lobby. Someone on his advance team asked me if I would represent the President on the welcoming podium as I was the only Assistant to the President in Dallas at that time. I said sure and he gave me the meeting time and place so that I could be introduced to the crowd. In the holding room, there were a lot of people going to be on the "welcoming podium." Jill and I waited our turn and then went up on the podium when introduced. Then the Veep and his delightful wife Barbara arrived; he said a few words and started off the stage and down the steps to work the rope line of cheering fans. I could tell that there was no way for him to get around us in the crowd and since we were closest to the stairs, Jill and I went down before him and stepped to the back of the pathway letting the Veep and Barbara work the line.

As they were doing so, I noticed that a female Secret Service agent was not watching the crowd. Instead, she had her back to Bush and was looking behind us, and she had both hands in the bag! The "bag" being the case in which the agents carried their fully automatic weapons. And when they had both hands in the bag, they were ready to shoot if need be. I saw this and I put my hand in front of Jill and moved her with me out of the way of whatever the agent was looking at. Except, the agent trained the bag on us as we moved! Jill or I was the target. I made eye contact with the agent and very slowly pointed out the security pin on the lapel of my blazer. The pin identified me as "one of the President's men." The problem was, the President was nowhere around there. He was in California. The Vice President was there. My security pin was blue. The Vice President's men had green security pins.

The agent was apparently not regularly on the Vice President's protective detail. She reached out with one hand and tapped another agent. When he turned around, she pointed to my pin. The agent recognized my pin immediately and told her it was OK. She dropped the bag and turned around to the crowd to resume surveillance.

Security was very tight at the convention. It was the first time a big event featuring the President of the United States had been held in Dallas in a long time and a lot of local folks were remembering the assassination of President Kennedy and they didn't want anything to spoil the event. That went double for the Dallas Police Department. Cars were stopped and searched blocks from the convention center. It seemed like there was a law enforcement officer on every corner. It all of a sudden got very personal.

As Jill and I were heading up to our room on the twenty-fifth floor of the hotel after the Vice President's welcoming ceremony, we found that the elevator had been blocked off at the twenty-fourth floor. We were told that we had to go through security on twenty-four and then walk up the stairs to the twenty-fifth. The President was due in later that day and he was staying on twenty-five also.

As we came around the corner, there was a secret service agent cleaning his automatic pistol by our door. He had ammunition all over the carpet and he obviously didn't realize that people were already on the floor. He started scrambling to clean up his workspace. Jill looked stunned. When we got into the room, she looked at me and said, "Those were real bullets." Sometimes you just gotta love 'em.

I assume that it was Mike Deaver working in concert with Nancy Reagan who decided who was going to stay on the twenty-fifth floor of the Anatole Hotel. The occupants looked like they had been picked because they were the safest, not from a security standpoint, but members of the staff who had been around the President for a long time. In addition to the President and Mrs. Reagan there was the President's brother, Neil (or as he liked to be called "Moon") and his wife; Mike and Carolyn Deaver; Ed and Barbara Hickey, Ed and Ursula Meese, Lee and Toni Verstandig and us plus a few personal staff. It was a very pleasant and comfortable group.

The convention was a week-long series of parties and evening sessions. As an Assistant to the President, I had full access to everything from the convention floor to the President's personal skybox. There really wasn't a lot of work done during the week. We had a full complement of staff in Dallas but it was as if the whole country had gone on a vacation for that week. The President's acceptance speech had been drafted by Ken Khachigian, in late July and the President had pretty much put it to bed the week before he was to deliver it.

On August 23, the night that the President accepted the nomination, we were sitting with the rest of the senior staff and their spouses looking out over the convention floor and watching history be made. NBC had set up a camera in front of Jill and me and all night long the little red light would periodically go on and Jill's sometimes smiling, sometimes teary face would be beamed around the world. Dick Darman, sitting just below us wanted to know who I had paid at the network for the extensive coverage.

After the convention, it was back to work. It was interesting how the President approached the campaign. He would go out and do events that Rollins and the campaign had set up for him and come right back into the Oval Office and pick up like he had never left. Of course, much of that can be attributed to traveling staff and up to date communications, but mostly I think it was just the way Reagan was. When he was running for reelection for Governor in California, he had done the same thing. He split his time between campaigning and running the state and he had a staff for each. He expected each staff to do its job and not interfere with the others.

That is the way it was in 1984. I continued to work on farm problems, steel problems, automobile problems, savings and loan problems, the elderly, the environment, the plight of small business, the fairness of the tax code, productivity, and planning for a domestic agenda for the second term. There was plenty to do without getting involved in the day to day activity of the campaign. When Reagan would return from a campaign trip, he was always in a good mood. The crowds, thousands of cheering, adoring Americans, could always bolster his spirits. As the year wore on, the rest of us were dragging but Reagan was happy—always looking for that pony.

The one downer in 1984 happened the evening of October 7 in a theater hall in Louisville, Kentucky. It was the first debate with Walter Mondale and it was on domestic policy. My debate.

Much has been said and written about that first debate with Mondale. It is clear that Mondale came out the winner. I was sitting just off the stage in a little room with Baker, Laxalt, Darman, Larry Speakes, and Stu Spencer, Reagan's longtime political advisor, when the debate concluded. The Mondale team was in the room next to us and they erupted into cheers. The "Louisville Slugger"* as his staff tried to brand him, was born. We were not so happy. Darman quickly said, "He did fine," but we all knew that was not the case. I jumped up and headed out the door and around the corner to the stage thinking there was something that I could do. I came head-on into the President and Mrs. Reagan as they came off the stage. I said, "You did great Mr. President!" He just looked at me and said, "No. I didn't." Nancy just looked shocked—or mad.

When we went back to the hotel, five or six of us went down to the spin room and tried to downplay what we all thought was a disaster. And right away, the knives came out to see who could pin the blame on whom. There is no question that the President was over-prepared for the debate. By general public acclamation, the blame fell on Dick Darman. Dick was not to blame. We all were. Baker, Meese, Deaver,

---

* Louisville is the home to Hillerich & Bradsby Co., the company that has been making baseball bats for major league ball players since 1884. Their signature bat is the "Louisville Slugger."

Darman, Fuller, Stockman, and Svahn. We all participated in the preparation of the President and we should have all shared the blame.

Years later after reading Paul Laxalt's memoir, I wrote Paul and told him that I thought his criticism of Darman was not well founded and that I thought Stockman deserved more of the blame. Paul wrote back acknowledging that Stockman may have been the culprit and that maybe "the folklore developed concerning Darman." The only one that I have seen who publicly acknowledged some responsibility for the poor performance was Jim Baker in his memoir. As Chief of Staff, of course he couldn't have denied responsibility unless he wanted to admit that he wasn't doing his job. But the only one who took full responsibility for the poor performance was Reagan himself.

The debate preparation for Louisville was much the same as that done for the 1980 debates with Jimmy Carter. Even down to where Stockman, who had played Carter in 1980 played the role of Walter Mondale in the six mock debates that we held prior to Louisville. It is true that Darman scheduled the times, Mike Baroody, Larry Speakes and I asked the questions, and Stockman played a brutal Fritz Mondale. The last practice session was up at Camp David in the Catoctin Mountains of Maryland.

For that session, we took a helicopter from the Vice President's residence up to Camp David and spent the day with the President. Everyone was there. The Veep, Nancy, Paul Laxalt, Stu Spencer, Dick Wirthlin, and those of us on the staff had been involved with the preparation to that point. The President was out horseback riding when we got there and set up Laurel Lodge for the mock debate. When he came into the room where the practice was to take place, Mike Baroody and I were at the debate podiums putting on a mock debate for the assembled crowd using Reagan/Mondale hand puppets. He laughed at the scene and seemed in a good humor, with no sign that he was concerned about the upcoming debate.

The practice went on for a couple of hours the same as the previous ones had. Stockman just ripped at the President, challenging each of his answers and attacking whenever he could. He couldn't have been more different than Mondale was in the real debate. Reagan was a very competitive person and throughout the preparations, he had tried to match Stockman's facileness with numbers and statistics. It would have been a tough task for any person to match Stockman when it came to numbers and statistics. As I look back on it though I think Stockman's approach and demeanor was more a case of Dave Stockman trying to show everyone how smart he was and how dumb Ronald Reagan was rather than trying to help Reagan prepare. Whatever it was, none of the rest of us recognized the effect that the whole process was having on Reagan. And because of that, none of us spoke up and tried to change the preparations. The night of the Louisville debate we all recognized it.

We spent the night in Louisville at the Hyatt Regency and boarded Air Force One the next morning to return to Washington. On the way, we made a stop in Charlotte, North Carolina for a campaign rally with Senator Jesse Helms who was up for re-election. There were thousands of cheering people at that rally, enough to bolster most people's spirits, but they did little for Reagan on that day. He was still quite depressed about the debate and it showed. His speech in Charlotte was flat as a pancake but the crowd didn't seem to notice or care. We left the cheering crowd behind and headed for Andrews Air Force Base.

At Andrews, we were going take a quick jaunt up to Baltimore to dedicate a statue of Christopher Columbus on the waterfront in Baltimore's Little Italy. I was going to quit the trip in Baltimore. Jill and the kids were going to meet me at the dedication and we would head home from there.

The schedule had me riding in Nighthawk 3, the staff helicopter along with Darman, Hickey, John Poindexter, and Stu Spencer. When the President is flying on Marine One, a few staff goes with him, the rest fly on Marine choppers which are not so opulent and are very noisy. When I ran up the ramp into Nighthawk 3, I saw that a friend of mine, Congresswoman Marjorie Holt, was already onboard. Marjorie was the Congresswoman who represented the district in which I lived and she was the ranking minority member on the House Armed Services Committee. More importantly on this day, she was the Chairwoman of the Reagan/Bush Committee for Maryland. She was sitting with Roger Stone, a partner of Charlie Black's, and the Reagan/Bush campaign coordinator for the East Coast. I said hi to them both and asked Roger how it was going. He unloaded on me. "How do you think its going? I'm sitting here with the Chairman of Reagan/Bush for Maryland and she is pissed!" I asked him why and he seemed a little put out that I needed an explanation. "She is mad because she is on this helicopter and not on Marine One."

They hadn't started the engines yet and Darman and I ran out the back ramp and over to Marine One. We quickly explained the situation to Mike Deaver. Deaver never hesitated; he got off Marine One and came over to Nighthawk 3. We put Marjorie on Marine One and I had made two people very happy—Holt and Stone.

During the motorcade from Ft. McHenry where the helicopters always landed when we visited Baltimore to the site in Little Italy, the streets were lined with well wishers and people cheering the President. As we zoomed along through the streets of Baltimore, I was waving at the crowd. Most of us on the staff, if we weren't engaged in some discussion, would wave back to the crowds when traveling in the motorcade. We knew that the crowd didn't know who we were but they were waving anyway and I always thought that they deserved a wave back. As we went fairly slowly by the restored inner harbor, I found myself waving at Jill and the children who were standing on the sidewalk! After the event was over, we found each other and drove home.

The next critical event in the campaign was the Vice President's debate against Congresswoman Geraldine Ferraro. This debate took place in Philadelphia between the two Reagan/Mondale debates. Gerry Ferraro was the first female candidate on either of the two major party's national ticket. As such, she was creating a lot of commotion in the media. I had known her when I was at Social Security and knew that she was a tough-speaking New Yorker.

To get the Vice President prepared to debate her, we had several of the same kind of practices that we had for Reagan. The major difference was that we used someone other than Stockman to be the opponent. Bush's practice opponent was Lynn Martin, a sharp Congresswoman from Illinois. Lynn knew Gerry pretty well and did a good job of imitating her in the practice sessions. I was the moderator in the practice sessions. I announced the rules and tried to keep the practices pretty much in line with what would happen in the real thing.

Bush was nervous about debating a woman and he was getting a lot of advice from a lot of people. Basically, we wanted him to be respectful, but to treat Ferraro just like he would treat any opponent on the national stage. The concern that his advisors had was that he would come across as condescending to the feisty woman from New York. His nervousness peaked during one practice session when I tried to enforce the agreed upon time limit on one of his answers. He became exasperated and rebuked me, letting me know for sure that he was the Vice President and he was going to take as long as he wanted to answer the question.

The debate itself was almost anti-climatic. Bush did well, only making one reference to Ferraro that seemed to raise the hackles of the pundits. She took full advantage of it and attacked as we believed that she would, but it didn't stick. Bush came out of it well ahead of the game, and it took some of the pressure off for the second Reagan/ Mondale debate.

The second debate against Mondale was held in Kansas City two weeks later. A different Ronald Reagan showed up for this one. He was his old self again. The preparation for this debate had been less intense than that for the first debate. Only a couple of rehearsals plus Nancy and Maureen had been working on him to relax. He knocked the ball out of the park when a reporter from the *Baltimore Sun* raised the issue of his age and stamina. Reagan responded to him, "Not at all, Mr. Trewhitt, and I want you to know that also I will not make age an issue of this campaign. I am not going to exploit, for political purposes, my opponent's youth and inexperience." Even Mondale had to laugh. We didn't know it then, but the race was over.

On November 1, I stood on the South Lawn waving goodbye as Marine One lifted off carrying the President on his last campaign swing before Election Day. He was going to crisscross the country for the next five days, ending the campaign in San Diego, California, the same place that the 1980 campaign ended. On election night Reagan won forty-nine states. We only lost Minnesota by the smallest of margins and Ed Rollins swears that if we had made one more stop there we would have won Mondale's home state. We did not win the District of Columbia either but that was a foregone conclusion. He got 59 percent of the popular vote and carried a whopping 525 electoral votes.

After the election we began to flesh out the second term agenda that we had sketched during the campaign. The year ended with a never ending series of budget meetings, most of them with the President. Ed Meese had decided that what was needed was a line by line review of all spending with an eye towards cutting where we could. Stockman was the chief staff person involved in putting together the material. Dave didn't have much use for either Ed or me in reviewing the budget, but because the President was involved, he had to go along with it. We made many recommendations between the election and the end of the year for budget reductions. In most instances, cabinet members accepted them without appealing the decisions to the President.

One other thing happened before the end of the year. A meeting was scheduled for December 14 on "Personnel" in the Ward Room of the White House Mess. The Ward Room was a little dining room in the Mess that could be reserved for group sessions. Every so often I used it to host a breakfast for the heads of independent agencies there. Many of them never got to come to the White House on any other occasion.

This particular morning I showed up at the appointed time and found John Herrington, the personnel director, Craig Fuller, the Cabinet Secretary, Joe Wright, the Deputy at OMB and I think Dick Darman all sitting around the table. Herrington ran through the agencies and the possible resignations, vacancies, and problem areas. It was fairly predictable—Jim Webb, then at the Navy, wanted the Veterans Administration; a Deputy had been selected at HUD—not Sam Pierce's candidate; maybe one of my staff, Randy Davis to take over EPA; we have two candidates for Education and need to pick one. Then the main subject of the personnel meeting was taken up and it turned out to be Margaret Heckler. They were developing a plan to get rid of her.

Ever since our unusual relationship began, I had been the subject of numerous news articles as having it out for Heckler. Most of them were put out by her handpicked staff. I knew she was making a shambles out of the department, but she was President Reagan's incumbent and I wasn't going to spend any time sniping at her. It wasn't good for my President so I was constantly trying to knock the news stories down. I told the guys in the Ward Room that I was not part of a conspiracy to get rid of her. They said I didn't have to be; the plan was to be simple. They were going to give her the "Haig treatment." I didn't know what that was and asked.

I was told that when Al Haig fell out of favor, the staff had dreamed up a scheme to get him replaced. Haig did not like his Deputy, Bill Clark and Clark had moved out of State and was serving as the National Security Advisor. The plan was to call Haig over to the Oval Office and have the President tell him that there was concern about his management of the Department and that he, Ronald Reagan was in charge of foreign policy and that he was sending Bill Clark over to the State Department to review what Haig was doing. When Haig objected and said he couldn't work under those circumstances, the President accepted his "resignation" on the spot and put out a press release. I don't know if this is how it really happened and everything you read about Haig's "resignation" seems confused enough that it could have happened that way.

This plan, the group told me, was similar. First, the various White House units would develop papers detailing the problems at HHS, the budget, personnel, relationships with Congress, etc. Heckler would be brought over to the Oval Office and told by the President that he had concerns about the reports of mismanagement going on at HHS and that he was ordering a management study of the department. He was going to tell her that I would head up the team that he was sending over there. Prior to her visit, a press release would be drafted announcing that the President had accepted her resignation. When she protested my being assigned to evaluate her tenure in the department, any indication that she wouldn't stay would result in the release of the press release. She would in effect not know that she had "resigned" until after it had happened.

I didn't realize it, but at the time there were a lot of people gunning for Heckler; so many in fact that they really didn't need me in the mix.

The Presidential Personnel Office (PPO) had put together a six page scathing indictment of her mismanagement at HHS. It outlined how she had reneged on her original agreement regarding departmental management; documented the exodus of Reaganites from the department; highlighted the large number of management positions that were vacant in HHS and explained how Heckler had thwarted PPO's attempts to recruit qualified candidates. PPO said of Heckler:

> "She seems to resist making decisions and delegating authority. She also seems to resist wanting knowledgeable, experienced people who have demonstrated support for the President's policies and budgetary goals. ... she has moved away from the concept of team work in managing the Department to the point of major communication breakdowns with key White House staff members; resistance to all personnel, policy and budget ideas not developed by her or her people; destructive management flaws which paralyze the President's overall initiatives as they relate to HHS; and vacancies and making budget decisions."

In the same paper when discussing my former position of Commissioner of Social Security, which had been really vacant since my departure in March of 1983 some twenty months before, PPO said that they had identified and sent to HHS over thirty-five highly qualified candidates to fill the position. Several of these candidates had been presented to Heckler for approval. One of them, the Chairman of a large publicly held corporation reported back to PPO that Heckler had told him that he was "overqualified for the position." The candidate was flabbergasted and expressed his dismay to PPO about the comment. Needless to say, he didn't take the position.

At the conclusion of the meeting, I told the assembled group that as long as everyone understood that I was not clamoring for her head, I would be glad to lead the review team. And that's how 1984 ended.

Chapter 17

Reagan's Biggest Mistake

On Tuesday morning January 8, 1985, I was sitting in my office in the West Wing thinking about the upcoming State of the Union speech and sifting through possible domestic initiatives for the second term. We had many ideas put together by the staff in the Office of Policy Development, but nothing with a global sweep.

Marty Anderson once told me that I had the toughest job in the administration because the major thrust of the Reagan Revolution, domestically, had taken place before I arrived at the White House. As I think back on it, I spent the first sixteen months of my tenure in the White House primarily reacting to activity generated by outside forces. The only domestic initiatives that we had underway were the development of a tax reform proposal, a department by department review of spending, and a comprehensive study of the welfare program.

The tax reform study was being run out of the Treasury Department by Secretary Regan. My role was to represent the President on Regan's task force. The spending review was being done in the White House with the President sitting in on the sessions. The welfare reform effort was being run directly out of my office. I had convinced the President and Ed Meese that the second term was the time to "end welfare as we know it," just like the second term in Sacramento. In 1981 we did most of the things that we thought needed to be done with the current program, the Aid to Families with Dependent Children Program. Bob Carleson at the White House had successfully gotten the changes enacted in the Omnibus Budget and Reconciliation Act of 1981 and Linda McMahon on my staff at Social Security had very quickly implemented them. But that was just the tip of the iceberg at the federal level. There were so many more programs and agencies involved that we thought that only a White House led effort could succeed.

Sitting there in my office on that Tuesday morning I felt very confident about the President's second term and my ability to contribute to its success. Then my phone rang. It was Ken Cribb, Ed Meese's assistant. Kenny said that Ed wanted me to hustle down to his office right away. When I walked into Ed's office, Ken was there with Bruce Chapman. Bruce had been the Commissioner of the Census before he came over to the White House on the OPD staff and was a good conservative. They were both giggling and I thought that I had been had. Ken had broken out a bottle of sherry and was in the process of pouring "a toast." Now working in the White House has driven a lot of people to drink, the author included, but not at ten o'clock in the morning.

When I asked what was up, Ken gleefully told me that the President was at that very moment walking into the press briefing room and announcing that Jim Baker, the Chief of Staff, and Don Regan, the Secretary of the Treasury were "swapping jobs." He said we were finally getting rid of the pragmatists in the West Wing. There wasn't anything like that on the President's schedule and I guess the look on my face caused Cribb and Chapman to come up short. I told them, "I'm not going to toast that. It's a disaster." I said, "You guys don't know Regan."

I had known Regan from the early days at Social Security. He was the "managing trustee" of the Social Security Trust Funds and I had had several run-ins with him during the financing fight. After I moved over to the White House, I had breakfast with Don once a week and usually saw him at Cabinet meetings or meetings of the Cabinet Council on Economic Affairs (CCEA). I had also participated as a member of the Task Group on Regulation of Financial Services which was chaired by Vice President Bush and had Regan as a Vice Chairman.

I never understood why Baker agreed to the swap. I guess it was just because he was tired of the West Wing and had to get out of there. One thing that I knew for sure about Regan; he was no staff guy and he was not shy about letting everyone know it. I knew the President and I knew Regan and I knew that this wasn't going to work. And I told Ken and Bruce just that.

My impression of Don Regan was that he was a blowhard; the type of guy who as a youngster was the bully of the playground. But also, like the bully, when really confronted would turn tail and run. He had a lot of money and lorded it over people who didn't. He once told me that my problem was that I didn't have "FUM" and he did. I had heard him use the challenge on others before he used it on me so it didn't have much of an impact. "FUM" per Don's definition was "Fuck You Money"; you used it when you didn't like what was going on. He had an ego that wouldn't quit.

As you might expect, the announcement hit the White House like a bombshell. Ed Meese was still embroiled in defending himself against the wild accusations that had been made against him and would probably be heading over to Justice as the Attorney General once it was all over. Mike Deaver was reputed to want to leave and make money on the outside as a government affairs professional and now Baker and presumably Darman would be leaving.

Interestingly, in his diary, the most telling comment that President Reagan made about the swap was that it hadn't leaked to the press. He made the decision on Monday the seventh and announced it the morning of Tuesday the eighth and he was very pleased that the three of them had kept the secret. It is not surprising that it didn't leak; three of the biggest leakers in the Administration, Regan, Baker and Darman, were personally involved in the outcome.

It is also interesting that Reagan didn't think much about the swap; he actually thought that it might solve some problems. That attitude was really indicative of how Reagan viewed the staff in general. When I finally told the President that I would be leaving the staff, he said what I had heard him tell fifty staff people during the years that I worked for him. "Well, OK." When I got back to my office, I called Jim Jenkins, a long-time Reaganite who had left the White House and moved back to Sacramento. Jim had been sort of a mentor to me over the years and I needed to tell someone that I had resigned. He asked me, "What did the old man say?" I asked him, "What do you think he said?" Jim replied, "I liked that one. Call Central Casting and get me another one just like him!" There was probably more truth than jest in his comment.

I was still walking around wondering to myself why in the world the President would do this, break up the winning team when I ran into Marlin Fitzwater. Marlin had been at Treasury before coming over to the White House Press Office. He was a career federal employee who had worked in a number of agencies and had a good reputation as a straight shooter. Marlin had moved over to the White House in 1983 like me and he served as the Deputy Press Secretary for Domestic Affairs. I liked Marlin and we worked pretty well together. Marlin was not one to use a lot of words when just a few would convey a message. I asked Marlin what he thought and he just rolled his eyes up in his head and laughed. I got the impression that he knew that this was not going to be a pleasant experience for any of us. As it turned out, Fitzwater left shortly thereafter to be the Press Secretary for the Vice President. I never asked him, but it sure seemed like Marlin was doing his best to stay out of the way of Donald Regan.

The swap wasn't to take place until after Jim Baker was confirmed as Secretary of the Treasury but folks started to jump ship almost immediately. Craig Fuller, a good friend and Cabinet Secretary became the Vice President's Chief of Staff. Fitzwater went over there as Press Secretary and John Herrington, the Personnel Chief worked himself into being Secretary of Energy.

In the meantime, all of the Assistants to the President were requested by Regan to put together transition papers outlining their current job, plans for 1985, issues that were likely to come up, and the like. We were also informed that we would each be interviewed by Regan presumably to see whether he wanted to keep us on or not. My personal staff was a little nervous about what was going to happen; I sensed this particularly in my two assistants, Betty Ayers and Jan Farrell, because if I were replaced, they would probably have to go too.

We put together a ton of transition material for Regan but just as in the 1980 Transition; most of it went unnoticed and unused. Regan's staff called and set up an appointment for our meeting. It was being done in Don's office. When the time came for me to go over to Treasury for my "interview" with Don, I had pretty well decided that I would move on whether in government or in the private sector. After I had waited in the outer office for an appropriate amount of time, I was ushered in and was surprised to see that we were going to do a "one on one" meeting without any witnesses or observers.

We exchanged pleasantries for awhile. Don had always impressed me with his knowledge of Wall Street and the economy and it was fascinating to hear him talk about it. But on this day he got right down to business. He asked me "I suppose that you want to stay?" I think he was a little surprised when I replied, "Not necessarily." I guess he figured that I would be begging to remain in my job or maybe that is what had happened with those staff who had already been interviewed by him. He asked me what I meant and I told him that whether or not I stayed depended on what he and the President had in mind for me to do. I told him that I was comfortable either way.

In addition to thinking himself an authority on the economy, Don Regan also fancied himself as quite a salesman. And I think that at that moment he felt some need to "sell" me on the idea of staying in the West Wing. We talked about his concept of a more organized structure. He felt that the troika was too diffused with no accountability and he wanted to establish clear lines of authority and responsibility. He was very critical of the "White House staff" and felt that all during the first term that the President had been undermined and underserved by all of the "leaks" and discord that came out of the West Wing. He said that he wasn't a proponent of the Cabinet Council system notwithstanding the fact that during the previous four years, as the pro tem head of the Cabinet Council on Economic Affairs, he had held more Cabinet Council meetings than the rest of them combined. He felt that the system took up too much of the President's time and wasted the time of Cabinet members who could otherwise be managing their departments.

He said that he hadn't settled on a firm structure for the staff yet and he asked me for my ideas. I explained that I thought we needed a simpler structure, with one office in charge of domestic policy and one in charge of national security. Don seemed to understand and he offered me the domestic policy portfolio. We talked for a while and he said he wanted me to stay. He asked me to go back and lay out a scenario that I thought would work. He talked a good game. I said, "OK."

As our meeting broke up, I said that there was one other thing that he should know. I told him that we had a plan going into place to get Heckler out, referring to the meeting that we had had in the wardroom in December where I agreed to head up the management review team on HHS. When I told him about it, he hit the roof. He said, "You leave her to me! That woman is a disgrace! I'll take care of her myself." As I walked out the door I thought to myself that the Heckler problem was solved and that I didn't have to participate in the execution. Little did I know.

Don was very active in the period leading up to his first day on the job. He recruited Pat Buchanan, the conservative author and media figure to be Director of Communications and he got Max Freidersdorf, who had led the legislative fight during Reagan's successful first year, to return as Assistant to the President for Legislative Affairs. He rounded out his recruitment by bringing Ed Rollins back to the West Wing as Assistant for Political and Intergovernmental Affairs. Rollins had successfully led the 1984 reelection effort. He also convinced Bud MacFarlane to stay on as National Security Advisor and Larry Speakes as Press Secretary.

He did a series of on the record interviews and in February right after assuming the job of Chief of Staff, he announced that he was setting up a more structured West Wing with five key Assistants to the President, Buchanan for communication, Freidersdorf for legislative affairs, MacFarlane as National Security Advisor, Rollins as political and intergovernmental, and me as domestic policy advisor. He said that there would be more accountability in the office; more definition to the roles each person would play; less distraction caused by internal struggles that had existed in the first term; and generally a more cohesive organization to serve the President. It was all BS.

Reorganizing the domestic side of the White House operation was not a new topic however. Shortly after Ed Meese's nomination to be Attorney General was announced, Ed asked Craig Fuller and me to give some thought as to how the White House domestic operation should be organized in the event that the President decided not to appoint someone as a replacement for Ed. Both Craig and I had expressed some level of frustration over the duplication and overlap that existed between the Office of Cabinet Affairs and the Office of Policy Development. We had previously suggested to Ed that some consolidation and streamlining of functions should occur but he had hesitated and decided in the end to do nothing. His leaving and the departure of David Gergan provided an opportunity to relook at the situation.

Some of the incentive to reorganize the domestic side of the house at that time was generated by the conservative community. As soon as Ed's nomination was announced, a firestorm erupted in the conservative community over a concern that the "pragmatists" in the West Wing were taking over. The conservatives coalesced around a candidate to replace Ed, the beer baron, Joe Coors. Joe was a long-time friend of the President's and was very active in conservative causes. The campaign to "Let Coors be Meese" (a play on the conservative's mantra to "Let Reagan be Reagan") and "Coors to You Ron" grew very rapidly and pitted long-time friends and colleagues against each other. Apparently, with support from Ed, Jim Baker, and Mike Deaver, the President had decided not to replace Ed. Urging him to do so was most of the kitchen cabinet, all long-time friends and supporters.

I put together a plan for Ed that basically split up the operation into two offices. In mine I had the Office of Policy Development, the Office of Cabinet Affairs, the Office of Planning and Evaluation, the Office of Drug Abuse Policy, and a new Office of Special Projects. In my plan, Craig Fuller was to take over all of the external contacts including the Office of Public Liaison, the Office of Private Sector Initiatives, the Office of Public Affairs, the Office of Communications, and the Office of Media Relations. We didn't recommend any changes to the Cabinet Council system. As so often happened during the first term, the plan leaked and John Lofton of the *Washington Times* did a column on it. Lofton reported that the Meese job was being abolished and the duties would be split between Craig and me. It was enough to cool the ardor of those pushing Joe Coors and no reorganization occurred. We maintained the status quo during the campaign year.

But in January of 1985, as part of the "getting to know you" phase, Regan asked me for my thoughts on West Wing organization. In doing so, he said that he felt that the current Cabinet Council system was too cumbersome, with a lot of overlap, and consumed too much of the President's time.

Feeling that we were in agreement on what needed to be done, I sent Don a memo on January 23, two weeks before he was to come over to the new job. In that memo I outlined the current structure and proposed reducing the seven Cabinet Councils to four and proposed a system similar to the National Security Council's National Security Decision Directive (NSDD) system to ensure that the President's decisions would be documented, communicated, and implemented.

We met a second time over at Treasury and fleshed out our agreement. Don agreed that OPD and OCA needed to be consolidated and that we needed to reduce the number of Cabinet Councils and other inter-departmental bodies that demanded the President's time. We settled on two councils, a Domestic Policy Council (DPC) and an Economic Policy Council (EPC). I was to be an ex-officio member of both. We quickly agreed that Baker, as Secretary of the Treasury would head up the EPC in the absence of the President. The DPC on the other hand required some finesse. I wanted Ed Meese to head it up. My rationale was that the Attorney General provided services to all of the Departments of the federal government and was the only department whose reach stretched to all domestic issues. My real reason for pushing for Ed was that I was concerned that we would lose his input and clout as he got more involved at the Department of Justice. Don finally agreed that Ed would head up the new Domestic Policy Council. That was just about the last thing during our relationship upon which we agreed.

As part of his transition, Regan brought over some of his staff from Treasury to serve in the White House. Baker had taken Darman and several other people with him to Treasury, Meese was taking his staff to Justice, Fuller and Fitzwater went to the Vice President's staff so there were a number of vacancies available for Regan to fill. As fast as he could Regan brought in people who were more loyal to him than they were to Ronald Reagan. He wanted people around him who would be "yes" men. The President wanted people who would give him their unvarnished opinions; Don wanted people who wouldn't buck him. And that is what he got; but it wasn't what he started out with.

Regan put off announcing any of the changes we had agreed to and every time I talked to him about it, he dissembled. First he wanted me to discuss it with one of the staff people he had brought from Treasury who he wanted to be the Cabinet Secretary. I met with the person and went over the agreement that Regan and I had reached. After the meeting I sent Regan a second package on February 19 with the agreed organization chart, a staffing plan, and a draft memorandum to the President making the case for a domestic policy directive system. Regan then wanted to hear what my deputy, Roger Porter thought about the structure. Roger had been with Regan for the first four years of the Administration as the Executive Secretary of the Cabinet Council on Economic Affairs. I thought it somewhat odd and realized that Regan was just stalling. I gave the plan to Roger and asked for his comments. His response to me was

> "The memorandum on "Organizational Structure for the Domestic Policy
> Function" outlines a number of changes that are absolutely essential."

On April 4 I resent the package to Regan with a note indicating that I had tried to see him on several occasions but had been rebuffed by his staff. I ended the note with

> "I would like to discuss organization and staffing with you as soon as you
> have time. I would be glad to come out to Santa Barbara next week if you
> like. Or I'll polish up my old Wilson staff irons. Or I'll be your caddy."

I got no response. Finally, on June 11, 1985, five months after we first started discussions, I got an unsigned note from Regan that said:

> "This is my own way of describing how I think we could set up your re-
> sponsibilities and those of (the Cabinet Secretary). I realize I have tarried
> quite a bit on this."

Attached to the note was a "preliminary draft" of Responsibilities and Staffing that repudiated the agreements that we had verbally made during discussions. I quickly replied

"The draft is in contradiction to our original agreement and subsequent discussions regarding domestic policy organization in the White House."

It was in the follow up meeting to our memo exchange that I learned by observation that Donald T. Regan did not like confrontation unless he was the confronter. Like the bully in the schoolyard, when a bullied kid stood him up, he ran. All of the talk and hyperbole about Regan as a decision maker and running the White House in a corporate fashion was just talk. He and I had a confrontation. He backpedalled some but in the end it was apparent to me that he was going to have his way with the organization and keep it bifurcated. It was also apparent that I could be "the last Californian in the West Wing" as long as I wanted to but without the portfolio that we had previously developed. I thought about going to the President but I realized that would be a futile gesture. Reagan routinely ducked personnel issues; at times it was almost like he didn't understand what was going on.

I was certain then that Regan was going to be a failure. He just didn't have the temperament or the capacity to be a staff guy. He wanted to be the boss. When the appointment was announced, I knew that the President was making a big mistake by making Don Regan the Chief of Staff. Even I didn't know at that point just how big a mistake he was going to prove to be.

Chapter 18

A Different West Wing

Life with Don Regan as Chief of Staff was difficult. Not only for me, but for just about anyone in the White House who wasn't brought in by Don or who refused to genuflect to him, morning, noon, and night. It was disastrous to have to sit there day after day and watch Regan ruin what Reagan had done for the country. Right from the day he took over, Regan tried to put his imprint on the White House. He didn't try to change any policies of Reagan; he was more concerned with his own position and the perception of it by the media. Many stories appeared in the media about what an organized person he was and how he was going to run the White House in a systematic, corporate manner. Most of it was the product of the Regan, Inc.* leaking machine.

One of Regan's first big tasks was to get the Congress to authorize continued funding for the MX missile system. There was strong sentiment on both sides of the issue in Congress and it wasn't totally partisan. Some Democrats felt the program should be continued and some Republicans were against further funding. Nowhere was the split closer than in the House of Representatives. I didn't normally insert

---

* "Regan Inc." was the headline on a cover of *Business Week* magazine, which featured a photo of Regan in 1985. It was a reference to Don and his minions.

myself in matters that were purely defense or foreign policy—except for matters involving Canada, Mexico and various trade issues. But I got involved in the MX fight quite by accident.

In the early 1980s the agricultural sector of the economy was suffering. Prices were down and drought conditions existed in several areas of the country. Family farmers were losing their farms and the 1981 farm bill had reduced several government subsidies and price supports. It was a problem that I had been working on ever since arriving at the White House. Governors in farm states were keen to get some relief.

The Chairman of the House Agriculture Committee was E. (Kika) de la Garza, a Democrat from Texas. I had met with the Chairman on a few occasions, looking for common ground. During a meeting with the Governor's of Iowa and Montana I was interrupted by a phone call from Chairman de la Garza. I answered jokingly and told him that I was right then meeting with some Governor's on the subject of agriculture. He responded quickly and directly. "Screw agriculture! I'm talking the MX vote. I call you and the President calls me. I call Lehman (then Secretary of the Navy) and he doesn't return my calls. The MX vote is coming up and Ortiz and I can tie the vote and let O'Neill break the tie." I was really taken off stride and asked him why he was calling me. He replied because I was the only one in the White House who would take his calls! I asked what he wanted and he said, "Me and Ortiz want a Navy homeport in Corpus Christi! It's difficult to go against the leadership; it's easier to go with them. Tell the President that we are undecided but I don't feel that I can support the Administration." He was really worked up and he said he was mad also because Regan wouldn't return his calls.

I called John Poindexter, at that time the Deputy National Security Advisor and relayed my conversation with Kika. Kika got the concessions he wanted and we won the MX funding on a razor thin vote. We needed both de la Garza and Ortiz. That's the way public policy is sometimes made—a horse trade or a sausage link.

My feeling is that Regan may have recognized early on that he might be in over his head. Nothing made him madder than to find out something was happening that he didn't know about in advance. He tried to centralize all things going to the President through his office. His minions put out the message that Don was in charge and that it was a one over one relationship— everybody reported to Don and Don reported to the President. It couldn't work and it didn't.

As surprising as it might seem given the rhetoric he was putting out to the press, I learned early on that you could do anything that you wanted to do as long as you gave Regan a "heads up" as he termed it. When it came to the economy and Wall Street, Don was truly a knowledgeable individual, but he had a narrow focus. He didn't understand politics and he couldn't recognize a non-economic issue if it tripped him. I used to joke that you could stick your head in his office (his door was almost always closed, even when he was alone) and say, "Hey Don. Just want to give you a heads up. We are taking the boss out on the south lawn and have him do a couple of sheep!" and his reply would be, "OK. Thanks for the heads up."

The public posture of his tenancy as Chief of Staff was that he was in total control of the White House. The Iran/Contra scandal proved that he obviously wasn't. I can say without qualification that I had more access to the President, more freedom to influence policy and more opportunities to do fun things during Regan's tenure than I ever did during the seventeen months I worked in the West Wing under the Meese, Baker, Deaver troika.

Under the troika, by mutual agreement, one of them was at every meeting and event that the President attended. When in July of 1984, the President requested a briefing on Social Security, I sat down with him in the Oval Office for about an hour, but we weren't alone; Ed Meese was sitting in the room working on some unrelated paper work. On another occasion I was to attend a meeting in the Oval Office on a budget issue. When I greeted Reagan's personal assistant,

Kathy Osborne, just outside the working door to the Oval, Kathy said, "They're in there." I opened the door and walked in and found myself with the President and the Vice President. And the White House photographer took several pictures of the three of us in conversation. Then a fourth person came in, Chief of Staff Jim Baker and more photos were taken. I have several photos of the four of us standing in the Oval but I was never able to find any of the photos that were taken of just the three of us. I have always harbored the suspicion that I wasn't supposed to be in there by myself and that Jim just told the photo shop not to print any of them!

On one occasion, the President was scheduled to do a Flag Day event at Ft. McHenry in Baltimore, Maryland. I was scheduled to go on the trip as was Regan. At the last minute, Regan cancelled and I found myself escorting the President and Mrs. Reagan to Marine One on the South Lawn. It never would have happened under Meese, Baker, and Deaver. On the helicopter the President sat in his seat facing forward on the left side, with Nancy sitting in front of him, facing aft. I sat in the seat on the right side of the aircraft facing both of them. Larry Speakes, the Press Secretary, sat in the back with the Secret Service detail.

On the trip up to Baltimore, the President was going over the speech he was to give. It contained the usual Flag Day ceremonials and it had a section on the tax reform proposal that we were trying to get Congress to pass. The President turned to me and said, "Jack, I don't think that I want to talk about tax reform here. This is a patriotic event." I was quickly pondering what was going to happen when Regan found out that I changed the speech when Mrs. Reagan said, "You have to stay on message." I looked at the President and said, "You're the President, if you want to take it out, we'll take it out." He promptly crossed out two pages of the speech. I could tell that Mrs. Reagan was not pleased. I was on a roll and decided to keep going. I said, "Mr. President, did you see where Earl Weaver is returning to manage the Baltimore Orioles?" He responded that he had seen it in the newspapers. I suggested that when he was doing the greetings, the Governor, Senators, the Mayor, etc., that when he got to the Mayor (Don Schaefer, whom we both new) that he say, "Don, I know that you are the mayor of Baltimore, but I understand that the Earl is back." The President liked it and penciled it in to his copy. Mrs. Reagan looked at me and said, "Why don't you rewrite the whole speech, Jack?" The line about "The Earl" got a great laugh from the predominately Baltimore audience at the event.*

When we landed I grabbed Speakes and told him what had occurred. He suggested that I tell Bill Henkle, the top advance man. Henkle just threw up his hands and muttered several oaths. Cutting two pages out of the speech reduced the time to give it by a couple of minutes and Henkle had a flight of jets set to do a flyover of Ft. McHenry based on the full speech. Henkle took off to find a way to delay the jets for a couple of minutes when Speakes dropped the bomb on me. He told me that he had already given the speech to the pool of reporters who were traveling with us and it had the two pages on tax reform in it. I thought about it for a second and said, "OK. We have to tell the President." Larry and I then walked a gauntlet of police and secret service agents to the holding room where the President and Mrs. Reagan were awaiting the start of the program. We walked in and I told the President the situation. Larry suggested that we could just tell the

---

* An interesting anecdote on that trip. I was on the Board of Governors of the National Aquarium in Baltimore at the time, having been appointed to the Board when I was Commissioner of Social Security. The Aquarium had a request for a permit to capture some Beluga whales for an exhibit. The request had been pending before the Marine Mammal Commission in the Department of Commerce for some lengthy period. I mentioned this to Michael Driggs, the guy on my staff who handled commerce and trade, and told him that I was going up to Baltimore the next day with the President and it would be great if we could take the permit with us. I don't know what Driggs did or what he told them, but I had the permits in time for the flight. When I told the story to the President he laughed and commented on the "pretty expensive way to deliver a whale fishing license."

press that we were running short of time and decided to shorten the speech. The President thought for a moment and then said, "No. Why don't we just tell them the truth? I read it and didn't think this was a proper forum to be discussing political things and I took it out." I said, "It sounds good to me." Larry and I walked out of the room and Larry whispered, "I guess you know we just took our life in our own hands." I knew.

So under the troika, there was always one of the three with the President. Under Regan that was not the case. After Don had been there a couple of months, I think that he had enough and decided to hand off some of the "tending to the President" to others. Of course he always attended the high visibility events where he could strut his stuff. Sometimes he went a little overboard like when the President and Soviet Union First Secretary Gorbachev had their first summit in Geneva. With the two of them seated on a couch, Regan was photographed between them hanging over the back of the couch. Whether it was Regan's incompetence or just lack of interest, he just didn't seem to focus on anything other than making sure Don Regan looked good. In the end, he even goofed that up.

One of the first things Regan decided to do when he arrived was to reduce the number of Assistants to the President. Regan was a person who had strong opinions and he didn't like people who questioned them. As it turned out he had a pretty long list of people that had angered him while he was Secretary of the Treasury and he set out to get back at them and in several cases to get rid of them.

His first victim was Lee Verstandig, the Assistant to the President for Inter-Governmental Affairs. But in a manner that I was to observe several times over the next fifteen months, Regan didn't fire Lee. He had someone else do it. In Lee's case, the message was given to him by Ed Rollins. Regan had appointed Rollins as Assistant for political AND intergovernmental affairs and his first assignment was to fire Lee. Lee never knew what hit him. Nor did he know why he was being dumped. In retrospect, it was pretty merciful. Regan's later "firings" were not nearly as clean and there was a long list of targets. Several were very high visibility like Heckler, while others were done with less publicity but similar results.

Robert C. (Bud) MacFarlane had taken over as the National Security Advisor in 1983 just after I joined the White House staff. Bud was a retired Marine and took his job very seriously. A quiet intense man, Bud worked longer hours and put more effort into doing his job than any other staff person.

Bud could be so intense that he could miss a point. One morning we were at the senior staff meeting and Bud was giving a report on a Middle East airliner highjacking. A group of terrorists were holding the plane and passengers hostage at the airport. Bud gave his up to date report as he had read it from the overnight intelligence summary. At the end of his report, he indicated that we didn't know how the incident was going to end. I spoke up and said, "The terrorists let the passengers go and blew up the cockpit of the aircraft with a grenade." Bud just stared and me and said, "We have no information to that effect." And I said, "I just watched it live on CNN before coming down here." It was the early '80s and our intelligence community had not yet begun watching 24/7 news.

Bud like the rest of us with the title of Assistant to the President worked for the President. When Regan came on the scene, he wanted everyone to report through him and Bud chafed at that, insisting that his responsibility was to the President and that he reported directly to him. I never saw Regan get as mad as when something got to the President from Bud without going through him and he really blew his top when Bud called the President directly to report on some international incident. The vibes between the two of them were not good.

Then the leaks began; personal, viscous leaks that Bud was having an affair with a female reporter. At first they were just around the

White House but then they began appearing in print. In his memoir, *Special Trust*, Bud said that his press assistant, Karna Small, told him that the leaks were coming from Don Regan's office. Bud said that he went to Regan and said, "Don I've been told that these false rumors are being put about by you or your staff." To which Regan replied, "Bud, that isn't true." But the rumors continued and the work situation became so bad for Bud that he resigned. I attended the reception that the President gave for Bud. It hurt me to see Bud standing there, bleeding (figuratively), while the President gave his usual speech about how he understands when a person has to return to the private sector. But you could tell from the look on Bud's face that he really didn't want to leave. He was being forced out.

Bud wasn't the only one who was to be the beneficiary of leaks from Regan, Inc. I was walking into a meeting in the Cabinet Room one afternoon when I was accosted by John Herrington, the former White House personnel director and at the time the Secretary of Energy. John accused me of being an anonymous "high White House official" quoted in the press saying that he was incorrect in his assessment of the mid-East oil situation. I had seen the stories and not only was Herrington trashed, but there were derogatory statements made about the Vice President with regard to the same issue. I told John that it was not me, but he insisted that it was. He said that he had been told explicitly that it was me. I was pretty shocked and upset. It was inconceivable to me that someone would think that I would leak anything let alone a personal slur.

The next morning at the senior staff meeting I mentioned the incident to Fred Khedouri, the Vice President's policy director and a friend. Fred just looked at me. I prompted him, "You know the story about Herrington and the Veep and oil." Fred just kept looking at me. Then it hit me and I said, "Wait a minute. You guys don't think that I did that? The Vice President doesn't think I did it?" Fred said that yes they had been told that the leaker was me. I immediately went to Craig Fuller, the Vice President's Chief of Staff and explained what was happening. Craig told me that the Vice President did indeed think that it was me. I asked Craig to arrange a meeting with the Vice President for me. I think that Craig knew me well enough to know that it wasn't me and he set the meeting up shortly thereafter.

When I met with the Vice President, it was a private meeting; photos at the start and then just the two of us. I explained to him what I understood the situation to be and about my run-in with Herrington. I told him that I didn't leak period—not the good stuff and not the bad stuff. I told him that the President abhorred the leaks and I was the President's guy. I looked him in the eye and told him that it wasn't me. He seemed to believe me and we ended the meeting on a cordial note. I assume that Craig had briefed him. Craig knew that I wasn't a leaker yet someone had told them that it was me. And that someone was either Regan or one of his lieutenants.

Unlike Bud, I didn't confront Regan. I figured that it wasn't worth the effort and that eventually it would blow over. Again I was wrong. Leaked stories continued during the first six months after Regan and his Mice* arrived. The *National Journal* had a weekly column entitled "White House Notebook." As early as February 23, 1985, the *National Journal* said:

> "John A. Svahn, a protégé of Edwin Meese III, presently holds the top domestic policy post, but it is by no means clear for how long. When Regan announced his appointments ... he said that Svahn too would be staying for a while. Since then, however, Svahn's name has surfaced as one of those who might be asked to step down from assistant to the President rank to that of deputy assistant."

The next month the *National Journal* headline read:

---

*Mice was the term the media used to describe four non-descript Regan aides brought from Treasury.

"Svahn Song for Lone Sacramento Survivor? ... Or Will Scrappy Policy Chief Hold Ground?"

By July, the *Evans and Novak Political Report* was less circumspect:

"Domestic Policy Chief <u>Jack Svahn</u> is going."

I never talked to any of these reporters. They were getting their information from "White House sources." And it was news to me that Regan appointed me to anything much less "for awhile." But the crowning leak, one that definitely changed my relationship with Regan occurred in August of 1985.

The President was out at his ranch in California during August for a much deserved rest after having had an operation to remove a large malignant tumor from his colon in July. The first week that he was there, Don Regan was the senior officer on site in Santa Barbara. I was scheduled to take over as the senior staff member when Don left and I was looking forward to it.

I took the first week off and went sailing with the family. At the Inner Harbor in Baltimore I picked up a copy of the *Baltimore Sun* to see what was going on in the world. My blood pressure immediately went up. There, prominently featured, was a story by Jack Germond out of Santa Barbara which implied that I was leading the charge to get Peggy Heckler removed as Secretary of Health and Human Services. I went back to the stand and found a copy of the *Washington Post*. There again was a front page story out of Santa Barbara by long-time Reagan biographer Lou Cannon spelling out in some detail the campaign that I was supposedly running to gun down Heckler! It was a bald face lie.

I found a pay phone and called the White House and asked them to get me Larry Speakes. Speakes was out in Santa Barbara and when I got him on the phone I said, "Larry, that story is bullshit. You get Cannon and Germond and tell them so. Knock that story down!" Larry replied, "I can't. Regan gave it to them. I was sitting right there." I couldn't believe what he was telling me. Regan was deliberately lying. I asked the operator to transfer me to Regan. He wasn't "available." I called Larry back and told him to tell Regan that I wanted to see him when I got out there. We were going to have it out.

I took the boat back and packed for Santa Barbara. I caught a plane out of Andrews Air Force Base. When I got to the Biltmore, I went straight for Regan but he wasn't there; he'd already left for a vacation on another aircraft! So I got Larry and asked him to find Cannon and Germond and get them into the office, the same office that Regan had used when he was there. For some reason, Larry couldn't find Germond but he did get a hold of Cannon and scheduled a meeting. I had known Lou for a number of years and had read his two biographies on Ronald Reagan. We were not friends, however, and I had never been interviewed by him.

I started the conversation with Lou by telling him in no uncertain terms that the story he printed was false. He quickly replied, "I had a source." I guess in the world of journalism that having a "source" is an absolute defense. I told Cannon that I knew he had a source; his source had been sitting in the very chair that I was now sitting in and that Larry had been there also and that Larry had told me that Regan had given it to him. Larry was standing in the room and Cannon knew that I had him. I told him again that the story was not true. I was not leading a charge against Heckler. He just said that he had a source.

While I was in Santa Barbara I tried to contact Regan a couple of times but he was "unavailable." I was accompanying the President back to Washington on September 2 and I decided to wait until I got back to have it out with Regan. When I got back to the White House I had calmed down some so I knew there would be no fisticuffs. Instead, I went to Regan's office, opened the door and walked in, closing the door behind me. I told him that I knew that it was he who gave the story to Cannon and Germond and that he knew that it was a lie. To my absolute astonishment, he denied it. He said, in a most sincere tone,

"It wasn't me." I laughed. Those few minutes changed our relationship entirely. Don knew that I knew.*

In his memoir, *For the Record*, Regan says that he curbed the leaks that plagued the White House during the first term by asking staff not to leak. "I asked them all to cultivate a passion for anonymity; and with the exception of Buchanan, the Thomas Paine of the Right, they complied so effectively that the press began calling them "the Mice." They were called "the Mice" all right, but the appellation had nothing to do with their passion. However, they, along with Regan, did cultivate anonymity. All of their leaks were anonymous.

After our little chat about the Heckler leak, Don actually became somewhat friendly. Occasionally, there would be a reference in the media about me still wanting to oust Heckler, but as time went on, most of it was actually put out by Heckler and her staff. On one occasion after Heckler left, I saw a story that was obviously generated by Regan, Inc. entitled "Stakes Must Be Well Done" in which it was said, "her mistake was that she didn't drive the wooden stake through the heart

---

* Canon never wrote anymore about me going after Heckler. But he didn't forget that Regan had used him. When Regan published his memoir *For the Record*, Lou called me up and asked if I had read the book. I said that I had. Lou asked me if there was anything that stood out for me as being untrue. I just laughed. But I told him that the symbol of all the BS in the self-serving book was Regan's description of the inauguration in January of 1981. He said, "January 20 fell on a Tuesday in 1981. It was a cold day, the view was poor, and the President's words were distorted by loudspeakers and carried away by the wind." I reminded Lou that the day was unusual for January in Washington; the sun was shining and it was abnormally warm. Lou did a column in the *Washington Post*. Cannon said, "In classic mysteries, the perpetrator of a crime often gives himself away with a little lie or accidental misstatement. Politicians and authors can be similarly revealed. ... Former White House chief of staff Donald T. Regan's provocative book also contains incontestable inaccuracies. Presenting a vivid picture of Reagan's inauguration Jan. 20, 1981, Regan writes that "it was a cold day, the view was poor and the president's words were distorted by loudspeakers and carried away by the wind." In fact, it was one of the warmest days of the winter, with temperatures soaring to 56. The view was good. The wind was light. Regan must have had some other occasion in mind." Cannon never admitted that he had been duped, but I took the column as an apology.

of John Svahn." The story went on to say that I had participated in "shoving her out the door." I sent Regan a note with the clip that read simply, "DTR - AW Gimme a Break – Jack." I got one back from him that said, "taking the rap for doing something that some one (sic) else did to herself is never easy ---DTR."

When Heckler finally left in late 1985, it was a messy departure. Instead of just firing her, Regan, Inc. continued with a barrage of leaks about her competence, demeanor, and a messy divorce she had with her husband John. It was death by a thousand cuts. In the end, she became U.S. Ambassador to Ireland. The daily briefing of the news media by Press Secretary Larry Speakes took on an almost comic refrain as the media asked "If she is doing such a good job at HHS, why does the President want to send her to Ireland?" The public humiliation surrounding her departure caused the President to join her in the White House Press Briefing Room to goofily exclaim that he wasn't firing her; she was getting a "promotion." Heckler stood solemn faced while the President tried to deflect the questions from the press. She was almost in tears. And Regan, the great leaker and the cause of the public humiliation of Heckler and now Reagan himself, was nowhere to be found. Just as when he engineered the departure of McFarlane and Verstandig, Regan went to ground when the deed was actually being done. It seemed that the messier one of his actions was, the longer he would stay out of sight.

Just after the announcement that she was being "promoted," as Heckler was leaving the White House via the West Wing basement entrance, Pat Buchanan and I were returning from lunch and waiting for the elevator next to the door. I didn't know what to say to Heckler; she looked like she had been crying. So out of my mouth popped, "Congratulations Margaret!" The next morning the episode was described verbatim in the *Washington Times*. I didn't leak it and I am pretty certain that Heckler didn't. The only other witness was the uniformed Secret Service agent at the desk and I am sure he didn't tell the *Times*, so that only leaves Brother Pat trying to do me a "favor."

Regan could be extremely petty about his position. When he took over as chief of staff, John Herrington was on his way to the Energy Department and the Assistant to the President for personnel was vacant. The Deputy in that office was Bob Tuttle and it was known that Bob wanted to move up into the top position but Regan didn't want him in the job. He wanted his "own person." One evening in late January I was attending a reception for Citizens for America (CFA) in the Blue Room of the White House. CFA was a group of like-minded citizens organized by Lew Lehrman, the New Yorker who created the Rite Aid drugstore chain. The membership of CFA was a who's who of wealthy conservatives. Many friends of Ronald Reagan were in attendance. As I was standing there, I saw Holmes Tuttle, a long-time friend and confidant of the President's, put his arm around Reagan and ask him to step out of the function and into the Great Hall. I was talking to Joe Coors at the time and I remarked "I guess that cinches who the next personnel chief will be." I was right.

Regan was mad. He was publicly quoted as saying that Tuttle wasn't his choice; that the President had told him to pick Tuttle. In private he was even more upset. So out of spite he demoted the position from Assistant to the President to Deputy Assistant. Even though the previous three personnel chiefs had a suite of offices in the West Wing, Regan kept Tuttle in an office in the Old Executive Office Building. Regan later commented that the personnel director had been given too high a visibility and that it wasn't that important a job. Reagan believed that "people **are** policy"; Regan just didn't get it. Bob, a very competent guy, finally gained Regan's confidence and after a period of penance in the OEOB, got an office in the West Wing.

Regan continued to move to eliminate or punish people who challenged his authority or angered him. And anyone could be a target. But it was never a frontal confrontation. When the speechwriting staff wouldn't heel on command, he directed Buchanan to fire the chief speechwriter, Bentley (Ben) Elliot. Buchanan finally did tell Ben that Regan was firing him. When it came time for the perfunctory going away party, Ben told the President that he wasn't leaving voluntarily. The President didn't seem to realize it and he did nothing to stop Ben from being run out of town.

Regan constantly trash talked people that he didn't like. In one personnel meeting in mid 1985, he started in on Ed Gray, then the Chairman of the Federal Home Loan Bank Board (FHLBB). The FHLLB and its sister agency the Federal Savings and Loan Insurance Corporation (FSLIC) regulated and insured the nation's Savings and Loan institutions. Gray had been on the Task Group on Regulation of Financial Services chaired by the Vice President. Regan, then Secretary of the Treasury was the Vice Chairman. Regan didn't like some of the things that Ed said during the meetings. Ed was hell bent on trying to sound the alarm about the financial crisis in the Savings and Loan industry and Regan didn't want to hear any of it. Regan didn't forget that Ed wouldn't keep quiet when Don made a pronouncement.

On this evening he made some derogatory comments about Gray and said he was going to get rid of him. Having watched him "get rid" of several people by this time, I knew that he didn't mean that he was going to call Ed in and fire him or have the President do it. It was going to be another death by a thousand anonymous cuts. I told Don that he couldn't do that; that Ed had worked tirelessly for Ronald Reagan in California and that he deserved better than a public lynching. I told Regan that I would go over and talk to Ed and convey the message.

I went over to Ed's office and we had a long talk. He explained to me the situation with the S & Ls again. (Ed was right. It was the biggest financial collapse in the United States when it happened) I told him that Regan wanted him out and what Don had done to others in similar situations. Leaks, rumor, and lies were all part of his repertoire. Ed said that the President would never fire him. I agreed but I told him that the President wasn't going to be involved, that Reagan wouldn't even know about it. That Regan would start a campaign of leaks to ruin his reputation. I told him as a friend that he had seen it before; some guy gets so much pressure that he is finally worn out and leaves and there is Ronald Reagan saying that he understands people want to get back to the private sector/spend time with their families/make some money/or just go home. Ed was a stubborn guy and he refused to bow to Regan and true to form, Regan started a campaign to wear Ed down. Regan finally got his way, but Ed didn't go out bowed; he put up a hell of a fight.

Regan showed his pettiness in many ways. He wanted everyone to acknowledge his position and power. And it wasn't just the staff; he also wanted Cabinet members to know who was boss.

When Olaf Palme, the Prime Minister of Sweden, was assassinated on a street in Stockholm on March 1, 1986, it was a shock that reverberated throughout the world. My grandfather was born in Sweden and I asked the President about the delegation going to the funeral. I assumed that the Vice President would lead the delegation but I told him that I was probably the highest ranking Swedish American in his Administration and that my father would be really proud if I were to represent the United States. He said OK. I then told Don Regan what the President had said and Regan didn't indicate he cared one way or the other.

As it turned out, the delegation was not going to be headed by Vice President Bush; instead it was headed by George Shultz, the Secretary of State. And incorporated into the funeral trip, there was to be a meeting with the Soviet Union.

The Swedish government knew that the funeral would be attended by a large number of leaders from around the world and they limited each official delegation from a country to just three individuals. Shultz objected to my being on the delegation because he wanted to take an Assistant Secretary of State, Roz Ridgeway, a skilled negotiator with the

Soviets. Our Ambassador to Sweden, Greg Newell, was to be an automatic member of the delegation. George made his objections known to the White House and it caught the eye of Don Regan.

With Regan, if a decision had been made to which he was a party, anyone complaining or challenging the decision had to be stomped on. And as far as Regan was concerned, the decision to have me as a member of the delegation had been made by the President and Don Regan was going to enforce that decision. Don sent word that if Shultz wanted Ridgeway on the trip, to get the delegation expanded to four people. When the State Department objected saying that the Swedish government said only three, the dispute escalated until Regan sent back the word through a subordinate that I was going on the delegation or Shultz wouldn't get an airplane.

Neither the President nor I knew anything about the disagreement or Shultz's reasons for not wanting me on the trip. Had he mentioned it to me, I would have given up my slot and I am sure that if George had mentioned it to the President I wouldn't have been on the plane.

Regan won. The U.S. delegation was expanded to four. The trip was a quick one. I had never been to Sweden but my grandfather had been a member of the Swedish King's Guard in the late nineteenth century so I was very interested in Stockholm. While at the White House, we had been invited to the residence of the Swedish Ambassador, William Wachtmeister on several occasions and he had encouraged us to visit Sweden. Unfortunately, there was very little sightseeing to be done on this trip.

We left Andrews Air Force Base at about 9:00 PM on March 14 heading for a refuel and crew change at Shannon Airport in Ireland. When I woke up the next morning we were landing at a U.S. Air Force base in Mildenhall, England. It had been too rough to get into the airport in Ireland so we had diverted to Mildenhall. Even though it was about five o'clock in the morning, I was fully awake and decided to de-plane and go into the operations building for a cup of coffee while the crew fueled the aircraft. As I exited the aircraft I met a Major General standing at the bottom of the stairs. He was the Wing Commander and inquired if George was on the plane. I replied that he was, but was asleep. The General had his private car sitting next to the plane and invited me to his residence for coffee. I felt I should stay with the plane but he assured me that his quarters were close-by and that the duty officer would call with plenty of time to get back.

When we got to his quarters his wife was fully dressed and smiling and a sergeant was just getting the coffee prepared. The next thing I knew, the local Member of Parliament and his wife showed up, dressed like they were going to dinner. And it was 5:00 o'clock in the morning! We had coffee and briefly chatted and then it was time to go back to the plane. Before I left, however, the General's wife had me sign their guest book which I gladly did and bid them good-bye.

When the plane landed at Arlanda Airport in Stockholm there was a lot of press to greet us. George made a brief statement and then we proceeded to the Sheraton Hotel to freshen up before the funeral. In each of our rooms there was a plate of cookies baked by our Ambassador Greg Newell's children. That was lunch.

The funeral was to take place in the Stockholm City Hall, a beautiful building with a very large great hall. The city and for that matter, the entire country, was in complete mourning. It reminded me of those days in the United States after President John F. Kennedy was assassinated in 1963. The streets were empty and everything was closed. Security was extremely tight. The entire country was watching television.

We got into a motorcade and headed for the funeral service. Dark suit and black tie was the uniform of the day per instructions from the Swedish government. When we arrived at City Hall, we entered through a side door. It was apparent that we had been waiting until almost all of those attending were in the hall and seated. I was behind George and he started shaking hands as we went by the first row of guests. I didn't know what we were doing but I followed suit shaking hands with each person as if it were a reception line. Then I began to recognize the people I was shaking hands with. They were all heads of state or foreign ministers. Rajiv Gandhi and Perez de Cuellar were the recognizable faces that tipped me off. George and I split up and I took my assigned seat in the very crowded auditorium next to the number two guy from East Germany. He should have stopped at the Sheraton to freshen up.

The Swedes had asked everyone at the end of the service to stay in their seats until Palme's casket left the Hall. Everyone but the U.S. and Soviet Union's delegations. They knew about the meeting and wanted to facilitate it taking place. So at the end, we jumped up and ran out to the waiting motorcade while the rest of those in attendance sat in their seats and watched. The city was deserted; no traffic either vehicular or foot. After awhile I noticed that we were going past some buildings for the second time. Upon inquiring, I was told that we were in fact driving in circles. We were doing that because the Soviets were not ready for the meeting with Shultz so the Swedes had decided that we should just keep driving in circles.

After regrouping at the hotel, we motorcaded to an evening reception at the Ministry for Foreign Affairs for all the delegations. It was very interesting. Cocktails and small talk with many heads of state. I even had the opportunity to chat with Bishop Desmond TuTu for a while. There was only one uncomfortable moment at the reception when I turned around and bumped into Daniel Ortega, the kingpin from Nicaragua. A person accompanying him pointed to the security pin on my lapel. It was a round blue pin with "USA" imprinted on it. At this period in time, it was well known that the United States was supporting the Contras in their fight against Ortega's brand of communism. I introduced myself but I was a little nervous that one of the Nicaraguans might decide to make a scene or worse.

Our final stop for the day was in the Swedish government building for an 8:30 PM meeting with the new Swedish Prime Minister Ingvar Carlsson and his Foreign Minister Sten Anderson. The meeting was very formal and served only to officially convey our condolences and pledge continued cooperation with the Swedish government. Then back out to the airport for a 9:40 PM departure.

Because we had stopped at Mildenhall that morning, we had to stop there again for fuel and to pick up the crew that we had left there to rest. When we landed around 11:00 PM, George, I and several others were sitting on the plane having a cocktail. As we taxied to a stop, I told George that it was likely that there would be a two star general waiting to greet us and that it would be nice for him to say hello. George agreed and put on an overcoat over his casual pants and headed for the door. I knew what was going to happen so I tightened up my tie and put on my suit coat. Sure enough, there was the general and his car beckoning us to visit his quarters for a nightcap. George was a little embarrassed because he was casually dressed. We got in the car and rode over to the house.

There was the General's wife, chipper and dressed in a different outfit than the one she had had on eighteen hours earlier. And there was the local Member of Parliament and his wife bubbling along about life in the area. We stayed for the short time it took to get the plane refueled and then bid our goodbyes. The general's wife pulled out the guest book; I had already signed it so I handed it to George. While George was writing, I was saying goodbye to the General and his wife. As we were shaking hands I leaned over and whispered to her, "We'll see you tomorrow morning." I thought she was going to faint. Wheels up and we headed for Washington, D.C. I was back home Sunday afternoon. The whole trip only took a day and a half. It was the only foreign trip that I took while at the White House.

One interesting event that occurred during 1986 had to do with drug testing. Drug testing of the President! The Office of Drug Abuse

Policy reported to me. It was directed by a very capable scientist and a Deputy Assistant to the President, Dr. Carlton E. Turner. Carlton had been in the office when I arrived and we hit it off pretty well. He ran his shop and I didn't interfere. If he needed some help or some advice he would come to me; otherwise he handled the program. It was a many-faceted operation and dealt with domestic drug problems as well as international activities, some of which I really didn't want to know about the details. But Carlton's most important job as far as I was concerned was to support Mrs. Reagan's "Just Say No" campaign against illicit drug use. And keep her happy.

One area that Carlton was always pushing was a drug-free workplace. On Monday August 4, 1986, at a Cabinet meeting the President announced his objective of a drug-free America and called for "a national crusade against drugs." In announcing his campaign he set a specific goal of a drug-free workplace, with the federal government setting the example for the private sector. In discussions with the President, we explained that there would have to be testing. He agreed and felt that drug testing should be voluntary or at least limited to critical or sensitive positions specifically citing law enforcement and air traffic controllers. I had been in a meeting with him when he was asked a slew of questions about fighting drugs and I knew that he had thought the issue through and was ready to proceed.

Carlton and I drafted a decision paper for the President and sent it through Don Regan on July 29, 1986. It came back to me from the President on August 4. The President said that he wanted drug testing for those applying for federal jobs that were sensitive positions and for current employees in sensitive positions. He didn't want mandatory screening for all employees, instead opting for a voluntary program. The one subject that he hesitated about was whether prosecutors should seek the death penalty for drug traffickers. The Justice department was very much in favor of it, but Reagan felt that to push for it would just complicate matters by bringing the anti-death penalty crowd into the equation. One thing that he didn't hesitate on was establishing a drug testing program for the White House staff. Right next to "RR" it said, "we will lead the way."

On Friday August 8, Carlton and I sent a memo to the senior staff explaining that we felt that the senior staff should lead the way by volunteering for testing and that we had arranged with the White House Physician's Office on the ground level of the residence to have samples taken on Monday August 11. On Monday, at the conclusion of the senior staff meeting at 8:30 AM we all trooped over to the medical office to give a specimen. First in line was Ronald Reagan.

Chapter 19

End Game

After the blowup with Regan over the Heckler story that he leaked in August of 1985, I came to the conclusion that there just wasn't a place for me in the White House. If truth be known, I was tired of government and of the constant snipping and games played by Regan's Mice. I could tell that they didn't understand Reagan and that they owed their very existence to Regan. Until Regan left, there wouldn't be any improvement. I wasn't the only one to come to that conclusion. Rollins left as did Max Freidersdorf and B. Ogelsby. They were followed by the Counsel, Fred Fielding. Regan replaced them with his own people.

About that time, I was approached by E. Pendleton James about a position in the private sector. Penn had been the personnel director for the transition in 1980 and had served as the Director of Personnel in the West Wing. Penn left the Administration after the first year and had established a recruiting firm in New York. He was then in the process of doing a search for the American Insurance Association (AIA), the group that is made up of the property and casualty insurance companies. They were looking for a CEO who knew Washington, D.C., and could move the group from its New York base to the Nation's Capital.

I went through the interview process, met with their search committee and then with members of their board. In the end, they offered me the position at roughly four times the salary that I was making in government. It was a very tempting offer and I accepted it. Then just as we were going to finalize the agreement, Brooks held his hearing calling for an investigation of me and the systems contract awarded two years earlier to EDS.

The GAO testified as to the "facts" that they found. They said that personnel from Deloitte (one of the subcontractors to EDS and the company for which I had worked for two years in the 1970s) had been housed in the Commissioner's Office and thereby received inside information. I didn't know what they were talking about. To show you the competence of the GAO "investigators" they didn't inquire as to where the Commissioner's Office was during my tenure. They just looked at what existed in late 1985 and concluded that must have been the way it was in 1982. As I learned later, my successor remodeled the whole space and expanded the Commissioner's Office substantially.

After the accusation was made, I couldn't leave. Even though in fact, the timing of the accusation and my leaving to go back to the private sector were not related, it would look like I was being run out of town on a rail. I told the AIA people that I would have to wait for the investigation to conclude and my innocence established before I could leave. They did not understand why I wouldn't leave and perhaps in hindsight I should have but I had spent a lot of time in government and had seen a lot of guys get attacked and turn tail. It usually ruined their reputation and I wasn't going to have that happen to me. The AIA wasn't happy about it but I stayed.

So in November of 1985, I settled down to await the results of the FBI review. Leonard Garment had explained that the FBI was very thorough and it was likely that it would be several months before they completed their review. I knew in my own mind that I was finished with government service; it was just a matter of time. Don Regan knew

I was done too; I had talked to him about the AIA opportunity and I was just about ready to talk to the President when Brooks started his circus.

The one good thing about knowing that I was leaving was that there was now nothing holding me back. I was free to do what I wanted to do until I did in fact resign. So as we entered 1986, I was a lot less inhibited than I had been throughout 1985. The President wasn't going to get rid of Don and even given the choice between Don and me; there was no question in my mind where the President would come down. I also concluded that Regan and his Mice were going to do what they wanted to do but they couldn't get rid of me. I don't know if Regan told his Mice to knock off the anonymous attacks in the press, but the attacks died down.

As 1985 ended, one more interesting piece of legislation was passed by the Congress, the Balanced Budget and Emergency Deficit Control Act of 1985, or as it was known around Washington, Gramm-Rudman-Hollings (GRH). It was named after its sponsors, all deficit hawk Senators, Phil Gramm (R-TX), Warren Rudman (R-NH) and Ernest Hollings (D-SC). Essentially GRH mandated that if the deficit exceeded certain pre-set limits, the President had to issue an order to "sequester" that is reduce spending by preset amounts across the board. Certain categories of spending were exempt, but it was apparent that if GRH were implemented, there would be fiscal chaos.

Several of us thought that the President might veto the end product and that we would certainly have the opportunity to advise him to do so. The President quickly decided to sign the legislation, conferring only with Don Regan. I was amazed that Don, whose knowledge of economics I had admired, would let the President make this mistake. But make it he did. The President had always wanted a "balanced budget amendment" and he viewed this as a vehicle going in that direction. On December 12, 1985, we did a quickie signing with the authors. Darman and Baker came over from Treasury and Dick remarked, "I wouldn't have missed the signing of the Tax Increase Act of 1985 for anything." Because there was no audience and we needed to somehow make it look like a ceremony, several of us on the senior staff sat in a row of chairs facing the President with the television camera shooting the back of our heads while the President signed the bill. It was all for show.

Several members of the administration were madder than hell that the President had signed it. George Shultz buttonholed me and said that he hoped that he was asked about GRH and if he was he was going to say it's a "catastrophe." I told him that the President was behind the legislation and that it would be unfortunate to have the Secretary of State be against the President. He was upset that the Cabinet had not been consulted before the President signed the bill. I passed the information about my exchange with Shultz to Regan in a handwritten note, suggesting that he might want to give Shultz a call. Regan responded, "It's not really his call – he's trying to protect for.(eign) Aid, new embassies, etc." Herbert Stein, a member of the President's Economic Policy Advisory Board and former Chairman of the Council of Economic Advisors under Nixon said, "Gramm-Rudman-Hollings is not sensible. I pray that it will be declared unconstitutional." Herb must have prayed hard because the U.S. Supreme Court did declare the law unconstitutional in 1986. It never went into effect.

In addition to the terrible destruction of the space shuttle Challenger on the scheduled delivery date, the 1986 SOTUS was notable in my mind for a couple of other reasons. First, it was really the first SOTUS planned, written, and delivered under the direction of Donald T. Regan. Regan had arrived at the White House just as the 1985 SOTUS was being delivered. He really didn't have any input to it other than the usual input from a cabinet member. But at the next SOTUS in 1986, he, and the cabal that he had brought over from Treasury, the "Mice" were in full charge and they set about making mischief.

Major speeches by the President took a lot of time developing and word-smithing. In the Reagan White House, we had a really crack group of speechwriters led by Bentley Elliot. Ben was supported by a staunch group of Reaganites that included Dana Rohrabacher and Anthony (Tony) Dolan. They were a bunch of hard line conservatives that fed the President the kind of raw meat rhetoric that he liked so well. Later on this group also included Peggy Noonan. During the first term, the SOTUS speech usually started with the writers meeting with the President to get a feel from him about direction. In the meantime, the senior staff would meet frequently to outline the initiatives that would be covered and to suggest a thematic construct to the writers. Part of this phase included sifting through the myriad of "must have in the speech" suggestions from the Cabinet departments.

In preparation for the 86 SOTUS I don't know how much early contact the speechwriters had with the President. I have read accounts that the Regan people restricted their access. What I did know is that they put together a draft stem-winder for which they were noted and forwarded it to the Staff Secretary for circulation to the senior staff for comment. All of the President's major addresses were circulated in this fashion. But in this instance the draft speech got a little "pre-circulation" to the Mice who rewrote the speech and forwarded it for review by the senior staff, implying that it was the speech was drafted by Ben Elliot and staff. Pat Buchanan tipped me off as to what was going on in Regan's suite. When the draft was circulated to the senior staff, it was the watered down version. It was pablum.

By this time my relationship with the Mice was guarded at best. I decided that rather than confront them with their mischief, I would respond to Ben Elliott directly, knowing that the draft that I was reviewing had been tampered with by Regan's staff. I sent Ben a note saying, "I am not a great speechwriter and you are, but this just doesn't sound like a Reagan speech." I went on criticizing the speech in a number of ways. I figured that since I was the only California Reaganite left in the West Wing, my saying the speech wasn't "Reaganesque" would get the Mice's attention. It did. The speech was returned to the speech-writers and re-drafted by Elliott and Josh Gilder more to the original draft, but the battle lines were drawn between the Mice and the speech-writers and the Mice occupied the inner sanctum. And of course the whole skirmish was leaked to the media and appeared in the press the next day. It was another nail in Ben Elliott's coffin and shortly thereafter Regan had him fired.

A second reason that the speech sticks out in my mind is that I had so much to do with what went into it. The two previous SOTUS that I was involved with as a White House staffer had been large collaborative efforts with suggestions for themes and initiatives coming from a variety of sources, both within the Administration and from the private sector. This one was different. Regan had tightened down so much that there was little input from outside and almost none from the staff. Instead, he seemed to be grasping at straws for something to put in the speech. Now granted this was the sixth SOTUS for Reagan and most would have said that he had said it all before but still, we wanted some new material. Seeing that Regan Inc. was not coming up with anything, I set out to develop some new initiatives for the coming year.

I discussed it with Pat Buchanan and we jointly came up with three areas which we knew would interest the President. The first was a comprehensive study of the welfare system to develop a plan to end it. Reagan had never forgotten that welfare was the issue that propelled him to the White House and that it was still on the table. Of course, I already had Chuck Hobbs on my staff working on a program, but we felt that a strong public commitment on the part of the President was necessary to push the rest of the Administration.

A second area was suggested by John McTague from the Office of Science and Technology Policy. McTague arranged for Buchanan and me to meet with a small group of scientists from NASA who had kept a small forward thinking project going despite budget constraints and space shuttle priorities. The project was the development of an aerospace plane; a plane so different that it would enter sub-orbital space and shrink the time it takes to fly from Washington, D.C., to Tokyo to less than two hours. We knew that Reagan couldn't resist it and he didn't.

The third area that I came up with was much more controversial and one which I had to push the President hard to get him to agree. It was the calling for a plan to address the problem of catastrophic illness in America including the need for Long Term Care. Reagan didn't want to get into the subject. He felt that if he opened the door that the Democrats would drive a massive new spending program through it. I argued that too many families were driven into poverty or bankruptcy because of health care costs resulting from one family member's illness. What sold him was when I told him that it was an issue that was going to have to be addressed and that the real question was whether we addressed it our way, with a solution that he could approve of or whether he wanted to pass that job on to a successor. Reagan thought for a moment and then approved the inclusion in the SOTUS of a call for a plan to solve the problem.

When the speech was finally delivered on February 4, 1986 (it was delayed a week due to the Challenger incident), it included a recitation of things that he had called for in the past—a Balanced Budget Amendment, the Line Item Veto, tax reform, free and fair trade, a security shield against nuclear weapons and other wants, but it only had three new domestic initiatives.

The day after the speech we had scheduled a Domestic Policy Council meeting at the Department of Health and Human Services (HHS). The purpose of the meeting was to follow up on the welfare reform study and on the SOTUS call for Secretary Bowen to develop a plan to deal with catastrophic health care costs for individuals. It was the first meeting of a Cabinet Council to be held anywhere other than at the White House. We were doing it at HHS, according to Regan, to show action. It was to be the first time that I would return to the Department since I left as Under Secretary.

The meeting itself was relatively short and the President spent most of his time talking about welfare reform. That may have been a mistake; we should have spent more time talking about Bowen's ideas about ways to address the issue of catastrophic health costs. Unbeknownst to us, that is Reagan, Regan, Meese and Svahn, old Doc Bowen had been looking at this issue for some time and already had a plan for solving it.

The Office of Management and Budget (OMB) had devised a plan during 1984 to increase the amount that a Medicare beneficiary paid for hospitalization as a way to save money —every hospitalized Medicare beneficiary would pay a coinsurance. In exchange, a new benefit would be available for beneficiaries who had long hospitalization. It was estimated that the new benefit would only be used by about a half a percent of all Medicare beneficiaries and that the savings would be approximately $745 million a year. OMB had planned to include the proposal in the President's fiscal year 1985 budget, which was to be released in February of 1984. At the last minute, I wrote a note to the President and recommended the he remove the proposal, dubbed the Medicare Cost Sharing/Catastrophic Protection proposal, from the budget. The President agreed. But the concept was out there and once something gets hatched in Washington, it rarely dies.

In 1981, Otis had chaired the Social Security Advisory Council, a statutorily constituted group charged with reviewing the current status of the program. At the time, Dick Schweiker and I decided that since Social Security was already a national priority and having another group looking at it would only cause more confusion than that which existed. We decided to have the Advisory Council focus on Medicare instead. Bowen used the time on the Advisory Council to develop a plan that provided for increased benefits for Medicare to the tune of almost $5 billion. It was this plan that became the basis for the recommendations that Bowen as Secretary of Health and Human Services made to the President in late 1986.

It was our intention that the study cover catastrophic costs to all Americans but Bowen focused primarily on Medicare beneficiaries. And his plan was a complete expansion of the role of government in administering Medicare at the expense of the private sector. The President's fears when we first talked about including the call for a catastrophic health proposal were realized. The Democrats loved Bowen's plan and they started to run with it. The proposal took on a life of its own. It was wildly popular and received the endorsement of many of the elderly interest groups. The Democrats loaded it up with additional benefits including mammography, respite care, and a prescription drug program. The potential costs were enormous but they were overshadowed by the package's popularity. It passed the House 302 to 127 and the Senate 86 to 11. Then the trouble started.

The programs under the Medicare Catastrophic Coverage Act of 1988 were, like the original OMB proposal, self-financing. Essentially, Medicare beneficiaries were going to pay extra taxes to pay for the new benefits. It was going to cost all Medicare beneficiaries more money each month for benefits they might never use. The backlash was unfathomable. Seniors staged protests all over the country and the more they found out about the new program, the more they protested. The *Chicago Tribune* reported on one such demonstration against the Chairman of the Ways and Means Committee and a strong proponent of the new law, Dan Rostenkowski:

> "Congressman Dan Rostenkowski, one of the most powerful politicians in the United States, was booed and chased down a Chicago street Thursday morning by a group of senior citizens after he refused to talk with them about federal health insurance .... Eventually, the six-foot four-inch Rostenkowski cut through a gas station, broke into a sprint and escaped into his car, which minutes earlier had one of the elderly protesters, Leona Kozien, draped over the hood."

Public opposition mounted rapidly and Congress, in its usual display of courage, repealed the legislation the year after it passed. The grand plan to address the problem of catastrophic illness and costs for Americans failed.

Which brings up a issue that continues to elude us as a self governing nation. The philosopher George Santayana is often quoted as saying, "Those who cannot remember the past are condemned to repeat it." And I am afraid that is ever so true where our government is concerned. When Congress repealed the Medicare Catastrophic Coverage Act of 1988, it cast aside the wisdom of history and replaced it with political expediency. Just as I told President Reagan that if he didn't solve the problem one of his successors would try and they wouldn't do it the way he might like. As it is, two of his successors, Clinton and Obama, have tried. Clinton failed and Obama has succeeded in passing health care legislation after a bruising battle only to have a majority of Americans want his program repealed. As new administrations come into office, instead of building on the lessons of the past, they routinely cast aside the work that has been done by their predecessors and boldly proceed to make the same mistakes.

Thirty years ago we faced the abyss in financing the Social Security system. We made the hard decisions and the system built surpluses. But we knew at the time that the program would have financing problems again when the baby boom began to retire. We knew then that action would have to be taken early in the twenty-first century to avert another crisis. That time has come but the current class of politicians has forgotten and has failed to take actions in a timely manner. It is a simple system. Current workers pay for the benefits of current retirees. The ratio of workers to retirees is decreasing; workers are retiring at an earlier age. Further raising the retirement age from its scheduled sixty-seven to sixty-nine for today's toddlers would avoid a lot of hand-wringing and scare-politics in the future. For someone to suggest that now would result in screams from organized labor and groups that make their money off the elderly. But in 1983 we raised the retirement age for full benefits from sixty-five to sixty-seven and there were no riots in the street. Remember, when Social Security was first passed in 1935 the average life expectancy for a person born that year was sixty-two and they set the retirement age at sixty-five. They were counting on most people not living long enough to collect it. Life expectancy of a person born in the United States this year is seventy-eight. If we set the retirement age like our forefathers did in 1935, it would be eighty-one. We don't need to do that of course, but it shows that there is considerable room for responsible action.

The examples are myriad. Social Security's data processing system was teetering on the brink in 1981. We spent a lot of capital, both fiscal and human, to bring it up to date. Then the agency promptly forgot about keeping it up to date. The cycle is nearing completion. Today the SSA is scrambling to keep ahead of a crumbling system. In 1981 they had over $100 billion in earnings reported but not able to credit to a valid Social Security number. Today the number is $840 billion.

We had a financial meltdown in the Savings and Loan industry in the 1980s. We were warned about it before it happened but did nothing. History is repeating itself today as we watch the banks go under and homes foreclosed. And in an age when anyone can immediately access satellites with a GPS and pinpoint their location to within ten feet, our Air Traffic Control system still relies on ground based radar. One wonders why our government can't remember the failures of the past and plan for the future to avoid them. Santayana was right.

But my time was running out. My immediate staff had already left. Lou Hays went back to HHS to help Bill Roper run Medicare and Medicaid and Jan Farrell had taken a job in the Press Office. It was just Maria White and me left. I had been cleared of the Brooks accusation by the FBI in July and I made up my mind that it was time to leave. I was tired of all the West Wing in-fighting and even though I had no idea what I would do when I left, I made the decision to depart. I talked to Regan and to the President. The President was not too happy, but in his usual gracious way he bid me well. In his diary on September 17, 1986, Reagan jotted:

> "A sad note then a farewell party for Jack Svahn. He's been with us since 1968 in Sacramento. With 2 children approaching college time he has to get out in the private sector & make some money. He's really been great & we'll miss him."

My last day in the employ of the federal government was September 26, 1986. It was a Friday and the President was going to Camp David for the weekend. I walked over to the residence to say good bye and met him and Nancy in the hallway just inside the Diplomatic Reception Room. He was surprised to see me there and said, "We already said good bye to you." I laughed.

Leaving the White House is somewhat of a come down. The government wants to make sure that you realize that you are going back to be a regular citizen. Just like in the military, you have a checklist of things that you have to do before you can leave. And for each task, you have to get some responsible bureaucrat to sign off that you have completed it. After saying good bye to Reagan I went about getting the appropriate people to sign off on my departure. The National Gallery of Art got their paintings back; the U.S. Navy got back the glass encased model of the USS *Hartford* (Perry's ship in the Battle of Mobile Bay that had graced my office for three years); and I went to the White House mess to get the Navy Chief Warrant Officer in charge, to check the box that said that I had paid all of my mess bill.

My last stop of the day was over in the Old Executive Office Building where I was to turn in my diplomatic passport. I walked into a small office that was staffed by a lone woman. She looked up at me and inquired as to what I wanted. I held up the black diplomatic passport and told her that I was leaving and had to turn in the passport. She asked me my name and I told her whereupon she turned to a little box with five by seven cards in it and began to thumb through the cards.

When she couldn't find my card, she asked me to spell my name and I did. A second trip through the deck and she turned to me and said, "You don't have a diplomatic passport." I sort of laughed and held the passport up to show her it was black and said "Diplomatic Passport" in bold gold letters on the front of it. I then opened it to show her it was my picture on the inside. She looked at it and checked the spelling. Then she went back to the card file and rifled through the cards. Again she said, "You don't have a diplomatic passport!" I didn't know what to do so I asked her if she would clear me. She said I was cleared. I left.

This final episode was so representative of the two decades that I spent in government that I laughed all the way home. I used that passport for the next two years. There really was a pony. Ain't government great?

Acknowledgments

I would like to thank all of those who encouraged me to complete this book, some at an early stage and others right down to the day of publication. I received a lot of help from Diane Barrie with the National Archives Ronald Reagan Presidential Library and from Joanne M. Drake, a fellow Reagan Alum and now the Chief Administrative Officer of the Ronald Reagan Foundation. In addition, Marlin Fitzwater, the only individual to serve as Press Secretary under two consecutive Presidents, provided early guidance. Patrick Cooke, former editor of *ForbesLife* was instrumental in the development of the final title and Phil Gambino, an old colleague at the Social Security Administration brought me up to date on some of the fine points of their great programs. Throughout the process I was consistently needled about the need to finish the book by my mother, Esther Svahn and long-time friends and associates Bruce Yarwood and John Shermyen. But the real credit for this book being in your hands goes to my best friend and devoted wife of thirty-three years, Jill. Jill lived through much of this story and never faltered in her desire to have me tell it.